Shakespeare
and the
Poet's Life

Shakespeare

and the

Poet's Life

GARY SCHMIDGALL

THE UNIVERSITY PRESS OF KENTUCKY

Copyright © 1990 by the University Press of Kentucky
Scholarly publisher for the Commonwealth,
serving Bellarmine College, Berea College, Centre
College of Kentucky, Eastern Kentucky University,
The Filson Club, Georgetown College, Kentucky
Historical Society, Kentucky State University,
Morehead State University, Murray State University,
Northern Kentucky University, Transylvania University,
University of Kentucky, University of Louisville,
and Western Kentucky University.

Editorial and Sales Offices: Lexington, Kentucky 40506-0336

Library of Congress Cataloging-in-Publication
Schmidgall, Gary, 1945-
  Shakespeare and the poet's life / Gary Schmidgall.
    p.   cm.
  Includes bibliographical references.
  ISBN 0-8131-1706-2 :
  1. Shakespeare, William, 1564-1616—Authorship.   2. Shakespeare,
William, 1564-1616—Contemporaries.   3. Poets in literature.
4. Courts and courtiers in literature.   5. Great Britain—Court and
courtiers.   6. Poets, English—Early modern, 1500-1700—Political
and social views.   I. Title.
PR2957.S34   1990
822.3'3—dc20   89-28667

For my parents,
Peggy and Robert

Contents

Acknowledgments

I WOULD LIKE to express my gratitude to the John Simon Guggenheim Memorial Foundation for the fellowship that supported my early research and to The Huntington Library for courtesies regularly extended to me over the last two decades, as well as for a summer research grant.

Note on Citations

EXCEPT where noted, all citations from Shakespeare's works are made from *The Riverside Shakespeare*, edited by G. Blakemore Evans and others (1974). Citations from the Sonnets are from the Stephen Booth edition (1977). Abbreviations for Shakespeare's works are those of the *Harvard Concordance* (1973). For certain authors frequently quoted, I cite in the text by page number from the following editions: John Donne, *The Complete English Poems*, edited by A.J. Smith (1971); Ben Jonson, *The Complete Poems*, edited by George Parfitt (1975) (all other Jonsonian citations coming from *The Works*, edited by C.H. Herford and Percy and Evelyn Simpson [1925-52] and made by volume and page number); Sir Thomas Wyatt, *The Complete Poems*, edited by R.A. Rebholz (1978); Sir Philip Sidney, *The Poems*, edited by William Ringler (1962). George Puttenham's *The Arte of English Poesie* (1589) is cited by book and chapter number. Because many of the contemporary works on which this study draws are not easily accessible, I provide for the more important ones their Short Title Catalogue (STC) number on initial citation. All quotations are reproduced exactly as printed in the editions cited except for normalization of *i, j, u,* and *v* and a small number of silent corrections of anomalous typography or punctuation.

Introduction

THIS STUDY is, above all, about the English Renaissance poet's life, his motivations for poetizing, his attitudes toward the economy of letters, and the attitudes of society (high society in particular) toward his profession. Paradoxically, it will focus on an author who appears to have entertained for a very short time the notion of being a dedicated (and dedicating), publishing, professional poet and will offer, from several perspectives, some answers to a highly speculative but important and fascinating question about his artistic biography: Why was it William Shakespeare's destiny as a poet to "Bud, and be blasted, in a breathing while"?

The facts are few and pointed. In 1593 and 1594, Shakespeare for the only time in his life published poetry (*Venus and Adonis* and *The Rape of Lucrece*) under his name and apparently with careful personal oversight. Both poems proved popular and were often reprinted. As for the Sonnets, most scholars assume they date from about the same time, though they did not become available for publication until 1609.[1] Barring either the unlikely discovery of other poems in manuscript or the appearance of hitherto-lost editions, we can say that Shakespeare devoted himself solely to writing for the stage during his last two London decades. Why did the blossoming young poet cease writing sonnets and epyllions, cease in his efforts to combine the professions of courting poet and dramatist, and turn more exclusively to the world of the theater?

We shall never know whether this cessation occurred by conscious choice or merely by default as the years passed. And we are also unlikely to learn what combination of personal and professional circumstances played a part. Neither can we possibly say with certainty *when* Shakespeare was a dramatist, a poet, or a dramatist-and-poet. We can only say that, sooner rather than later, he stopped being a poet. This is enough, it seems to me, to make it worthwhile contemplating the *professional* considerations that might have caused Shakespeare—or any poet of the time—to feel impelled (as one man wrote in a dedication to Southampton) "to be freed from a Poet's name."[2] The five chapters of the present book thus converge, from widely varying directions, on a general professional question with Shakespeare particularly in mind. Organized accordingly, this study is intended to hang together in two ways: One is as a study of poets and poetizing in Shakespeare's canon. Though I cast a wide net among Renaissance poets— referring often to Wyatt, Spenser, Sidney, Greville, Donne, Jonson, and the sonneteers of the 1590s, each chapter employs evidence in Shakespeare's poems and plays as a rhetorical point of departure or arrival. Every one of Shakespeare's works figures at some point in the discussion, and a half-dozen are given extended attention. Obviously, then, I welcome readers who come with a primary interest in Shakespeare; but to my mind the second way the book hangs together is dominant, namely, as a meditation on the nature of the Renaissance poet's life. Keeping this priority firm saves me from the onus of appearing to assert the unprovable about Shakespeare's *actual* personal career choices and the onus of seeming to desire to justify them.

Lacking certain knowledge, we can scarcely expect to arrive at a simple answer to the provocative question. What is more, several aspects of the turn away from poetry ("complexifiers" in economists' parlance) urge us to conclude that a clear explanation may be too much to hope for. First is the sheer surprise of it. If several editions of *Venus and Adonis* and *The Rape of Lucrece*, and the well-known praise from Harvey, Meres, Weever, and the *Parnassus* plays are any indication, Shakespeare gained some considerable fame from his early poetical exertions—"fame," as the King says in *Love's Labour's Lost*, "that all hunt after in their lives." Richard Barnfield's praise published in 1598, when Shakespeare was working on his seventeenth play, describes this fame and must strike us as startlingly specific: "And *Shakespeare* thou, whose hony-flowing Vaine, / (Pleasing the World) thy Praises doth containe. / Whose *Venus*, and whose *Lucrece* (sweete, and chaste) / Thy Name in fames immortall Booke have plac't."[3] Why did he walk away from such fame? Cheeky callowness, indifference, supreme artistic boldness, or shrewd calculation of the main chance? Whatever the answer(s), it is rare for authors to renounce success, rare enough to give the question in Shakespeare's case an air of puzzle and mystery.

A second complicating element of the question is that it adjoins the primal query underlying all authorial effort: Why write? Many bold critics have made asses of themselves trying to answer this question which, perhaps, hath no bottom. But it is not a question we can ignore. Richard Poirier insisted in *The Performing Self*, "We must begin to begin again with the most elementary and therefore the toughest questions: what must it have felt like to do this—not to mean anything, but to do it?"[4] The question Why write? was not ignored by the wisest Renaissance poets: "Come, let me write, 'And to what end?'" Thus Sidney begins his psychomachia-inverse, *Astrophil and Stella* Sonnet 34 (quoted in full on page 25). Renaissance poets had frequent occasion to whisper this question in real life, though few—Sidney and Shakespeare chief among them—asked it "aloud" in or between the lines they wrote. Few poets exhibited the questing self-consciousness of their identity and methods as poets that is bared in Sidney's question. The ways it was answered, we shall soon see, at once illuminate and complicate our understanding of Shakespeare's willingness to abjure verse.

A third complication derives from the fact that our question requires us to focus on the most complex part of a writer's career, its beginnings, when the pressures and anxieties experienced are most volatile. All writers, Shakespeare surely included, are keenly subject at the inception of their careers to the kind of preoccupation described in a letter by Robert Frost: "My whole anxiety is for myself as a performer. Am I any good? That's what I'd like to know and all I need to know."[5] Such anxiety often leads to unpredictable extremities—sometimes electrifying, sometimes merely egregious. One can find passages to fit both epithets from the opening of Shakespeare's career when, clearly, an exuberant literary upstart was testing in numerous ways whether he was any good. It is tempting to think of Shakespeare arriving from the Midlands, Lancashire, or wherever in the cultural cynosure of London just as Lucentio arrives at Italy's "nursery of arts" in *The Taming of the Shrew* (possibly, the Arden editor suggests, Shakespeare's first London play): "I have Pisa left / And am to Padua come, as he that leaves / A shallow plash to plunge him in the deep, / And with satiety seeks to quench his thirst" (1.1.21-24). And *satiety*—whether of taffeta phrases in *Love's Labour's Lost*, blood in *Titus Andronicus*, preposterous hijinks in the two farces, or villainy in *Richard III*—is an apt word for the works that came from Shakespeare's youthful pen.

Shakespeare's sonnets and long poems in particular are remarkably full-dieted performances, and are generally accepted as calculated, extrovert, virtuosic vanities of a just-fledged poet's art. As the following pages urge, these performances say much about the poet and his self-image. I use the term *performances* advisedly. Poirier has also written, "Performance is an exercise of power, a very curious one. Curious because it is at first so furiously self-consultive, so even narcissistic, and later so eager for publicity, love, and historical dimension."[6] There is, as we shall see, much eagerness of this kind in Shakespeare's poetry. Indeed, it might be said that in his early years Shakespeare consulted several plausible selves; the focus of the present study will be his self-as-poet.

A beginner's anxiety was shared by all those nonarmigerous persons who presented themselves as performers on the Renaissance literary stage, as Richard Helgerson has noted: "In those crossings of the threshold, when the author first appears before his audience, the pressure on self-presentation is greatest. To some extent, each beginning . . . brings a renewal of self-presentational pressure."[7] This self-consulting performance was exacerbated by the complex, rigid etiquette that governed all modes of social and artistic self-presentation or self- fashioning in the Renaissance. Some of this etiquette may seem to have worked on primitive levels because, with Miss Manners and her Gentle Reader, we have progressed far beyond Giovanni Della Casa's *Galateo, A Treatise of Manners* (1576), wherein the reader is advised: "when thou hast blowne thy nose, use not to open thy handkerchief, to glare upon thy snot, as if [thou] hadst pearles and rubies fallen from thy braines." Or, "let not a man to . . . lie tottering with one legg so high above the other, that a man may see all bare that his cloathes would cover."[8] But the etiquette facing the upstart courting denizen also took highly sophisticated forms. Authors were thus induced into various elaborate forms of indirection, deference, masking, and politesse, which led to very complex socioliterary transactions (studied most notably by Frank Whigham and Arthur Marotti). These will also make it harder to arrive at a clear answer to our question.

A last complication worth noting is more specific to Shakespeare's beginnings as an author: His turn from poetry apparently came at a time when he had yet to discover his artistic identity and was gamely covering all his careerist bets. Jorge Luis Borges has observed, "The fate of a writer is strange. At first he is baroque—ostentatiously baroque—and after many years he may attain, if the stars are auspicious, not simplicity, which in itself is nothing, but a modest and hidden complexity." Elsewhere he made his point more prosaically: "I think a writer always begins by being too complicated. He's playing at several games at the same time."[9] Though Borges was thinking of his own career, his view applies emphatically and poignantly to Shakespeare. One need simply describe some of the works from his first few years on the literary scene to recognize that he was playing several games at once: a vast historical trilogy with its pendant "tragedy" of Richard III, a comic and a tragic epyllion, a Plautine farce (*The Comedy of Errors*), a sonnet sequence, a domestic comedy of manners

(*Taming of the Shrew*), a Senecan tragedy (*Titus Andronicus*), and an aristo-cratic comedy of manners (*Love's Labour's Lost*). There is an irresistible parallel here with the young pianist who exults in a spectacular technique, but without having much "to say" about the music that is specific to the musician's not-yet-matured creative personality. Thus, our question posi-tions us to focus on Shakespeare at his most baroque, when his work was rife with ostentation—much of it "delightful," some of it "maggot" (LLL 5.1.111; 5.2.409). Peering behind Shakespeare's lines is always risk-laden, but especially so when, as in his early years, he was performing the literary corantos and capers that he perceived as suitable to the decorum of several established genres.

Enough has been said to make clear that the explanation offered here for Shakespeare's digression from what Drayton called the "nice and Narrow way of Verse" will be multifarious and not without internal contradiction.[10] The reader should also be forewarned that the picture painted in the following pages will be a darkly shadowed one, as a thesis proposed not long ago by Alvin Kernan in *The Playwright as Magician* can conveniently suggest. Kernan sees the Young Man of the Sonnets as "the Muse of courtly lyric poetry: open, clear, idealized, beautiful, changeable rather than complex in nature, polished in manners, the inheritor of a great tradition, aristocratic and male." He finds the muse of the theater repre-sented by the Dark Lady: "illicit, darkly mysterious, sensual, infinitely complex, beautiful and ugly, common and public, the source of pleasure and pain." Kernan then speculates that Shakespeare finally chose the latter muse.[11] This thesis has its obvious attractions, but I shall argue, converse-ly, that the poet's life was by no means the idealized one presented by Kernan. More to my purposes are the following: the bitter complaint of Ovid Senior in Jonson's *The Poetaster* (recall that Shakespeare launched his poetical career as an Ovidian), "Name me a profest *poet*, that his *poetrie* did ever afford so much as a competencie" (4:211); Donne's reluctance to produce some verse for the Countess of Huntingdon: "That knowledge which she hath of me, was in the beginning of a graver course, then of a Poet, into which (that I may also keep my dignity) I would not seem to relapse. The Spanish proverb informes me, that he is a fool which cannot make one Sonnet, and he is mad which makes two" (*Letters*, 103); or the colloquy from a play of the 1590s in which Surrey says, "Oh, my Lord, you tax me / In that word poet of much idleness: / It is a studie that makes poore our fate," and Sir Thomas More replies, "This is noe age for poets."[12]

It should be clear that in speaking of "the poet's life" I refer to the class of Renaissance authors who produced primarily recreational, nondramatic verse—what George Puttenham (defining "Lyrique poets") classed as "songs and ballads of pleasure." My interest is thus to inquire how Shakespeare's early experience of such a poet's life, and his observation of others who lived it as well, might have affected his achievement in that vastly larger universe created by the Folio's "Scenicke" poet. "I have endeavoured to prove," wrote Coleridge, "[that Shakespeare] had shown himself a *poet*, previously to his appearance as a dramatic poet," and the present study attempts to explore how the former identity might have been diffused in the latter.[13]

This purpose can be phrased more atmospherically. Oscar Wilde wrote in "Shakespeare and Costume Design" (1885) that "nobody, from the mere details of apparel and adornment, has ever drawn such irony of contrast, such immediate and tragic effect, such pity and such pathos, as Shakespeare. . . .He was the first to see the dramatic value of doublets, and that a climax may depend upon a crinoline."[14] Wilde's aperçu aptly reminds us of the Renaissance notion of the "garment" of poetic style. It was, for instance, Puttenham's purpose in his *Arte of English Poesie* to "apparel" the "good Poet or maker [in] all his gorgious habilliments." My purpose is thus not to search for "Shakespeare's poets"—a task, in any event, that Kenneth Muir was able to perform nicely in a short essay[15]—but to learn something of his sensitivity to the "apparel and adornment" of poetic style, to consider how he may have felt in the poet's gorgeous habiliments, and to explore how (in his later years) they became merely another, but often a quite useful, part of the tiring-house wardrobe.

Finally, let me say that, while arriving at several uncomplimentary conclusions about the Renaissance poet's life, I do not intend to suggest that the life of a playwright and actor was necessarily less demeaning. Surely there was much discomfort in a life of stooping to the tastes of a Globe Theater "general" and in coping with the constraints of censorship, the hostility of London's city fathers, and the hazardous economics of public playing. But Shakespeare's experience as a dramatist has been studied hitherto by numerous scholars from Bentley, Bradbrook, Harbage and Bethell to Rabkin, Gurr, Wickham, Weimann, and Barish, to name but a few of the more prominent. I have therefore excluded the risky life of the London theater from consideration here. The blunt fact remains that Shakespeare's canon displays a clear professional preference; it is for us to account for it as plausibly as we can without making unnecessary, invidious comparisons between poetry and drama.

Something should be said about the place the present study occupies in the current critical landscape. My evidence is drawn primarily from contemporary letters, courtesy books, rhetorical treatises, front matter, and biographies; my catalyzing question is one of Shakespearean biography. To some, this will seem passé in the light of recent critical fashions. But it has been my desire, employing methods dusted but surely not exhausted by "antique time," to work outward from the central locus of Shakespeare's canon in the direction of several important critical enterprises of recent birth. While I have not partaken of the paradigms or terminology of the "new" historicism or deconstructive theory, for example, I believe the present study complements several studies in these fields. The focus of one of the founders of new historicism, Stephen Greenblatt, has been summarized as "the forces of containment as a means of describing the paradoxical relationship of texts to society."[16] The reader will find frequent occasion in this study of the paradoxical relationship of *poets* to society to recall the insights of Greenblatt and those who have followed him. An important study, which appeared after mine was completed, underscores the complementarity I have hoped for: Joel Fineman's *Shakespeare's Perjured Eye: The Invention of Poetic Subjectivity in the Sonnets* (1986). Though Fineman indulges an extremely dense discursive style and eschews reference "to an actual or biographical Shakespearean personality . . . of a kind that historical critics look for in literary and extra-literary archives" (82) precisely my metier—I was surprised and pleased at how often his assertions ramified what I have to say: beneath our radically different methodologies are important shared premises and conclusions.[17]

Several valuable recent books (behind which loom such names as Burke, Foucault, Goffman, Elias, and Geertz) have explored exciting new paths but, tantalizingly, have only reached the Shakespearean threshold. I have tried to move toward them from the opposite direction. I am thinking, for instance, of Daniel Javitch, whose focus on the "association between court conduct and the poet's art" in *Poetry and Courtliness in Renaissance England* (1978) and other works figures often in the following pages. Richard Helgerson's concern, in *Self-Crowned Laureates* (1983), with "self-definition and self-presentation" among Renaissance poets often reflects on the less exalted professional poet's life, too. (The term *laureate*, incidentally, never occurs in Shakespeare.) Especially contiguous with my study is Frank Whigham's *Ambition and Privilege: Social Tropes of Elizabethan Courtesy* (1984), an exploration of "rhetorical semiotics at court" and "tropes of promotion and compliment . . . combat and rivalry" employed at court. The implications of Whigham's study for the newly arrived lyric poet at court are daunting, and I have sought to draw some of them into the context of Shakespeare's London life and his imagined courtly lives. My historical-biographical focus also bears some similarity to that of Arthur Marotti's frequently speculative but illuminating *John Donne, Coterie Poet* (1986). Also valuable is Eckhard Auberlen's *The Commonwealth of Wit: The Writer's Image and His Strategies of Self-Presentation in Elizabethan Literature* (1984), which explores in several suggestive ways the "writer's self-representation as an attempt to influence social evaluations of his position." Unfortunately, Auberlen excludes authors principally known as dramatists; Shakespeare is mentioned but a few times in passing. However, several of Auberlen's observations pertinent to the playwright-poet will be pursued here.

My study of Shakespeare's self-consciousness as a poet and his self-conscious deployment of poetical style also draws upon recent linguistic and rhetorical approaches. Richard Lanham's *The Motives of Eloquence* (1976) figures in the opening of chapter 1, and the relevance of Marion Trousdale's *Shakespeare and the Rhetoricians* (1982), which rests on the assumption that "poetic language to the Elizabethans was always a conscious language," will also become clear. Keir Elam's Shakespeare's *Universe of Discourse: Language-Games in the Comedies* (1984), combining the disciplines of linguistics, the philosophy of language, language-oriented sociology, and semiotics, is "a study of the self-consciousness of Shakespeare's language" and "the intense linguistic awareness" of Shakespeare's age. Further evidence of these characteristics appears often in my study.

A third area of scholarship toward which my approach has seemed to impel me is metadrama, spawned as long ago as Anne Barton's *Shakespeare and the Idea of the Play* (1962). Though metadramatic criticism often veers into discourse on the hermeneutics and ontology of the theatrical experience, the genre's less theoretical and more sociological manifestations will be found relevant to much that I have to say. James Calderwood in *Shakespearean Metadrama* (1971), for example, says of a play to which I devote much attention, *Love's Labour's Lost*, that it focuses on "language and the durability of art" and on "the poet's relations to society and language." This same reflexive awareness is much in evidence in my discussion of the poet's self-identity. It might be more accurate, though, to say my quarry is more specifically the manifestation of a metapoetics in Shakespeare's plays.

Chapter 1 sketches some of the general features of the poet's courting life, offering first a reading of *Venus and Adonis* as a parable of both the courtier's and the courting poet's experience "in waiting," then turning to other images of this experience in *Love's Labour's Lost* and the Sonnets. Chapter 2 addresses the strategies of front matter. Title pages, dedications, and epistles to the reader were the bibliographical and typographical forms of "courtesy" during the Renaissance; here I explore authorial courting from this peculiar, often exasperating, sometimes amusing part of the literary terrain. Chapter 3 focuses first on the patron-client relationship and on various attitudes toward the writer's profession as they are conveyed in Shakespeare's diction, then on his changing presentations of patronage in *Love's Labour's Lost*, *Timon of Athens*, and *The Tempest*. Because poetic virtuosity and courtly dexterity were then perceived as intimately related, chapter 4 explores the illuminating intersections between the courtier's and the courting poet's lives. Central here is a canvass of the half-dozen roles of the poet to be found in Shakespeare's imaginary courts. The chapter closes with a look at the ways two of Shakespeare's richest creations, Falstaff and Iago, combine all of these shadow roles of the poet. Chapter 5 shows, through close consultation with the Young Man sonnets, that the private goals and circumstances of a neophyte suitor are deeply ingrained in these poems. G.K. Hunter has called Spenser's *Amoretti* in a limited sense "the history of a courtship," and in a similarly limited sense I argue that the Young Man sonnets present the history of a courtiership.[18] As an envoi and summary of my speculations, I offer in the epilogue a brief allegorical reading of *Antony and Cleopatra*.

Chapter One

"Thou Thing Most Abhorred"
The Poet and His Muse

I wish not there should be
Graved in mine Epitaph a Poet's name.
—Sir Philip Sidney

VENUS, Shakespeare's first masterly comic character to appear before the public in print, has—like virtually all his subsequent protagonists—evoked reactions wildly at variance with each other. C.S. Lewis, decidedly immune to her charms, wrote that she reminded him of those corpulent older women with expansive bosoms and moist lips who harassed him when he was a boy. Others have more recently nominated Venus genetrix of eloquence, predatory Freudian mother, protean temptress, a forty-year-old countess with a taste for Chapel Royal altos, and the embodiment of infinite desire. One critic, wishing to encompass all of Venus's many facets, has suggested that Helena in *All's Well That Ends Well* "nicely catalogues" them: "A mother, and a mistress, and a friend, / A phoenix, captain, and an enemy, / A guide, a goddess, and a sovereign, / A counsellor, a traitress, and a dear" (1.1.167-70). Commentators on *Venus and Adonis*, which announced Shakespeare's arrival on the poetical scene and was the work most often reprinted in his lifetime, have transformed Venus many times in their effort to demonstrate what the voluble heroine and her poem (hers it assuredly is) are about. Several of the most illuminating interpretations have been unabashedly tendentious, as, for instance, when Richard Lanham asserted in *The Motives of Eloquence* that *Venus and Adonis* and the other narrative poem, *The Rape of Lucrece*, are "*about* rhetorical identity and the strategies of rhetorical style."[1] In this exordium for a study of the poet's life in Shakespeare's time, I will approach *Venus and Adonis* in the same narrowly focused way, namely, with a view of the poem as being "about" the poet's identity and his strategies in the lists of patronage and clientage.

The poem at first blush is about coitus: what Shakespeare in Sonnet 20 calls "love's use." This is the consummation for which Venus so devoutly pleads. But the poem is also about the more complex, multifarious "love" that the speaker himself pleads for in Sonnet 20: the courting suitor's politic love, without which one did not survive long or prosper in the corridors and side chambers of a Renaissance court. Sex and the Goddess of Love may dominate the drama of the poem, just as the author's complete mastery of ornament and meter may dominate one's first experience of reading it. And this initial experience might leave one purely admiring what Jonson called the "neat and clean power of Poetrie." But we learn from the same poet that this power often lay at the disposal of a "most abhorred" muse who would "betray" the poet into the service of some "worthless lord" ("To My Muse" 54). In the shadows behind Shakespeare's exuberant sexual comedy, one can discern the presence of such a cunning courting muse—a difficult, exasperating lady. It is she, I believe, who is responsible for the curious dissonance beneath the happy din of the poem's lavish auricular figures— the poem's subtle "Melodious discord, heavenly tune harsh-sounding" (431). In the following pages I shall suggest that there is much in the poem to subvert the notion that poetry's, or the poet's, power is "neat and clean" when deployed amid the pressures of ambitious suit. Rather, this power is hard to manage, compromising, and more effective in ingenious than in ingenuous hands.

In Donne's first satire the acerbic speaker demands from his "uncertain" friend a promise not to abandon him in the street for a "gilt" captain, a "brisk perfumed pert courtier," or some "velvet Justice." He warns his friend not to "grin or fawn" on such a personage or "prepare / A speech to court his beauteous son and heir" (155). It is possible, I think, to see in the seductive speechmaking to which this warning alludes, the drama (wittily masked by the Ovidian vehicle) of *Venus and Adonis*. The vigorous excursions of an aspiring suitor ("Love is a spirit all compact of fire," Venus boasts, "Not gross to sink, but light, and will aspire" 149-50) and the self-protective aloofness of a targeted patron are mirrored often in the poem. The more specific poetical context of this antagonism is caught as well in Jonson's typically pungent image of "one of these beggarly Poets . . . that would hang upon a young heyre like a horseleech" (6: 302). It is ungallant to associate Shakespeare's charming though resistible goddess with a horse-leech. But this is a usefully jolting way to open consideration of Venus as a type of the suitor-poet at court, Adonis as an avatar of any "beauteous son and heir," and Venus's 150-line spree of suasive ingenuity as broadly evoking all poetical eloquence produced for ulterior purposes at court. The tug-of-war between the "sick-thoughted" and "bold-fac'd suitor" (5-6) and the "tender boy" (32), in other words, is suggestive of many aspects of the contemporary relationship between poet-clients and potential patrons that this book will explore in detail.

Venus exists in a thinly disguised Renaissance suitor's world pervaded by an unceasing tension between the suitor's instincts to besiege, possess, and exploit and the patron's instincts to fortify, repel, and husband riches from expense. Realities of the suitors' pressure on the few patrons ripe for exploitation were plain enough. No doubt these realities were partly responsible for the elaborate decorums that developed over the centuries to mask, however transparently, the intense friction along class lines. The courting "love" necessary to breach these decorous restraints had to be shrewd indeed. Precisely therefore, Venus—intent on a most indecorous carnal triumph—purveys her "cunning love" to foil Adonis's various reprehensions. Transforming one's own ambitious agenda into "love" required such "wit" as Venus impressively displays: namely, artifice, rhetoric, and the poet's "making" art. Venus's love is courtly in its purposeful sophistication and encroaching vigor. Like all love that is called to an "audit by advised respects" (SON 49), it leads not to a calm peace that passes understanding but to the extreme fretfulness of Sonnet 129's "expense of spirit in a waste of shame." Venus, we can reasonably imagine, wears the face of a "courtier practike" who "hath not toucht the *puntilio*, or point of his hopes," as it is described in Jonson's *Cynthia's Revels*: "a most promising, open, smooth, and over-flowing face, that seemes as it would runne, and powre it selfe into you" (4: 71).

The special torture of hoping that one's love will be accepted as genuine, and yet fearing that it will be accounted feigned, is a hallmark of much Renaissance love-suasion. Wyatt's poetry is rife with such civil war,[2] and Sidney's speaker announces this conflicted awareness in the very first line of *Astrophil and Stella*, with its fine pun on *feign:* "Loving in truth, and faine in verse my love to show." Shakespeare's sonnets are rich in similar anxiety, which is expressed at a climactic moment in Venus's *pro et contra* apostrophe to Death. Here Venus, beside herself with fear that the boy in whom all her hopes are freighted may be dead, expresses (for present purposes) a suitor's fear of the death of his suit. Behind this stanza is the ever-tentative, mercurial ethos confronting the ambitious at court:

> O hard-believing love, how strange it seems
> Not to believe, and yet too credulous!
> Thy weal and woe are both of them extremes:
> Despair and hope makes thee ridiculous:
>   The one doth flatter thee in thoughts unlikely,
>   In likely thoughts the other kills thee quickly. [985-90]

Flattered by "unlikely" hope for success and gored by "likely" fear of failure—such was the Renaissance suitor's emotional métier. And not a small part of Venus's ridiculousness is her reflection of the affected and vulnerable courtly suitor: She is not-so-distant kin of Armado in *Love's Labour's Lost* and Viola-Cesario, Malvolio, and Aguecheek in *Twelfth Night*. The couplet above also reminds one of another suitor who dwells on the razor's edge of courtly ambition, the speaker of Sonnet 87: "Thus have I had thee as a dream doth flatter: / In sleep a king, but waking no such matter."

(Perhaps a historical point can be made apropos of Venus's overripe, cathartic apostrophe to Death: Prince Henry died suddenly at the age of eighteen in 1612. Like Adonis, he possessed charisma, promised much, and died elaborately lamented. Venus's effusion is distinctly in the style of the numerous mortuary verses elicited by his death. Most of them were in the vein of her "If he be dead,—O no, it cannot be" [937]. Many of Henry's mourning poets stood in Venus's position of having suddenly lost a choice object for exploitation.)

We are given remarkably few hints about the landscape of *Venus and Adonis*. Even these (for example, "Witness this primrose bank whereon I lie" [151]) sound formulaic. But aspects of the suitor's courtly world are implicit everywhere. Court, for instance, was no place for the aging. John Chamberlain observed in a 1601 letter to Dudley Carleton: "Here is much justling and suing for places in the privie chamber, by reason that most [courtiers] being growne old and wearie of waiting, wold faine bring in a successor, as Master Killegrew his sonne, Sir Thomas Gorge his cousen Ned, Sir Ed: Carie his sonne Phillip."[3] Courtly suit was rather for the young and vigorous, as Venus urges:

> Were I hard-favour'd, foul, or wrinkled old,
> Ill-nurtur'd, crooked, churlish, harsh in voice,
> O'erworn, despised, rheumatic and cold,
> Thick-sighted, barren, lean, and lacking juice,
>   Then mightst thou pause . . . [133-37]

Consider eyesight too. When protocol often required "tongue-tied" patience from those in waiting (see SON 85, 140), much depended on eye contact. Thus, Castiglione urges his courtier to employ all possible "devises, apt posies, and wittie inventions that may draw unto him the eyes of the lookers on as the Adamant stone doth iron."[4] Venus employs just such gallant ocular weaponry in the poem, where, as with the Sonnets, eye contact is a prominent theme: "Oh what a war of looks was then between them! / Her eyes petitioners to his eyes suing, / His eyes saw her eyes, as they had not seen them, / Her eyes woo'd still, his eyes disdain'd the wooing" (355-58). Such "dumb play" (359) often masked eager strife to serve among the surrounding entourage. Many stood ready to say, as Venus does: "Bid me discourse, I will enchant thine ear" (145). Adonis weeps, and the sun and wind—like attendants lunging to perform courtesies—"strive who first should dry his tears" (1092). Such "smiling strife / Of climb-fall court," as Sidney phrased it, was commonplace among the numerous parties besieging the powerful. Needless to add, the most useful siege machine was the well-filed tongue ("the engine of her thoughts," 367); the most valuable skill, the ability to "insinuate" (1012).

Venus's irresistible passion ("she cannot choose but love") is natural, for the advantages of favor from the powerful at court were great. With reason the speaker of Sonnet 52 calls the Young Man his "sweet up-lockèd treasure"; similarly Venus: "Alas, poor world, what treasure hast thou lost!" (1075). The fierce competition for the troves at court engendered a compelling urge to thrust through all obstacles into the inner sanctum and intimacy: "Were beauty under twenty locks kept fast, / Yet love breaks through, and picks them all at last" (575-76). Arrived there, the urge was to isolate, capture, imprison, and exploit the patron: "Her lips are conquerors, his lips obey, / Paying what ransom the insulter willeth; / Whose vulture thought doth pitch the price so high / That she will draw his lips' rich treasure dry" (549-52). This was the supreme fantasy of the Renaissance suitor. It was almost always, as it is for Venus, only a fantasy: "All is imaginary she doth prove" (597). Suitors were forever urging with varying degrees of tact, as Venus urges Adonis, "Be prodigal" (755), but patrons rarely answered the call.

Many disagreeable traits of suitors figure in the poem. Their grasping eagerness is drolly captured when Venus "courageously" plucks Adonis from his horse, immodestly attempts to "govern" him "in strength" (42), and yokes her arms around his neck (591). The courting "love" of suitors easily turned into highly proprietary jealousy, making them "full of fear / As one with treasure laden, hemm'd with thieves" (1021-22). Jealousy and envy were frequent courtier's sentiments, and it is not surprising that Venus's discourse on jealousy (643-60) is cast in phrases from the dramatis personae of actual court life: the "sentinel," "sour informer," "bate-breeding spy," and the "dissentious . . . carry-tale" who "sometimes true news, sometimes false doth bring." Resentment, too, lurked in the breasts of those from whom the patron attempted to escape. "What bare excuses mak'st thou to be gone!" (188) exclaims Venus, echoing the hurt speaker of Sonnet 92: "But do thy worst to steal thyself away." And corruption lay inevitably in the suitor's way. Venus speaks more truly than she knows when she warns of the danger of the boar: "Rich preys make true men thieves" (724). The boar, whom Venus imagines making rival love to Adonis with his tusk, it might be added, is yet another avatar of the aggressive Renaissance suitor.

At the end of her amorous career the distraught heroine delivers her prophetic "morality" on having loved (1135-64). These rich stanzas not only accurately prophesy the love intrigue in many a Shakespearean play but also accurately describe the main qualities of politic love at court. Indeed, these stanzas can easily be read within the tradition of the dispraise of, or farewell to, courtly life, so often does Shakespeare's diction carry courtly connotations: Sorrow will "attend" on love; it will be "waited on" by jealousy, and "full of fraud"; it will "ne'er be settled equally, but high or low"; love will be whimsically "merciful, and too severe" and "subject and servile to all discontents."

Many of Venus's prophetic specifics reverberate against the reality of Tudor-Stuart courtiership, also against the client-patron relationship evoked in the Young Man sonnets. Her warning that love will "find sweet beginning, but unsavory end" well summarizes the experience of the Young Man's suitor . . . and many in real life. Her fear, expressed in Shakespeare's finest affectation of the letter, that love will "bud, and be blasted, in a breathing while" (1142) is also apt for the fashionably changing, factional world of the court. Her observation that love's "bottom" is "poison," its "top o'erstraw'd" introduces the prominent Shakespearean theme of duplicity at court: the "beauteous wall" that "doth oft close in pollution" (TN 1.2.48-49) and the courtier who honors his lord only with his "extern" (SON 125; OTH 1.1.63). When she says that love's "sweets" shall "the truest sight beguile," one is reminded of the "compound sweet" of courtly luxury in Sonnet 125 that draws the suitor from "simple savor" and from simple truth.[5]

The unsuccessful suitor's end (if his wealth still afforded him a country seat) was a quiet if bitter rustication. This is what Venus chooses for herself. She retires to her seat at Paphos, after first tucking between her breasts a souvenir of courtship's "gaudy spring" (SON 1). Many a Renaissance suitor turned his back on the court with Venus's sense of exhaustion and emptiness, but it is doubtful whether many departed with her grace:

> Thus weary of the world, away she hies,
> And yokes her silver doves, by whose swift aid
> Their mistress mounted through the empty skies,

In her light chariot quickly is convey'd,
  Holding her course to Paphos, where their queen
  Means to immure herself and not be seen. [1187-94]

What, then, of the object of Venus's "tributary gazes" in this parable of the suitor's fretful life? Most readers find Adonis a disagreeable adolescent: narcissistic, complacent in his sententious wisdom, and—with his "frowns," "louring brow," and "heavy, dark, disliking eye"—altogether too wintry. This physiognomic rhetoric of disdain was, of course, a prominent feature of interaction among clients and patrons, and we will arrive at a more balanced assessment of Adonis by considering him briefly as a reluctant patron, rather than as an unwilling sexual partner. From this perspective Adonis's "dull disdain" becomes more shrewd. Venus becomes but one of many potential "bold-fac'd" suitors; allow *her* to impale the aristocratic dear and many others will surely follow, eager to oppress. Give a small token of favor (for example, the kiss Adonis offers at line 536 in exchange for his freedom) and the suitor will but hunger for more: "having felt the sweetness of the spoil, / With blindfold fury she begins to forage." Imagine Adonis as a potential patron and certain lines take on special force, as when in perfect aristocratic form he sours his cheek and cries, "Fie, no more of love! / The sun doth burn my face, I must remove" (185-86). Doubtless many a patron answered the suitor's cajoling "What great danger dwells upon my suit?" (206) with variations on Adonis's "'Tis much to borrow, and I will not owe it" (411). Perfectly aristocratic, too (and reminiscent of James's regnal style), is Adonis's preference for hunting over the oppressive ambience of the privy chamber, which (primrose bank notwithstanding), is the poem's implicit "scene."

The patron's continual challenge was to keep reasonably civil and at bay the predators who stalked him. For this skill Venus eulogizes Adonis: "The tiger would be tame and gently hear him. / If he had spoke, the wolf would leave his prey, / And never fright the silly lamb that day" (1096-98). But the more bold a suitor's "vulture thoughts," the more urgent the taming remonstrances had to be: "Remove your siege from my unyielding heart, / To love's alarms it will not ope the gate. / Dismiss your vows, your feigned tears, your flatt'ry. / For where a heart is hard they make no batt'ry" (423-26). It will chasten our criticism of Adonis to think, as we read this rejection of false-hearted courting, of Henry rejecting Falstaff in *2 Henry IV* or the King rejecting Wolsey in *Henry VIII*.

The present approach should not leave Adonis or the typical Renaissance patron unscathed. The climactic aspersion in Venus's oration—"Fie, lifeless picture . . . / Well-painted idol, image dull and dead" (211-12)—ought to remind us of many a Tudor aristocrat's impassive portrait. His suitor's love Adonis laughs to scorn, and scorn appears to have been the suitor's usual fare. Alvin Kernan ventures, "There is not . . . a single case of a totally satisfactory poet-patron relationship in the time of Elizabeth and James."[6] If this is accurate, Venus's ridicule, "Art thou obdurate, flinty, hard as steel?" (199), takes on a certain historical verisimilitude. For the purpose of Ovidian melodrama, Adonis's behavior betrays callow youth; for the purposes of my parable, it betrays the basic posture of what Autolycus in *The Winter's Tale* calls "court-contempt."

The Renaissance suitor was typically regarded as Adonis regards Venus: more as a wearisome nuisance than as a danger. The Renaissance poet was a species within this large genus. We can begin to consider his identity and status more directly by casting back over the poem for hints that among Venus's protean identities is that of the poet-at-court. An apt point of departure is George Puttenham's description of the poet's role in *The Arte of English Poesie:* "Our maker or Poet is appointed not for a judge, *but rather for a pleader,* and that of pleasant and lovely causes and nothing perillous." He adds that "lovely causes" ought to be spoken only "in the eare of princely dames, yong ladies, gentlewomen and courtiers, being all for the most part either meeke of nature, or of pleasant humour."[7] On this orthodox view of the poet's métier and proper audience Shakespeare founded the comic role reversal of *Venus and Adonis.* Venus is emphatically Puttenham's pleader: "impatience chokes her *pleading* tongue" (217); "love-sick love by *pleading* may be blest" (328); "Her *pleading* hath deserv'd a greater fee" (609). And Adonis is effeminized into the type of a meek young lady ("bashful shame" causing a "maiden burning" in his cheeks [49-50]) into whose ear Venus urges her "lovely cause." Thus, the muscular dame is thrust into the male world of "suit" (206), "theme" (422), and "treatise" (774), while Adonis is thrust into the grass, from whence many a maid arose with green sleeves and something else.

Venus's extemporal performances dominate the action: the *suasoria,* the lecture on poor Wat, the address to Death, and the prophecy on Love. And yet . . . the Goddess of Love's labors are lost. One reason for this is clear: She is also Dame Poetry and her ends are therefore perceived as dubious, her methods suspect. Puttenham explains why in the same chapter "Of Figures and figurative speaches," from which I just quoted. "Figures," he says, are "abuses or rather trespasses in speech, because they passe the ordinary limits of common utterance, and be occupied of purpose to deceive the ear and also the minde, drawing it from plainnesse and simplicitie to a certain doublenesse, whereby our talk is the more guilefull and abusing" (3:7). Venus's very first stanza, an ecstasy of "false compare" and "loud lying," identifies her as a purveyor of "figurative speaches" not to be trusted. Adonis calls her immodest, and this immodesty is, throughout the poem, bound up with ornate stylistic excess. Venus, like the ornate style, always errs on the side of overmuchness. Her theme is not merely handled but "over-handled" (770). Her grieving ululations become "tedious" and outwear the night (841), and her "copious stories" end "without audience, and are never done" (845-46).

Venus tries to tailor her plea to her audience ("to a pretty ear she tunes her tale" [74]), but Adonis quotes her bombast as guile and abuse. He dismisses it, as poetry was often dismissed in Shakespeare's time, as mere "feigned" emotion, "flatt'ry," and "deceiving harmony" of "mermaid's songs" (777, 781). Later, he rejects Venus's "idle" talk with phrases that recur in antipoetical literature: "I hate not love, but your device in love" (789); "Love is all truth, lust full of forged lies" (804).

The apostrophe to Death also excites suspicion, for it identifies Venus as a two-faced pleader: "Now she unweaves the web that she hath wrought" (991). She is clearly one of those described by Thomas Heywood in his defense of drama as part of a university curriculum: "It teacheth audacity to the bashful Grammarian . . . and makes him a bold Sophister, to argue *pro et contra* . . . [and] to defend any *axioma*."[8] Venus is such a bold sophister, and Shakespeare expected his readers to follow her figurative and logical audacities not only with pleasure but with Adonis's skepticism as well.

The difference, then, is that Shakespeare's audience was certain to relish Venus's magnificently unfeigned immodesty, just as it would take with salt the author's studiously feigned artistic modesty in the dedication to Southampton. Adonis, on the contrary, is of a different party—the solemn party of Egeus, Theseus, Olivia, Henry V, and all such as look down their noses on poetical stuff. He typifies the aristocrat with a tin ear for poetry and lacking any sense of verbal play. He smiles but once, and then only in disdain at Venus's suggestion (214) that, in the modern phrase, they "make out." As for "making" in the Renaissance sense of poetizing, Adonis proves a wretchedly inert audience. His disdain is "dull" (33) and in the presence of eloquence, he is as unmoved as Constable Dull is by the "great feast of language" in *Love's Labour's Lost*. His speeches, moreover, are tellingly plain and ridden with commonplaces, worthy of no one so much as Polonius. To Adonis, Venus's pleas merely display, in the phrases of Sonnet 82, rhetoric's "strained touches" and "gross painting."

The spirit of Venus and of poetry is "not gross to sink, but light" (150); Adonis's spirit is earthbound, phlegmatic. "What see'st thou in the ground?" Venus implores, "hold up thy head" (118). In this, Adonis is curiously like the boar that kills him: "this foul, grim, and urchin-snouted boar, / Whose *downward eye* still looketh for a grave, / Ne'er saw the beauteous livery that he wore" (1105-7). Adonis does not look up to poetry and reacts joylessly to the "beauteous livery" with which Venus apparels her emotions. It has not the aesthetic power to hold him, and so he breaks from its "sweet embrace" and pursues what is in effect the rival of Dame Poetry. Adonis is thus also like the despisers of poetry in Sidney's *Defence*, who "have so earth-creeping a mind that it cannot lift itself up to look to the sky of Poetry."⁹ Adonis's death represents especially poetic justice, for the boar thus becomes kin to Spenser's Blatant Beast in *The Faerie Queene*, yet another enemy of poetry: "Ne spareth he the gentle Poets rime, / But rends without regard of person or of time" (6.12.40).

As a mere juvenile too addicted to the outdoor life and too solemn for the "lovely causes" of a poem like the one he inhabits, Adonis is perfectly cast for Samuel Butler's famous aspersion: "Were I a schoolmaster I should think I was setting a boy a very severe punishment if I told him to read 'Venus and Adonis' in three sittings."¹⁰ Adonis cannot sit still for either the dalliance or the poetic virtuosity Venus has to offer. It is just as well that the boy was not destined for her. Had he lived, it seems he would have become an Egeus (who thinks of "rhymes" along with "gawds, conceits, / Knacks, trifles") or a Henry V (for whom a "rhyme is but a ballad")—a paramour with whom Venus would have been perfectly miserable.

Venus's poetical exertions are ultimately in vain. Her failure to achieve her desired end anticipates the experience of many poetizing figures in Shakespeare whom we shall consider in the following pages. Is it coincidental that these figures, indeed *all* figures in the canon who assume consciously or discernibly poetical postures, shoot wide of their mark and in one way or another prove "a motley to the view" (SON 110)? And is it coincidental that Shakespeare himself—at an early but now undiscoverable point in his London career—ceased to appear among the ranks of publishing professional poets and ceased taking part in the social economy of clientage, thereafter becoming by default what Holland called in the Folio a "Scenicke Poet"? This study will explain why I believe the answer to these questions is no.

The preceding pages disclose my thesis: In *Venus and Adonis* and (as we shall see shortly) in *Love's Labour's Lost* and the Sonnets, Shakespeare was creating, whether consciously or with gathering rue, imagined versions of the poet's life and methods that were far from sanguine. They constitute a "satire to decay," that is, a satire on "time's spoils" of the poetic tradition that was losing its hegemony on England's Parnassus in the early 1590s. The phrases just quoted are pertinently from Sonnet 100, in which the speaker says his muse is becoming "forgetful" and "resty." He is becoming doubtful of the expense of his "fury" on "some worthless song." Has he been "Dark'ning [his] pow'r to lend base subjects light"? Has his time been "idly spent" producing "gentle numbers"? Sonnet 100 is about its speaker's loss of poetic energy, concentration, direction, and confidence, just as the present study is, in its broadest measure, about the reasons why *any* Renaissance poet—not Shakespeare alone—might experience a similar sense of loss.

That some such loss occurred in Shakespeare's case is certain, unless we wish to venture hypotheses of either continued, but strictly private, circulation or lost editions of other poems. *Why* it occurred is another matter. S. Schoenbaum has observed that Shakespeare's life record is "destitute" of "intimate relations" and "seems to offer no insight into how the transient stuff of life was metamorphosed into transcendent achievements of art."[11] We shall never know precisely through what combination of domestic, psychological, artistic, political, financial, and serendipitous causes Shakespeare stopped writing ornate poems and sonnets and began concentrating more exclusively on works for the stage. Nor can we overlook a possible epidemiological cause for the early spurt of poetry: the severe plague of 1592-94 that curtailed public playing. But while the salient facts have been thoroughly besmeared by sluttish time, we need not be deterred from gathering what evidence we can from Shakespeare's works and from the contemporary literary scene in order to understand better the Renaissance poet's place, reputation, and self-image. The overarching purpose is, thus, to convey something of the professional, rather than the personal, reasons why any poet in Shakespeare's time (writing poetry as Shakespeare did early on) might have been impelled toward a crisis of confidence such as Sonnet 100 describes.

Though poetical self-confidence (the goddess's or the author's) is scarcely lacking in *Venus and Adonis*, the text nevertheless reflects on the poet's profession in several disconcerting ways. Most obviously and importantly, the poem forces us to confront a harsh fact: It indicates unambiguously that the world of Shakespeare's imaginary poet had little to do with the humanists' idealized version received from Cicero and Horace. John Day gives us a flavor of this ideal in *The Parliament of Bees* (circa 1608):

> The true Poet indeed doth scorne to guilde
> A cowards tomb with glories, or to build
> A sumptuous Pyramid of golden verse

Over the ruins of an ignoble herse.
His lines like his invention are borne free,
And both live blamelesse to eternity.[12]

These sentiments are of course rehearsed from Sidney's *Defence of Poesy*, where the poet is cast as "disdaining to be tied to any . . . subjection" and as "freely ranging within the zodiac of his own wit" (100). Sidney gave this poet a moral impetus by calling him to urge the reader's mind "forward to that which deserves to be called and accounted good" (112). The age's supreme humanist poet, Jonson, reiterated this view often; for example, when he described the true poet as able to "conceive, expresse, and steere the soules of men" (6: 282).

Venus and Adonis, however, does not take us in this noble direction. Comedy rarely does. Shakespeare delivers here a world brazen in more ways than one, not Sidney's golden world. The poem falls within the category Sidney disparaged as traveling "under the banner of unresistible love," and one imagines Venus herself as appearing remarkably like Sidney's "honey-flowing matron eloquence apparrelled, or rather disguised, in a courtesan-like painted affectation" (138). Shakespeare clearly intended to address his audience for the first time in print as Sidney's "good-fellow poet," who promises the reader only that he will be delighted.

Shakespeare succeeded primarily because he recognized that poetry, in the capital at which he had arrived, was a trivial pursuit—a view that a careful reading of the *Defence* along with the *Arcadia* and *Astrophil and Stella* would serve to corroborate.[13] If anything, Shakespeare's poem is a send-up of the highfalutin pretensions of the humanists who took poetry under their protection. His spirit is rather that of Folly, in Erasmus's mock encomium, when she utters her witty gibe at poets—a gibe nicely subversive of Day's glowing lines. Shakespeare's voluble goddess peers through the lines of this locus classicus from the antipoetical tradition: Poets' "whole aim is nothing but to pamper the ears of fools, and to do it with sheer trifles and absurd fables. And yet, relying on such trifles, it is wonderful to see how they promise immortality and a life like that of the gods, not only to themselves but also to others. Beyond all others this group is on intimate terms with *Philautia* [self-love] and *Kolakia* [flattery], and no other class of mortals worships me with more single-minded fidelity."[14] Vending her trifles and fables, Venus is on intimate terms with self-love and flattery, but Shakespeare's first public literary performance suggests that he too was on good terms with them. Richard Poirier, we have noted, has written that the performing poet is "at first so furiously self-consultive, so even narcissistic, and later so eager for publicity, love, and historical dimension."[15] This observation applies with special force to the author of *Venus and Adonis:* He is performing here very much as his heroine-alter ego does, furiously consulting his own motives, eager for publicity, and pressing to gain his historical dimension on the literary scene.

Important though the young poet may have perceived this performance to be for his budding career, he could have had no illusion about the audience it would please. We have heard Puttenham's testimony that poetry was not for "perillous" matters such as those "for the triall of life, limme, or livelyhood" but rather was destined for an audience—"Ladies and young Gentlewomen, or idle Courtiers" (3: 10)—disinclined to "sour and severe" contemplations. Shakespeare surely recognized that the poet, amid all the "perillous" machinations of the Tudor court, was bound to be numbered among its gauds and trifles. Jonson registered this point in one of his last masques, *Love's Welcome to Bolsover* (1634): "Rime will undoe you, and hinder your growth, and reputation in Court, more then any thing beside. . . . If you dable in Poetrie once, it is done of your being believ'd, or understood here" (7: 813). The career of at least one erstwhile poet aside from Donne bore out Jonson's observation. For it was only after John Davies ceased writing poetry around 1600 that his soaring fortunes elevated him to the posts of Solicitor General (1603) and Attorney General (1606) of Ireland and King's Sergeant (1612).

In his *Satyrical Essayes* (1615), John Stephens reiterated Jonson's view when he observed that "the deepest Poets have neglected verse, I meane the polished forme of verse." He then delineates the poet's typical métier in a way neatly descriptive of *Venus and Adonis:* "The relish of Poetry is a candied barke: an elegance so sweetned with apt phrase and illustration, as it excludes rough harshnesse and all mystery: controversies and Philosophicall questions bee therefore improper arguments for a Poeticall tractate."[16] Like many a youthful first performance, the poem is virtuosic but thoroughly conventional. The aesthetics Shakespeare inherited observed the axiom that nothing succeeds like excess, and excess he produced. He was willing, for the moment, to be written down among the crew of "*Venus*-brokers, and loves-shifting mates" (Samuel Rowlands), a producer of "ink-wasting toys" (Sidney).

Sidney says that the genuine poet disdains subjection; Day, that his invention is born free. Both views inform a golden age. Posterior literary criticism to the contrary, most English Renaissance observers looked about and concluded that their age was by no means golden: "these unhappy times" (Peele); "this ambitious age" (Burghley); "these times . . . most part sicke of the sullens" (Florio); "this apostate age" (Markham); "O ingratefull and damned age" (Meres); "the present jarre of this disagreeing age"

(Fletcher); "this *Wane* and *Crisis* of the world" (Reynolds); "this backward Age (too much declining from Vertue)" (Cornwallis); "this malicious age" (Drayton); "this iron and malitious age of ours" (Puttenham).[17] Poets in an iron age could not scorn subjection. The zodiac of their wit was likely centered on the sun's "sovereign eye" (SON 33) or the eye of some other powerful patron. In his dedication for *Venus and Adonis* the poet revels in subjection and explicitly acknowledges that his invention is born to humble servitude: "If the first heire of my invention prove deformed, I shall be sorie it had so noble a god-father." Venus herself, cloven to Adonis in her involuntary passion for incorporation, offers a brilliant image of the typical Renaissance poet's inability to disdain subjection. Her addiction to "the object [keen diction!] that did feed her sight" (822) reflects as well on the eagerness with which hungry clients sought nourishment from the powerful. After the catastrophe, Venus is filled with the failed suitor's feelings of loss. In this she is oddly but tellingly like Wolsey, the last of Shakespeare's proud but doomed suitors:

> O how wretched
> Is that poor man that hangs on princes' favors!
> There is, betwixt that smile we would aspire to,
> That sweet aspect of princes, and their ruin,
> More pangs and fears than wars or women have. [H8 3.2.366-70]

The second subject that *Venus and Adonis* opens to consideration concerns the motivation for poetizing. Why did poets write? and secondarily, why did they publish? The latter question is perhaps the easier to speculate about, as William Barley does in his *New Booke of Tabliture* (1596): "Bookes . . . that are compiled by men of divers gifts are published by them to divers endes: by some in desire of a gainefull reward, some for vaine ostentation, some for good will & affection, and some for common profit which by their workes may be gotten."[18] All these motivations are plausible; all of them probably played a part in Shakespeare's decision to risk opprobrium through publication and the enrollment of his name among a class of authors popularly "subject to scorne and derision" (Puttenham, [1: 8]).

The more difficult and complex question, Why write? is posed brilliantly by Sidney, a sonneteer who never dreamed of publishing. His *Astrophil and Stella* Sonnet 34 is cast in the form of a miniature debate or psychomachia between the poet-speaker and his common sense, or reason. Sidney conveys the poet's mixed feelings dramatically, but the poem's overall effect remains elusive. This is because the sonnet (which follows) displays the same "protracted ambiguities" about the poet's pastime that Ronald Levao observed in "Sidney's Feigned *Apology*":

> Come let me write, "And to what end?" To ease
>   A burthned hart. "How can words ease, which are
>   The glasses of thy dayly vexing care?"
> Oft cruell fights well pictured forth do please.   4
> "Art not asham'd to publish thy disease?"
>   Nay, that may breed my fame, it is so rare:
>   "But will not wise men thinke thy words fond ware?"
> Then be they close, and so none shall displease.   8
>   "What idler thing, then speake and not be hard?"
>   What harder thing then smart, and not to speake?
> Peace, foolish wit, with wit my wit is mard.
> Thus write I while I doubt to write, and wreake   12
>   My harmes on Ink's poore losse, perhaps some find
>   *Stella's* great powrs, that so confuse my mind.[19]

The poet is on the defensive here and must end the debate by main force (line 11). His responses to the interrogation, though, are worth rehearsing, for they offer some of the possible premises for a Renaissance poet's endeavor. The first suggestion, that poetry has a therapeutic value, would have struck sixteenth-century readers as dubious and as a fair warning of the sonnet's comic slant. Donne floated the notion with tongue also in cheek in "The Triple Fool": "I thought, if I could draw my pains / Through rhyme's vexation, I should them allay" (81). The desire to compose a poem virtually always preceded the emotion described in the poem (this leaves aside, of course, palpable authorial emotion unconsciously pervading some Renaissance poems—notably, certain of Wyatt's). The second response, that grim material can be rendered delightful by art, is more orthodox. We meet it also in the *Defence*: "As Aristotle saith, those things which in themselves are horrible, as cruel battles, unnatural monsters, are made in poetical imitation delightful" (114). The next responses are perhaps most to the point of *Venus and Adonis*. Sidney's poet will risk publication to gain renown for his cause. Just so, Venus lavishly publishes her passionate "disease" to Adonis, hoping thus to win his "great powrs" to her will. Unfortunately, Adonis—who plays the role of Sidney's "reason"—hears only "words fond ware." The offer (line 8) to keep the verse in aristocratic private circulation is, of course, too late for the extrovert goddess. Such an offer was perhaps also unthinkable to a young poet of "public means" from Stratford on the make in London.

    Sonnet 34 reaches a false climax in line 10, where the poet arrives back at his first argument. Then, the triple pun in line 11 not only acknowledges that the poet's cleverness has marred his senses, causing him to silence peremptorily the voice of reason, but also nicely conveys the impression that he is powerless to restrain his wittiness. That the speaker calls the voice of reason "foolish" is a perfect (and damning) Erasmian irony. This line is at once triumphant and ignominious: triumphantly captivating in its dexterity, but ignominiously specious in its evasive tautology. As a poem reflecting on the poet's life, *Venus and Adonis*, I have already urged, is likewise triumphant and ignominious. Indeed, Sidney's line 11 parallels one that summarizes the epyllion's action with similarly punning wit: "She's love, she loves, and yet she is not lov'd" (610). And many a wise critic has valued it merely as "words fond ware." The poet's methods of argument in Sidney's sonnet are like those of Venus: agile, witty, but transparent. When these methods fail, Venus must resort to a desperate trick to silence her interlocutor: at Adonis's harsh look, "she flatly falleth down" (463).

The actual climax of Sidney's sonnet belongs not to Venus's realm (self-doubt is not among her defects) but to that of her creator. The poet perseveres though the argument leaves him in a quandary: "Thus write I while I doubt to write." Much of the best poetry of the Renaissance was produced by poets who were critically aware of their dubious identity as poets—Wyatt, Sidney, Donne, and Shakespeare chief among them.[20] They, like the poet in Sonnet 34, were confused by the challenge of poetizing and suspicious that the loss of something more than mere pen and ink was bound up with the act. Shakespeare addressed his poetry to "great powrs," for example, though in the case of his sonnets we are not sure precisely who the powerful person was. That he wrote this poetry while "doubt[ing] to write" I am convinced. The first hints of this doubt heard in *Venus and Adonis* are perhaps not stentorian, but, as we shall see, they grow louder in subsequent works.

The goddess-poet's motive for producing her elaborate *suasoria*, however, is never in doubt; rather, it is richly impugned in her first three stanzas, a potpourri from the Petrarchan lover's "book of words" (ADO 1.1.307) that conceals a decidedly un-Petrarchan sex drive. Her beauteous speech o'erflourishes a predatory intent, as when, in lines 163-74, she follows Duke Vincentio's noble argument in *Measure for Measure:*

> Thyself and thy belongings
> Are not thine own so proper as to waste
> Thyself upon thy virtues, they on thee.
> Heaven doth with us as we with torches do,
> Not light them for themselves; for if our virtues
> Did not go forth of us, 'twere all alike
> As if we had them not. [1.1.29-35]

But what sinks Venus in Adonis's and the reader's minds is the Duke's next line: "Spirits are not finely touch'd, / But to fine issues." Venus's motive is not a fine one; nor was Shakespeare "finely touched" in the Duke's sense when he wrote *Venus and Adonis*.

In *Henry VIII* Wolsey ascribes his fall to "high-blown pride"—the same vainglorious urge to ostentation which I believe lies behind the poem. But the "pride" displayed is more complex, encompassing all of the senses in which Shakespeare was apt to employ this richly connotative epithet. First, there is the libidinous pride that superheats the poem's drama (cf. "The flesh being proud" [LUC 712]; "salt as wolves in pride" [OTH 3.3.404]). Also present, but for the sake of comedy not emphasized, is the darker "foul pride" (SON 144) of the seductress Eve. The poem's setting is one of vernal, fecund "pride" (see SON 104): "sappy plants" and "earth's increase." Additionally, "proud titles" (SON 25) of queen, god, and goddess figure in *Venus and Adonis*, as does "youth's proud livery" (SON 2): "never did he bless / My youth with his" (1119). And finally, there is the pride of the ornate-style poet, which the speaker of Sonnet 21 appears to abjure:

> So is it not with me as with that muse,
> Stirred by a painted beauty to his verse,
> Who heav'n itself for ornament doth use,
> And every fair with his fair doth rehearse—
> Making a couplement of *proud* compare
> With sun and moon, with earth and sea's rich gems,
> With April's first-born flow'rs, and all things rare
> That heaven's air in this huge rondure hems.

A similar mock renunciation occurs in Sonnet 130, where the speaker ostentatiously refuses to belie his lover with "false compare." *Venus and Adonis* itself is evidence enough that its author shared much of this multifarious pride, but with a self-consciousness that Venus as a comic figure does not betray. Shakespeare knew (and knew his audience would recognize) that his "compare" was both "proud" and "false" . . . and all the more to be relished.

Venus and Adonis has drawn our attention to two reasons why a Renaissance poet might have been impelled to a crisis of confidence: his habitation in a distinctly brazen world and his dubious motives for poetizing. But the poem also draws our attention to a third reason why Puttenham might have concluded that many would-be poets "have no courage to write and if they have, yet are they loath to be knowen of their skill" (1: 8): the resistance that the ornate style by its very nature elicits. Centuries earlier, Longinus described this resistance in his treatise *On the Sublime:* "The cunning use of figures is peculiarly subject to suspicion, and produces an impression of ambush, plot, fallacy. . . . [The hearer] at once feels resentment if, like a foolish boy, he is tricked by the paltry figures of the oratorical craftsman. Construing the fallacy into a personal affront, sometimes he becomes quite wild with rage, or if he controls his anger steels himself utterly against persuasive words."[21] This exactly captures Adonis's response to Venus's performance.

In *Astrophil and Stella* Sonnet 58, one of his finest, Sidney expresses just this danger of the ornate style:

> Doubt there hath bene, when with his golden chaine
>   The Oratour so farre men's harts doth bind,
>   That no pace else their guided steps can find,
> But as he them more short or slacke doth raine,
> Whether with words his soveraignty he gaine,
>   Cloth'd with fine tropes, with strongest reasons lin'd,
>   Or else pronouncing grace, wherewith his mind
> Prints his owne lively forme in rudest braine.

The sonnet ends with the speaker's mighty speech gaining him the opposite of his intentions: He woos "woe" but his sad words gain him only "ravishing delight." Venus suffers the opposite irony, wooing delight but suffering woe in the end. She risks the same strategic dangers of the ornate style as the speaker of Sonnet 58 and fails to heed Longinus's more discreet observation: "A figure is at its best when the very fact that it is a figure escapes attention." But Venus is supremely incapable of such self-conscious concealing discipline, just as she is incapable of reasoning as Bassanio does when he rejects the "gaudy gold" casket (and by extension the aureate style):

> So may the outward shows be least themselves—
> The world is still deceiv'd with ornament . . .
>
> . . . ornament is but the guiled shore
> To a most dangerous sea. [MV 3.2.73-74, 97-98]

As a result, Venus elicits from Adonis just the sort of hostility that Longinus predicts. Her style is quoted as "device" and—like a suddenly backlighted stage scrim—becomes perfectly transparent, thus submitting her fallacious arguments to Adonis's view: "O strange excuse, / When reason is the bawd to lust's abuse!" (791-92). Shakespeare himself, of course, remains unscathed, his stylistic "golden chaine" (to revert to Sidney's sonnet) being so obviously ornamental rather than fettering.

Venus and Adonis and The Rape of Lucrece are twin peaks of Shakespeare's ornate style. He never again repeated their richly "strained touches" because his heart, one is tempted to believe, bent away from them and prevented him from mining for very long such veins of "gaudy gold." Moving now from the long poems to Love's Labour's Lost and the Sonnets, we can begin to sense that Shakespeare may have shared the view expressed in one Renaissance courtesy treatise: "words would be plaine."[22] His impetus was away from the "compound" (see SON 76.4, 118.6, 125.7) and toward the "simple" (SON 66.11). His instincts led him, it appears, toward the conveyance of artistic and humane truth "without all ornament, itself and true" (SON 68). There can thus be but one truly melancholy footnote to Shakespeare's most insouciant, complexly modulated—indeed, Mozartean—work: our sense that once he left the ornate, youthful vanity of Venus and Adonis he could never return.

⧼⧽

The first indubitable sign that he would not return is Love's Labour's Lost. It may be, as C. L. Barber concludes, that Shakespeare created this play "out of courtly pleasures" or, as G. K. Hunter suggests, that it "exposes to our admiration the brilliant life of a highly civilized community."[23] But if we look at the play carefully, keeping in mind the identity of the contemporary poet, we shall come away questioning the wisdom of admiring the poet's art. "Are we betrayed thus to thy overview?" the King asks Berowne after the latter has whipped royal hypocrisy a while. I will urge in the following discussion that the playwright in his first great comedy similarly betrays the ornate-style poet to a caustic overview.

Viewing Love's Labour's Lost as we have viewed Venus and Adonis is not novel. Some time ago Walter Oakeshott wrote, "the play, in both plot and sub-plot, is about the writing of love poetry," and others have pursued this path.[24] But I believe the play's extensive textual and subtextual comment on the contemporary poetical scene warrants further attention. A suggestive way to begin is to notice that the play's premise can be found readymade in a chapter from Puttenham on "figures, and how they serve in exornation of language." Here Puttenham reminds us of poetry's intended audience ("Ladies and young Gentlewomen, or idle Courtiers") and purposes: "to become skilful in their owne mother tongue, and for their private recreation to make now and then ditties of pleasure." The ultimate purpose is to learn "beau semblant, the chiefe profession as well of Courting as of poesie"; Puttenham then adds—and here the humor of the play begins: "to such manner of mindes nothing is more combersome then tedious doctrines and schollarly methodes of discipline" (3: 10). Berowne knows that courtiership and study are as fire and ice, but the academy is established in spite of his warnings.

The humor of the oxymoronic notion of a courtiers' academy was well founded in stereotypes of literary tradition and historical reality. Philibert de Vienne, in his satirical *Philosopher of the Court* (1575), observed that good courtiers will scorn "that Academicall Goddess" Pallas; and Dekker and Chettle wrote in *Patient Griesill* (1603) of "those changeable Silke gallants" who "in a verie scurvie pride, scorne all schollers, and reade no bookes but a looking glasse."[25] On the other hand, Berowne's aspersions about those who "painfully . . . pore upon a book" and "continual plodders" who ransack "others' books" are part of a long tradition of condescension toward the collegiate enterprise that stretches back to Chaucer's Clerk. If to feed on the "dainties that are bred in a book" (4.2.24) causes one to become a Holofernes, then one is almost happy to remain of Constable Dull's party. "He hath not eat paper," says the curate Nathaniel of him with ghastly poetic license.

In *Love's Labour's Lost* the comic concept of an academy presumes a view much like that expressed in Gosson's *Schoole of Abuse:* "If it be the duety of every man in a common wealth, one way or other to bestirre his stoomps I cannot but blame those lither contemplators very much, which sit concluding of Sillogismes in a corner, which in a close studye in the Universitye coope themselves up xl yeres together studying al things, & professe nothing . . . To continue so long without mooving, to reade so muche without teaching, what differeth it from a dumbe Picture, or a dead body?"[26] The four men of the play propose to become such anchorite "bookmates," and the play's action centers (in Gosson's *déclassé* phrase) on the very tardy bestirring of their stumps in several ways . . . most pertinently by facing up to the constraints of the ornate style's golden fetters. Puttenham's treatise discourses pertinently on the ways a poet's labors can be won and lost, and is the period's most expansive, important such document. Therefore, I shall briefly explore several ways that *Love's Labour's Lost* reflects on, and is illuminated by, *The Arte of English Poesie*.

Poetizing figures in the play all appear to have arrived—as the ornate tradition in sixteenth-century poetry itself had arrived—at Oscar Wilde's conclusion: "The first duty in life is to be as artificial as possible." (He adds: "What the second duty is no one has as yet discovered.")[27] One hopes, with little conviction, that the men might have discovered more important duties during their three-year sequestration. Their unlooked-for education under the ladies' tutelage, however, leads them to the brink of several renunciations: of self-indulgence, of idle withdrawal from a world filled with "speechless sick" and "groaning wretches," and of rhyme and "three-pil'd hyperboles." Indeed, Shakespeare works as hard to typecast the men as poets as he does to cast them as "*beau* semblant" courtiers. They are, as Puttenham categorizes them, among the breed of poets who have "sought the favor of faire Ladies, and coveted to bemone their estates at large, and the perplexities of love in . . . pitious verse" (1: 11). Nothing captures the notion that these courtiers are as their poetry is better than Puttenham's description of the way "amorous affections and allurements" ought to be penned. This, he says, "requireth a forme of Poesie variable, inconstant, affected, curious and most witty of any others" (1: 22).

Berowne, whose gifts are manifestly like those of the author of *Venus and Adonis*, leads the way in this poetic métier. His "sweet and voluble" discourse we may for brevity's sake accept as the quintessence of all that the King and other lords strive for. His voice consistently reiterates the Petrarchan axiom that loving and poetizing are conjoined. The precedence in his capitulation to Rosaline is telling:"Well, I will love, *write*, sigh, pray, sue, and groan" (3.1.201). "By heaven, I do love," he swears, "and it hath taught me to rhyme" (4.3.12). As he overhears the poetry of his cohorts, he exclaims "O! rhymes are guards [embroideries] on wanton Cupid's hose" (4.3.56). Later in the scene infatuation is made the sine qua non for poetry: "Never durst poet touch a pen to write / Until his ink were temper'd with Love's sighs" (4.3.343-44). This equivalence is wittily conveyed when the King asks Berowne if the "lines" he has just shredded betrayed "some love." Berowne retorts "Did they?" and in a just-listen-to-this fashion uncorks a sample worthy of light and aspiring Venus:

> Who sees the heavenly Rosaline,
> That, like a rude and savage man of Inde,
> At the first opening of the gorgeous east,
> Bows not his vassal head, and strooken blind,
> Kisses the base ground with obedient heart?
> What peremptory eagle-sighted eye
> Dares look upon the heaven of her brow,
> That is not blinded by her majesty? [4.3.218-25]

This not only leaves the King in no doubt about Berowne's amorous and poetic fury but also obviates the need for us to suffer through his flaccid sonnet again.

Berowne's achievements in this vein are variable. For example, we learn from Rosaline that he has had his triumphs, and he certainly has some fine moments during the action which put the best face on the ornate style.

These epitomize the "last and principall figure of our poeticall Ornament" that Puttenham discusses, namely, *exargasia*, or the "Gorgious." This figure "polish[es] our speech . . . with copious and pleasant amplifications and much varietie of sentences" (3: 20). Puttenham even suggests that it is not so much a figure as "a masse of many figurative speaches, applied to the bewtifying of our tale or argument."[28] In this sense, we can happily call "gorgeous" Berowne's arguments against the academy in the first scene, his soliloquy on love, his "salve for perjury," and his mock renunciation of fancy words.

But exponents of the gorgeous style always risked the danger of going too far. Venus is blithe about this risk, but Puttenham and Shakespeare were not. Berowne, unfirm in this knowledge, suffers some ignominious moments. For example, at the end of his envoi to the gorgeous style, he can't help employing the gallicism *sans*, and Rosaline cuts him dead: "Sans 'sans,' I pray you." Berowne apologizes, "Yet I have a trick / Of the old rage" (5.2.416-18). This throwaway exchange, one might say, encompasses the whole play: It is no easy task to learn not to mar either reason or integrity with wittiness once one has mastered the modes of ornate-style wit. The ladies appear to think that calming the "old rage" will take at least a year.

The risk of going too far can be more specifically explored if we look at the figure of *periphrasis*, or "ambage," where "we go about the bush, and will not in one or a few words expresse that thing which we desire to have knowen"; Puttenham notes that this is "one of the gallantest figures among the poets so it be used discreetly and in his right kinde" (3: 18). What, then, are we to make of this periphrastic binge performed by Berowne?

> This wimpled, whining, purblind, wayward boy,
> This signor junior, giant-dwarf, dan Cupid;
> Regent of love rhymes, lord of folded arms,
> The anointed sovereign of sighs and groans,
> Liege of all loiterers and malcontents,
> Dread prince of plackets, king of codpieces,
> Sole imperator and great general
> Of trotting paritors. . . . [3.1.176-83]

Either we can follow our evil exargastic angel and admire its exhilaratingly immodest show of imagination, or we can follow our good Baconian (nay Hobbesian) angel and say this is too much, and condemn it as an example of Sidney's "swelling phrases" of the love poets.[29] This is the auditor's or reader's choice, but no one will deny that it is a close call. Berowne here risks that his *periphrasis* (like *any* figure so flogged) will shade into two of the "vices and deformities" of poetry that Puttenham particularly condemns. The first is *periergia*, or "Over labour," which occurs when the poet displays "overmuch curiositie and studie to shew himselfe fine in a light matter" (3: 22). The second carries the impressive title of *bomphiologia*, or "Pompious speech," the result of "using such bombasted wordes, as seeme altogether farced full of winde" (3: 22). Not a few times, the men aim at the gorgeous only to hit the overlabored and pompous: The King's worst hour comes at 5.2.730-41; Berowne's, at 5.2.759-66. Their efforts are thus quite properly rated by the ladies, in keeping with Puttenham's diction, as "bombast" (5.2.771)—a noteworthy epithet that figures in Greene's famous 1592 attack on Shakespeare as supposing he could "bombast out a blanke verse as the best of you." [30]

The foregoing are aesthetic hazards attending the ornate style. More disconcerting are the play's allusions to its ethical hazards. Shakespeare forces us to view the men as poets; he also forces us to view poets as corrupters. The ornate balloon Armado proclaims early in the action, "My love is most immaculate white and red," to which the plain-style pin Moth replies: "Most maculate thoughts, master, are masked under such colours" (1.2.86-88). Of the poet's maculate thoughts and masks much will be said in chapters 4 and 5, but here we may observe that Moth's "colours" are at once those of cosmetics, of love's irresistible banner, and of ornate rhetoric itself. [31] The poetical "colours" of the men in *Love's Labour's Lost* hide "maculate" thoughts. The thread that runs through the advance publicity for Longaville, Dumain, and Berowne is the way their verbal skills disguise dangerous traits. Longaville's "soil" is a blunt and sharp-edged "will"; Dumain has a poor knowledge of "ill" and a habit of twisting it into goodness by his "wit"; some ears "play truant" to Berowne's tales, while others are "ravished." By play's end, when Berowne admits that "love is full of unbefitting strains; / All wanton as a child, skipping and vain," we have been carefully prepared for a shock of recognition: the ornate style has behaved in exactly the same way. The men have madly come to believe what they have so facilely expressed in auricular figures: "Vows are but breath, and breath a vapor is" (4.3.65).

One might conclude, in a generous spirit, that the men have blithely slipped into such folly unconsciously. But hints abound of their awareness of the unbefitting strains of their language and vows. The Princess says to Berowne, "you can cog [cheat]" (5.2.235), and cheating is perhaps the plainest word for their attempt to change reality through language. Berowne exemplifies this posture when he tries to "prove" Rosaline fair rather than dark-skinned simply by the force of assertion (4.3.271). Elsewhere, Shakespeare's diction reveals such seriousness when, in succession, the King asks Berowne to "prove / Our loving lawful, and our faith not torn"; Longaville requests "some tricks, some quillets, how to cheat the devil"; and Dumain, with greater candor, implores "some salve for perjury" (4.3.281-86).

Puttenham stands ready with the kindest possible term for the weaseling these requests elicit. This is the figure of *meiosis*, or the "Disabler." "We use it," he says, "to excuse a fault, and to make an offence seeme lesse then it is, by giving a terme more favorable and of lesse vehemencie then the troth requires. . . . [It is for] making a great matter seeme small, and of litle difficultie" (3: 19). The logic and diction of all the men's poems are thus "disabling," and we find the men hard at it up to the very end, performing further variations on the theme of their awful poems and trying to convince the ladies that "falsehood, in itself a sin, / Thus purifies itself and turns to grace." This is Berowne's poetical and moral nadir. Of course, the glory of the denouement is that the ladies judge the men to be *literally* disabled as suitors by their attempts to make a great matter (the breaking of "heavenly oaths, vow'd with integrity") seem of little difficulty.

The action does not end with the facile multiple coupling of "an old play" (5.2.864) because, aesthetically speaking, the poetic styles of the men and the women differ so radically. The men expound the gorgeous style of *exargasia*; the women (though capable of *exargasia* when mirth is becoming) expound the more Demosthenic style of *energia*, which Sidney praised for conveying passions more forcibly than the "fiery speeches" of love poets (*Defence*, 137). These stylistic twain cannot supply the basis for a "world-without-end bargain" (5.2.779). Puttenham describes the style of *energia* as "wrought with a strong and vertuous operation" and as producing "speaches inwardly working a stirre to the minde" (3: 3)—an apt summary of the virtuous but spirited seriousness with which the women comport themselves on their embassy to Navarre. The gorgeous style "invegleth the judgement of man, and carieth his opinion this way and that" (Puttenham, 1: 4), but the women are too perspicuous to be inveigled. Their ear is for matter from the heart and for "telling true." They therefore resolve: "to their penn'd speech render we no grace" (5.2.147).

The women are sharp critics of the ornate style, with its "huge translation of hypocrisy, / Vilely compil'd, profound simplicity" (5.2.51-52). They are sensible enough to recognize that, as Giles Fletcher observed in a preface to a sonnet sequence, "a man may write of love, and not bee in love."[32] But the women's attack on poetry finally goes deeper—and far beyond the unquestioning bounds of the affable Puttenham. For an attack more in tune with the women we must turn instead to this suspenseful period from Sidney's *Astrophil and Stella* Sonnet 15:

> You that do search for everie purling spring,
>> Which from the ribs of old *Parnassus* flowes,
>> And everie floure, not sweet perhaps, which growes
> Neare therabout, into your Poesie wring;
> You that do Dictionerie's methode bring
>> Into your rimes, running in ratling rowes[;]
>> You that poore *Petrarch's* long deceased woes,
> With new-borne sighes and denisend wit do sing[:]
>> You take wrong wayes, those far-fet helpes be such,
>> As do bewray a want of inward tuch.

Of this same want of inward touch the men are convicted in the play. They take "wrong ways" not only with their academy but also with language and vows. They are indiscriminate in their "fairing" of reality with the "bedecking ornaments" of praise. Indeed, the word *fair*, played on constantly by the men, occurs a Shakespearean-record fifty-six times in *Love's Labour's Lost*.[33] But the women finally challenge the men for this idle and conceited "heresy in fair" (4.1.22), this subjection to the ornate ethos. Their objections to this style are thus akin to those of Nietzsche: "By images and similes we convince, but we do not prove. . . . It is easier to learn how to write the grand style than how to write easily and simply." And Nietzsche then adds the ethical observation that is everywhere implicit in *Love's Labour's Lost*: "The reasons for this are inextricably bound up with morality."[34] The women set the men to learn this hard lesson.

There is nothing in *Love's Labour's Lost* of more illuminating and far-reaching consequence for the rest of the canon than its systematic anatomy of what Puttenham called the "vices and deformities" of the Parnassan style. For in his succeeding plays, Shakespeare on countless occasions—some memorable, others by-the-way—deployed the bombasted, exargastic style quite calculatedly, often setting it in tension against the plain, energetic (and usually virtuous) style. Numerous such occasions will be noted in subsequent chapters, but it is worth offering a few examples at the outset. In the companion play to *Love's Labour's Lost*, Romeo exults just before his marriage ceremony in a style purloined from the aesthetic of *Venus and Adonis*:

> Ah, Juliet, if the measure of thy joy
> Be heap'd like mine, and that thy skill be more
> To blazon it, then sweeten with thy breath
> This neighbor air, and let rich music's tongue
> Unfold the imagin'd happiness that both
> Receive in either by this dear encounter. [2.6.24-29]

Juliet's response, implying that Romeo is still courting "by the book," echoes the Princess's many deflations: "Conceit more rich in matter than in words / Brags of his substance, not of ornament." Unlike Romeo, Lucentio in *The Taming of the Shrew* never breaks out of his Petrarchism (for example, "I saw her coral lips to move, / And with her breath she did perfume the air" [1.1.174-75]), Shakespeare intending him as a foil for worldly wise Petruchio's plain-style vigor. Similar stylistic counterpoise underlies more momentously the speeches of Goneril and Regan (who not only wear what is "gorgeous" but speak gorgeously) and those of Cordelia in *King Lear's* first scene.

Holofernes, that tipsy imbiber of ink, and Armado, so heavily perfumed by the "oderiferous flowers" of rhetoric, deserve our pause at this point. For if the four courtiers are the *reductio ad absurdum* of the ornate style, then these two figures represent its *reductio ad nauseam*. They are Shakespeare's most flamboyant contribution to the tradition of satirical attack on "rude rhymers." Puttenham notes that anyone who is "studious in th'Arte or shewes him selfe excellent in it, they call him in disdaine a *phantasticall*" (1: 8), and both Holofernes and Boyet call Armado a "phantasime" with such disdain (4.1.98; 5.1.19). Though these characters are easy both to disdain and to enjoy, their style and artistic premises shadow those of the four aristocrats with remarkable consistency. And many a fine small touch ties together the merely absurd and the nauseating in poetical style, for example when both Armado and Holofernes desire to be the "extemporal" performer that Berowne truly is (1.2.174; 4.2.49) or when Holofernes prefigures Berowne in affecting the word *sans* (5.1.81).

But the essence of Holofernes' and Armado's comedy is a kind of ornate-style slapstick. The pedant's credo is a parody of standard Renaissance literary theory: "This is a gift I have, simple, simple; a foolish extravagant spirit, full of forms, figures, shapes, objects, ideas, apprehensions, motions, revolutions: these are begot in the ventricle of memory, nourished in the womb of *pia mater*, and delivered upon the mellowing of ocasion" (4.2.66-71). This is laughably mechanical, but such is the nature of Holofernes' folly. For him words are things in themselves, not means of communicating. He stands at the opposite end of the spectrum from the other men, taking language and words with deadly and tedious literalness. It would never occur to him to *play* with language, and indeed he never indulges in the play's primary mode, the pun. Even Constable Dull does that, if only once (4.2.64).

In Holofernes and Armado the snobberies of the ornate style are also vastly inflated: Holofernes rises in profound grandeur over the "unpolished, uneducated, unpruned" Dull; Armado assures the pedant, "We will be singled from the barbarous" (4.2.7; 5.1.76).[35] The two seek to rise, if not by blood, then by "high-born words" (1.1.171). Puttenham expressed disgust at the use of "ink-horne termes" and such "straunge and unaccustomed wordes" as *audacious* (Nathaniel actually uses the word), *egregious*, and *compatible* (3: 4); imagine his reaction to *remuneration, preambulate, intituled, enfreedoming,* and *peregrinate!* In the poetical jargon uttered by Armado *(l'envoi, enigma, epilogue, catastrophe, epitheton)* and by Holofernes *(epitaph, staff, stanze, verse, accent, canzonet, figures, apostrophus)* there is also satire on the newly ordained tradition of English theory. These two have read their Gascoigne, Webbe, and Puttenham.

One finds Holofernes and Armado's habits everywhere in Puttenham's discussion of the "vices" of the poet's craft (3:22): *metalepsis,* or "Farrefet" ("when we had rather fetch a word a great way off then to use one nerer hand"); *sinonimia,* or "Store" ("when so ever we multiply our speech by many words or clauses of one sence"); *cacozelia,* or "Fonde affectation" ("when we affect new words and phrases"); *soraismus,* or the "Mingle mangle" ("when we make our . . . writinges of sundry languages"); *tautologia,* or "Selfe saying" ("too much delight . . . with wordes beginning all with a letter"); and most generally, *pleonasmus,* or "Too full speech" ("the Poet or makers speech becomes vicious and unpleasant by nothing more than by using too much surplusage").

Finally, though, Shakespeare thrusts beyond the diffident, ingratiating *Arte* of Puttenham (whose ideal poet, in any case, would perform very much like the Princess's "please-man" Boyet) and achieves a more perspicuous, indeed Sidneian gravity. Armado, the "little academe's" prospective *machine à plaisir,* asks in soliloquy, "How can that be true love which is falsely attempted?" One of the play's several serious answers to this question is translated into aesthetic terms. (And we shall soon see how this question, similarly translated, animates the Sonnets as well.) The women answer in unvarnished terms: true love cannot be falsely attempted. The men's falsity is principally suggested through their identity as poets.[36] Like Sidney, they have adopted the role of poet, but unlike him they have lost conscious (and self-conscious) control of this role. It has overwhelmed their true selves or, rather, has inhibited the growth of their true selves. The men lack Sidney's ironic, self-critical detachment and are therefore unable to mount anything like a Sidneian defense against the women's indictment. "Dear guiltiness" is the final judgment to which they must answer.

Love's Labour's Lost can thus be viewed as a spectacular comic second to the motion of Sidney's few paragraphs in which he rejects the "lyrical kind of songs and sonnets" and all "such writings as come under the banner of unresistible love." For Sidney, such poetical exertions "miss the right use of the material point of Poesy," and, having isolated in his oration poetry's right use, he urges the reader in his peroration, "no more to laugh at the name of poets, as though they were next inheritors to fools, no more to jest at the reverent title of a rhymer" (138, 141). But, because the men of *Love's Labour's Lost* are very far from knowledge of poetry's proper use, Shakespeare urges his audience precisely to laugh and jest at poets. As he wrote, though, he must have savored the Erasmian irony of dispraising poetry virtuosically on poetry's own ground, with many a taffeta phrase, many a well-culled *epitheton*, and more than a thousand lines of rhymed couplets— by far the Shakespearean record. In this play, as Granville-Barker succinctly observed, "Shakespeare the poet had his fling."[37]

I hasten to add that the laughter and jests at poetry's expense ought to be projected with a sense of balance between the acerbic and the amiable. Is the play's ostentation "maggot" (5.2.409), or "delightful" (5.1.106)? A performance will succeed insofar as it allows the audience to arrive at both conclusions simultaneously. We should harbor a sneaking desire to be a Berowne, but we should not be ashamed, amid all the trivial flippancy, to see ourselves as Constable Dull too. Holofernes says of Dull, "Thou hast spoken no word all this while," to which he sensibly and honestly replies, with the play's funniest line: "Nor understand none neither, sir" (5.1.144-45). *Love's Labour's Lost*, as many have observed, ends on a note of balance with the "dialogue" of the spring and winter songs, but we can venture a more general conclusion: The play as a whole is a remarkably balanced dialogue about the pleasures and pitfalls of the ornate style, just as, in broader measure, it presents a dialogue between the voice of Roger Ascham ("Ye know not what hurt ye do to learning that care not for words but for matter") and the voice of Sir Francis Bacon ("The first distemper of learning [occurs] when men studie words and not matter").[38]

Many vignettes from *Love's Labour's Lost* lead one to think of moments in the Sonnets. Armado's frequent *sweet*-ening of his conversation reminds one of the many *sweets* in the Sonnets. Constable Dull reminds one of the speaker who excuses his "tongue-tied muse" in Sonnet 85 and worries that "blunt invention" is "dulling [his] lines" in Sonnet 103. Berowne overhears Longaville's sonnet and hoots, "pure, pure idolatry"—which echoes Sonnet 105's "Let not my love be called idolatry." Berowne's very last Petrarchan gasp—"Behold the window of my heart, my eye"—draws the mind forcibly to the preposterously exacerbated image in Sonnet 24: "my bosom's shop . . . That hath his windows glazèd." And many have noticed similarities between the speaker's and the men's persuasive tactics. Some points of comparison, however, go beyond these superficial touches to significant characteristics of the ornate poetic style that, I believe, are identifiable in the Sonnets. These deserve our attention now. (In chapter 5 we shall return to the Sonnets to explore how the poet, his self-identification with ornate techniques consolidated, behaves amid the social premises and processes of courtiership.)

The most obvious feature exhibited both in *Love's Labour's Lost* and in the Sonnets is the vulnerability to corruption of a style whose *raison d'être* is essentially paradiastolic, or praise giving. Puttenham describes the figure of *paradiastole*, or "the Curry-favell," as the employment of any "moderation of words" that tends "to flattery, or soothing, or excusing" (3: 17); within these three categories, the four men spend all their loving labors. However, these labors are lost because the women—unlike the Young Man—are not "fond on praise" (SON 84). Indeed, they submit the men's soothing flattery and excuses to a wilting attack worthy of Bacon's pronouncement (aptly, in his essay "Of Fame") that "we are infected with the style of the poets." This infection is the play's true plague. It is not too much to say that *Love's Labour's Lost* presents an extended meditation on the corruption of the favor-currying ornate style. After all, in many important respects, the play centers on the Princess's somber thoughts on the great, inevitable fact of courtly life: the aristocrat's "giving hand, though foul, shall have fair praise" (see 4.1.21-35).

The speaker of the Sonnets shows on many occasions the Princess's keen awareness of that "monarch's plague," flattery. The premises of her speech on the dangers both to the praiser and the praised are especially richly evoked in Sonnet 96, its simile reminding us so well of Queen Elizabeth's powerful and often corrupting sway over her courtiers: "As on the finger of a throned queen / The basest jewel will be well esteemed, / So are those errors that in thee are seen, / To truths translated, and for true things deemed."[39]

Frequently the speaker presents himself in the posture of the Berowne who bends his aureate skill to dubious ends: "Myself corrupting salving thy amiss" (SON 35), "proving" the Young Man "virtuous" though he is "forsworn" (SON 88), and making his "faults" into "graces" (SON 96). Indeed, one might well describe the speaker of the Sonnets as possessing the rhetorical gifts of Berowne and the self-awareness, or "conscience," of the Princess. The inevitable result of this combination, as we shall see in chapter 5, is the Sonnets' more complex, conflicted presentation of the courting poet's experience.

In more elaborate ways the Sonnets render other troubling consequences of the poet's style, which are but lightly touched in *Love's Labour's*

Lost. One is the sheer, sweaty effort of writing "letters full of love" in the Petrarchan style. Although Shakespeare does not present the men's struggles to write their poems, the strain of composition is amusingly apparent in their lines. Longaville hints at his own difficulties: "I fear these stubborn lines lack power to move . . . These numbers will I tear, and write in prose" (4.3.53-55). Dumain soon enters with his poem, his mind still whirring with leftover shreds of false compare, but he too lacks confidence in his work and says he will send "something else more plain" (4.3.119).

In the *Arcadia*, Sidney allows us to peer over the shoulder of an ornate stylist in the throes of poetical creation, and I think the picture is a plausible one for imagining the four courtiers—or any Renaissance poet—aiming with pen in hand "for the numbers that Petrarch flow'd in" (ROM 2.4.38). Dorus is here composing in the elegiac mode for Pamela:

Never pen did more quakingly perform his office; never was paper more double-moistened with ink and tears; never words more slowly married together, and never the Muses more tired than now with changes and rechanges of his devices; fearing how to end before he had resolved how to begin, mistrusting each word, condemning each sentence. This word was not significant; that word was too plain: this would not be conceived; the other would be ill-conceived: here sorrow was not enough expressed; there he seemed too much for his own sake to be sorry: this sentence rather showed art than passion; that sentence rather foolishly passionate than forcibly moving. At last, marring with mending and putting out better than he left, he made an end of it and being ended, was divers times ready to tear it.[40]

Shakespeare's sonnets are rich in glancing allusions to this anxiety-ridden task of transferring emotions, ideas, arguments, even truth from *pia mater* into poetry without perversion or loss of life. Three times (SON 17, 83, 86) Shakespeare puns on the notion that his pen is producing not so much a *tome* as a *tomb*, an idea that was to return in *All's Well That Ends Well*: "The mere word's a slave / Debosh'd on every tomb" (2.3.137-38). The speaker in Sonnet 38 implies that the Young Man's living "argument" cannot be so much expressed as merely "rehearsed" when it assumes the form of ink on "vulgar paper." In Sonnet 53 the speaker admits that to capture the Young Man's beauty in the usual ornate fashion ("Describe Adonis . . . ") is to achieve but a "poorly imitated" counterfeit. And Sonnet 100 conveys a sense of the ornate-style poet's harsh self-criticism in the cold light of dawn, after poetic fury has evanesced. Has the speaker merely produced "some worthless song"?

The self-doubt of Sidney's Dorus, too, is often and famously present in the Sonnets: the speaker "laboring for invention" (SON 59); depressed that his lines are "barren of new pride" (SON 76); and blaming his "pupil pen"

(SON 16), "poor rude lines" (SON 32), and "slight muse" (SON 38). But there are more than a few hints that in the speaker's heart of hearts lies Longaville's urge toward prose, and Dumain's toward "something else more plain." For example, when the speaker rejects "barren rhyme" (SON 16) and "stretched meter" (SON 17) or prefers "simple truth" (SON 66), "true plain words" (SON 82), and "simple savor" (SON 125).

The second troubling aspect of the poet's life introduced in the play and carried further in the Sonnets is the recognition voiced memorably some years later by the Clown in *Twelfth Night:* "Words are very rascals . . . words are grown so false, I am loath to prove reason with them" (3.1.21-25). *Love's Labour's Lost* is not only about the frailty of the men's oaths but about the frailty of words themselves. Many have made this point, notably James Calderwood, who observed (apropos of the Princess squelching the King for nicknaming virtue) that the play "calls attention to the dissolution of language."[41] This dissolution occurs when words run away—or are stolen by a punster—from their speakers. Many of the play's comic wild-goose chases focus on the antics of rascally words: *remuneration, haud credo, fair, big,* and others. Behind this fun, though, lies a searching awareness of the worthlessness of words *(rascal* was the hunting term for a lean, worthless deer), especially words from the pens of honey-tongued poets most likely to "dally nicely" with them and "make them wanton" (TN 3.1.14-15). The implied question here and so often elsewhere in Shakespeare is Sidney's "What may words say, or what may words not say?" (*Astrophil* Sonnet 35).

In his play Shakespeare was able to convey with much gaiety both the richness ("a great feast of language") and the hollowness ("the alms-basket of words") of the ornate style. Sidney's rhetorical question does not impinge Jaques-like on the play's ebullient spirits and language, but it does loom to more melancholy effect in the back of the speaker's mind in the Sonnets. Perhaps it is even paraphrased by the question that opens Sonnet 108: "What's in the brain that ink may character . . . ?" This question was particularly pressing for a poet "doing" his mind "in character" (SON 59) in a sonnet sequence, because from his vantage point the richness and hollowness of the style were both clearly visible.[42] Sonnet 85 eloquently expresses these potently mixed feelings about the ornate style that are so effectively neutralized by the comedy of *Love's Labour's Lost.* The octave elaborately describes "richly compiled" verse that is "polished" by a "well-refinèd pen"—poetry, we might imagine, like *Venus and Adonis* or Sonnets 18, 30, or 55. Yet in the sestet the speaker condemns it all as mere "breath of words" and in effect prefers the honest silence of a Costable Dull to the "glozes" of a Berowne.

This oscillating attitude toward the ornate style permeates the Sonnets. For example, one of them accounts as "lean penury" a poet's inability to lend "some small glory" to his subject (SON 84); another accounts all display of poetic "glory" as vanity: "O let me true in love but truly write" (SON 21). In one sonnet the speaker proudly declares in perfect plain style (not once but twice), "you are you" (SON 84), but in many other sonnets he prefers the "virtuous lie" of dubious similes over the plain style's "niggard truth" (SON 72). What could the ornate style say? and what could it not say? The speaker's answers to these questions are extravagantly, almost schizophrenically, variable. The ornate style nourishes him as fitfully as do his thoughts of the Young Man: "Thus do I pine and surfeit day by day, / Or gluttoning on all, or all away" (SON 75).

The paradox of this couplet is the paradox of the ornate style, which is very rich and can be truly enjoyed as *Venus and Adonis* must be enjoyed: by surfeiting. But the "compound sweet" of the style is hardly nourishing. Indeed, the end of *Love's Labour's Lost* suggests that the men's frailty issues precisely fom the richness of their language. Their banishment to a "for-lorn and naked hermitage, / Remote from all the pleasures of the world" where they will have to fast is also a banishment from the ornate-style feast. As Rosaline makes clear, the men will have to learn to subsist on something more substantial than the "mocks," "comparisons," and "wounding flouts" of the courtly style; their attention span will have to lengthen to include contemplation of a world-without-end marital bargain . . . and of death.

The sequence reaches a similar climax in Sonnet 146 ("Poor soul, the center of my sinful earth"), its exhortation "Within be fed, without be rich no more" applying not only to the moral but also to the aesthetic onus under which the four men bow at play's end. The women urge them toward its speaker's renunciation of all the world's vanities, among them the vanity of the ornate style. The question "Why dost thou pine within and suffer dearth, / Painting thy outward walls so costly gay?" can take us in many directions; for example, to the "beauteous wall" that often encloses "pollution" in *Twelfth Night* or, further off, to Lucifera's flimsy palace in Spenser's *Faerie Queene*. But this question also takes us to the frailty and ephemerality of the ornate style, which requires that "simple truth" be decorated in "the most excellent Ornaments, Exornations, Lightes, Flowers, and Formes" of rhetoric.[43]

"Why so large cost, having so short a lease . . . ?" the speaker of Sonnet 146 asks, and in an artistic sense the cost of the ornate style in concentration and creative energy was great. The lease conceit gives the question, for our purposes, an intriguing allusive edge, for Renaissance courtiers and poets most assuredly worked on "leases of short-numb'red hours" (SON 124). Many "hours of dross" were wasted by such persons, whether in waiting, suing, or writing sonnets or epyllions. Sonnet 146, I am suggesting, is but another shadowed representation of the courting poet's abandonment of the luxury of court and its exargastic impositions on his energies.

A third source of discouragement present in *Love's Labour's Lost*, but figured more richly in the Sonnets, is a consciousness that courting poetry—like the suddenly popular flame-colored taffeta, yellow cross-garters, or great crop doublets—was subject to the mercurial rule of court fashion. This sway of fashion is mentioned often in Shakespeare's plays, as when Parolles remarks on the old courtier who wears his "cap out of fashion, richly suited, but unsuitable" (AWW 1.1.156-57), or when Falstaff says he will eke enough fun out of Shallow to keep Hal "in continual laughter the wearing out of six fashions, which is four terms [that is, one year]" (2H4 5.1.79-80). The rule of fashion was granted by Eustache Du Refuge when he observed that only "such spirits are fit for the *Court* [who are] conformable and flexible to all sorts of humours and fashions."[44] And such is life in *Love's Labour's Lost*. Thus, Rosaline with her usual edge says of the Princess, "My lady, to the manner of the days, / In courtesy gives underserving praise" (5.2.365-66); and Armado, the absurd quintessence of courtiership, flaunts himself as an obsessed creature of fashion. To the King, Armado is "A man in all the world's new fashion planted," and Berowne calls him "fashion's own knight" (1.1.163, 177). But he is only one among many courtly fops in the period's stage literature; Boyet, Sir Andrew Aguecheek, and the nameless fellow who angers Hotspur on the field of Holmedon are his Shakespearean kin.

Poets did not escape the levy of fashion. Their work also aged and—like Parolles' aging courtier—was apt to become "richly suited, but unsuitable." At court, Puttenham warned the ambitious poet, "all old things soone waxe stale and lothsome, and the new devises are ever dainty and delicate" (3: 10). John Davies makes this point in his epigram, "In Ciprium," where we meet a "tierse and neate" courtier who seems perfectly à la mode, wearing a hat "of the flat crown-block" and "treble ruffes." But in the last line, the "new-fangled youth" gives himself away by praising "olde Gascoi[g]ne's rimes."[45] Sidney, in Certain Sonnet 17, amuses himself at the expense of poets who cannot muster innovation: "[They] thinke themselves well blest, if they renew / Some good old dumpe, that *Chaucer's* mistress knew." Samuel Daniel casts the problem of fashion more soberly in his *Defence of Ryme* (1603). Discussing the "strange presumption" of men to introduce neologisms, "free-denizens," into the language, Daniel draws attention to "that perpetuall revolution which wee see to be in all things that never remaine the same" and concludes that poets, like all men, must submit "to the law of time, which in few yeeres wil make al that, for which we now contend, *Nothing.*"[46]

This recognition of time's inescapable law overwhelms the Young Man sonnets and requires no further explanation here. But evidence in the Sonnets of time's corollary operation on the poet's psyche and work is worth noting. In Sonnet 17, for instance, the speaker imagines the time when his papers will become "yellowed with their age" and scorned. What is now for him "a poet's rage" will some day, like old Gascoigne's rhymes, be accounted no more than the "stretched meter of an antique song." In Sonnet 32 the speaker imagines that, after his death, his "poor rude lines" will be compared unfavorably with "the bett'ring of the times" and be "out-stripped by every pen." With flattering conceit, the speaker of Sonnet 38 calls the Young Man his tenth muse and asks his help in creating "eternal numbers." But the sonnet's reality is clear: the speaker's "slight muse" is having difficulty pleasing "these curious days." Sonnet 76 captures especially well the dilemma of the Renaissance poet: whether to follow the path of fashion or to become centered in a personal style and risk seeming arrogant or, worse, lacking in invention:

> Why is my verse so barren of new pride,
> So far from variation or quick change?
> Why with the time do I not glance aside
> To new-found methods, and to compounds strange?
> Why write I still all one, ever the same,
> And keep invention in a noted weed,
> That every word doth almost tell my name,
> Showing their birth, and where they did proceed?

The conceitful answer to these questions is that the speaker's "argument" is the Young Man's unchanging worth. But again the reality of the ornate poet's life, the struggle to invent and seem not merely to be "dressing old words new," is what vitalizes the poem. Poetry in the late sixteenth century was far from eternal. It may be, as the speaker apostrophizes Time in Sonnet 123: "We admire / What thou dost foist upon us that is old." But last season's or last generation's poetry was surely not sufficiently dusted with age to evoke much admiration. Shakespeare could not have expected many in his audience to share Duke Orsino's antiquarian taste for productions of "the old age."[47]

Accepting the dubious invitation to be fashionable was risky for all classes of courtly denizens. Fashion, like so much in the courtier's life, presented a Janus face, first beckoning with the promise of enjoying the "smiling pomp" of favor, then repelling with the fear of suddenly suffering the "thrallèd discontent" of disfavor (SON 124). In Sonnet 125 the speaker renounces this fashionable dwelling on "form and favor." Perhaps there is in this gesture, too, a premonitory renunciation of the form and favor of the ornate style.

∽

Just when the speaker of the Young Man sequence begins to notice signs that a lasting relationship is unlikely, he makes the necessary and obvious concession: "I grant thou wert not married to my muse" (SON 82). The marriage of true minds, which is the climax of Spenser's *Amoretti* sequence, is clearly not going to occur here. And a divorce of kinds—from youth, beauty, court, and the "strained touches" of the ornate style—is achieved in the final Young Man poems. In the preceding pages, I have sought to discover in a cluster of Shakespeare's early works (which could have been expanded to include *The Rape of Lucrece, Richard III,* and *Romeo and Juliet*) some hints why Shakespeare's own courtship of Erato, the muse of lyric poetry, did not result in a world-without-end bargain and why he eventually divorced himself from her to court Melpomene, Thalia, and Clio more exclusively on the other side of the Thames.

These hints, I think, make it easier to accept some of the obvious reasons one might adduce for Shakespeare's decision. Certainly, one of these was the weariness of the tradition. As early as 1578, John Florio concluded that "we need not speak so much of love, all books are full of love, with so many authours, that it were labour lost to speake of love."[48] Another reason was the difficulty of making ends meet. Ben Jonson's Ovid Senior in *The Poetaster* surely speaks for Ovidians of the 1590s, including Shakespeare, with some historical accuracy: "Name me a profest *poet*, that his *poetrie* did ever afford so much as a competencie . . . you'le tell me his name shall live; and that (now being dead) his workes have eternis'd him, and made him divine. But could this divinitie feed him, while he liv'd? could his name feast him?" (4: 211-12). Yet another reason may simply have been the author's eventual recognition (akin to that of the ladies in *Love's Labour's Lost*) that one cannot smell forever of the *flores rhetorici* of April and May. Or, as a madrigal text puts it: "O that the learned Poets of this time, / Who in a Love-sicke line so well can speake, / Would not consume good Wit in hatefull rime, / But with deepe care some better subject finde."[49]

In a 1607 speech King James made a similar point in terms that are for us even more pertinent: "Studied Orations and much eloquence upon little matter is fitte for the Universities, where not the Subject which is spoke of, but the triall of his wit that speaketh, is most commendable."[50] With *Venus and Adonis*, *Love's Labour's Lost*, and the Sonnets, the career-opening trial of Shakespere's wit was more than sufficiently achieved. Happily, in the works that followed them, "the Subject which is spoke of" came to bear the full force of the playwright's genius.

The works that have occupied us in this chapter dazzle us primarily by the brilliance of their surfaces, rather than by their pathos or emotional force. Not surprisingly, it is often by small but very engaging details of their ornate style that they can be most suggestively linked with each other. Berowne tells us, for instance, that "Love's feeling is more soft and sensible / Than are the tender horns of cockled snails" (4.3.334-35), and this reminds us of the superbly outrageous simile that occurs when Venus sees the body of Adonis: "Or as the snail, whose tender horns being hit, / Shrinks backward in his shelly cave with pain, / And there all smother'd up in shade doth sit, / Long after fearing to creep forth again" (1033-36).

To take another example, the speaker in Sonnet 27 pictures the Young Man in his dreams as "a jewel hung in ghastly night." The conceit suffers a horrible sea-change with Holofernes: "who now hangeth like a jewel in the ear of *coelo*, the sky, the welkin, the heaven" (4.2.4-5). But it scores a triumph in *Romeo and Juliet*: "It seems she hangs upon the cheek of night / As a rich jewel in an Ethiop's ear" (1.5.45-46). These are all touches of the honey-tongued poet Shakespeare, for whom the penetrating exploration of "the Subject which is spoke of" was not yet a principal concern.

In *Venus and Adonis* the moments of pathos are highly mannered, thrown off almost casually. As I have already ventured, there is but one speech in *Love's Labour's Lost* that carries substantial emotional and philosophical weight, namely, the Princess's meditation on false praise and the heart bent toward "fame." And, though some readers may disagree, I have found few instances of emotion convincingly expressed in the Sonnets; Sonnet 120 is perhaps for me the exception that proves the rule. The Sonnets generally seem the work of a shrewd and sober craftsman, not a person seeking, in Sidney's phrase, "to ease / A burthned hart" (*Astrophil* Sonnet 35). If it is fair to say, as William Fennor does in his "Description of a Poet," that "A true Poet can / Describe the inside of an outward man," then Shakespeare was not yet a true poet.[51]

To become a true poet, the "honey-tongued" Shakespeare had to transform himself into a "Scenicke" poet and move away from the style with which he had made such a notable first impression. He was, in a fascinating way, like Proteus in *The Two Gentlemen of Verona*. Sick-thoughted in *amour courtois* agony over Julia, Proteus (at the outset) listens to his friend Valentine urge him to venture out into a world elsewhere:

Home-keeping youth have ever homely wits.
Were't not affection chains thy tender days
To the sweet glances of thy honor'd love,
I rather would entreat thy company
To see the wonders of the world abroad,
Than (living dully sluggardiz'd at home)
Wear out thy youth with shapeless idleness. [1.1.2-8]

As Shakespeare's achievement shows, he did not remain "dully sluggardiz'd at home" in the ornate style, but ventured forth—if only to go as far as the other bank of the Thames—to discover the wonders of a larger world . . . and the Globe.[52] (Shakespeare appears to have changed lodgings, moving to the Bankside just after producing his notably ornate poems and plays.[53]) Hints we have already discovered and others pursued in the following chapters, I believe, suggest that to make this journey Shakespeare had to relinquish the poet's name. He may never have uttered so explicit a sentiment as Astrophil's in this chapter's epigraph, yet it is worth recalling that the word *poet* is in fact engraved in neither of the epitaphs in Holy Trinity Church.[54]

Finally, that Shakespeare's retirement from the ranks of "profest" poets was a sine qua non for his subsequent achievements can be suggested by noting a passing comment in *The Schoolmaster*: Ascham remarks that the Roman Sulpicius could never have achieved his reputation as a brilliantly theatrical orator *(tragicus orator)* if he had not "studied to express *vim Demosthenis* [rather] than *furorem poetae.*"[55] Shakespeare, eventually to be a *tragicus et comicus scriptor*, stood at a similar crossroad early in his career. It is clear that he made the same choice as Sulpicius, aligning himself with the women rather than the men of *Love's Labour's Lost*.

Chapter Two

"Dedicated Words"

The Strategies of Front Matter

> Ingenuous honourable Lord, I know not what blinde
> custome methodicall antiquity hath thrust upon us, to
> dedicate such books as we publish, to one great man or
> other.
> —Thomas Nashe to Southampton

STUDENTS of the Renaissance—inured to the nuisance of negotiating the few pages of bombasted, furbelowed prose or the conspicuously bad sonnet with which so many volumes from the period begin—have good reason to wonder, as Nashe does, at this "blinde custome."[1] For once one has read a few dedicatory epistles and addresses to the reader, one can almost say one has read them all. The elaborately deferential salutations, the clichéd imagery of self-deprecation (barren "leaves" and the lump of flesh licked into bear-cub form were favorites), and the many captious gestures aimed at backbiting Zoiluses and carping Momuses all wear thin quickly. So the modern reader soon learns to skip the front matter and go immediately to the text.

There were, to be sure, contemporary expressions of impatience with front matter. Not surprisingly, these often came from the age's premier scribblers, whose itch to bestride the press was always being scratched and who had, therefore, to be especially imaginative in their preliminary strategies: prolific second- and third-raters like Brathwait, Breton, Churchyard, Dekker, Greene, Markham, Munday, Nashe, Rich, Taylor, and Wither. Early in his career Anthony Munday struck the reasonable (and modern) note: "It were needlesse gentle Reader, to use a large preamble in so breefe a purpose: or to trifle the time in tediousnes, when a woord or twaine may suffise." But then he continues, "It is a custome, and I would be loth to break it, to desire thy friendship, in reading this little fancie."[2] More than three decades later John Taylor is more brusque in a letter "To the knowing Reader": "Now sir, it is a common customary use in these times, to salute you with somewhat; as Honest, Kinde, Curteous, Loving,

Friendly, or Gentle: but all these Epithites are over-worne, and doe, as it were, stinke of the fusty garbe of Antiquity."[3]

One response to the more lugubrious manifestations of the custom was satire. For one of the highpoints of Elizabethan garrulity, *Have with you to Saffron-Waldon* (1596), Thomas Nashe prepared a twenty-one-page "Epistle Dedicatorie" with a salutation stretching to eighty-eight words! He writes belatedly, expressing at the end what ought to be the first concern for all writers of front matter: "I both can and wilbe shut presently of this tedious Chapter of contents, least whereas I prepared it as an antipast to whet your stomacks, it cleane take away your stomackes, and you surfet of it before meate come." In a more rambunctious vein, Thomas Dekker begins his address to the reader of *The Wonderful Yeare* (1603):

And why to the *Reader?* Oh good Sir! theres as sound law to make you give good words to the *Reader*, as to a *Constable* when hee carries his watch about him to tell how the night goes. . . [T]o maintaine the scurvy fashion, and to keepe *Custome* in reparations, he [the reader] must be honyed, and come-over with *Gentle Reader*, *Courteous Reader*, and *Learned Reader*, though he have no more *Gentilitie* in him than *Adam* had (that was but a gardner), no more *Civility* than a *Tartar*, and no more *Learning* than the most errand *Stinkard*, that (except his owne name) could never finde any thing in the Horne-booke.[4]

The Renaissance penchant for mediation between text and reader through preliminary matter was most resoundingly detonated, though, with the appearance of *Coryats Crudities* in 1611. This volume's front matter comprised the following: a title page stuffed with 171 words; a six-page epistle to Prince Henry; a three-page "character" of the author by Ben Jonson; an acrostic "on the Author" by Jonson; an introduction to a group of "encomiastick and panegyrick Verses of some of the worthyest spirits of this Kingdome"; about a hundred pages of these verses by, among others, Harington, Goodyear, Donne, Holland, Drayton, Davies, Campion, and (with an emblem of course) Peacham; the translation of a twenty-six page essay on traveling; and an "Elogie of the Booke" by Laurence Whitaker. In the 1905 Glasgow edition the text commences on page 152!

Impatient though we may be with front matter, it provided one of the many possible venues for the observation of ritual, and in Renaissance England one could not hope to rise or prosper without such ritual. Sending forth a volume with social or political ambitions but without front matter was comparable to going naked. Thomas Heywood confided in his note to the reader for *The Golden Age* (1611): "I was loath . . . to see it thrust naked into the world, to abide the fury of all weathers, without either Title for acknowledgement, or the formality of an Epistle for ornament." Front matter provided an arena, like the lists of a fancy-dress barriers at court, wherein one was able to perform elaborately decorous feats that scrupulously combined deference with self-advertising. In this arena, as we shall see, some fine lines of distinction had to be observed—a process that sometimes caused authors to twist themselves into very odd, often laughable postures. These postures are sometimes revealing, for at no time was the Renaissance author more intensely absorbed in fashioning his public image than in the composition of front matter. Though the observation of formalities was often by the leaden rote of an Armado (*Love's Labour's Lost*) or an Aguecheek (*Twelfth Night*), or merely plagiarized from "methodicall antiquitie," there is much to learn from this crucial self-fashioning by authors eager to be on their best cross-gartered formal behavior.

Front matter is the bibliographical and typographical form of "courtesy," and Renaissance courtesy treatises (enchiridions) have recently become an important source of illumination for scholars studying the social economy of letters. The purpose of the present chapter, then, is to observe the realities of courtesy and courtiership by undertaking expeditions into this strange part of the period's literary terrain, drawing mainly from titles published during Shakespeare's active years. (I will be ignoring the front matter of ecclesiastical volumes almost completely.) Afterward, I shall turn first to some of the strategies authors developed to present themselves to the public and their patrons, then to the psychological and social implications of these strategies. Turning from authors to the objects of their attention, we shall consider what might be termed the dedicatory lifetime of certain prominent Elizabethan and Jacobean dedicatees (for example, Lucy, Countess of Bedford; Prince Henry; and the Earls of Bedford, Oxford, Pembroke, and Southampton). From their perspective, we shall attempt to reconstruct the experience of the custom of front matter over a lifetime. Finally, we shall arrive at a detailed consideration of the front matter from Shakespeare's career and what it suggests about the shape his authorial life assumed. Thomas P. Roche, considering the political and social ramifications of front matter, has written recently, "We know too little about the niceties of dedications."[5] The present chapter, while more narrowly occupied with the professional and commercial implications of front matter, is founded on the same impression.

The single most important publishing event in the history of sixteenth-century English poetry—excepting, perhaps, the appearance of Tottel's *Miscellany* in 1557—was the publication in 1591 of no fewer than three editions of Sir Philip Sidney's *Astrophil and Stella* sonnets. The publication of a sequence from so prestigious a hand made it more difficult to accept the Spanish proverb that condemned the author of a second sonnet to Bedlam, more difficult to see the composition of love poetry merely as a trivial way to evaporate wit. Nonarmigerous poets were emboldened to follow in Sidney's distinguished train, and the poetical floodgates of the 1590s were opened.[6] Among the first down the chute was Samuel Daniel, whose *Delia, contayning certayne Sonnets* appeared in 1592 (Stationers' entrance was made on 4 February), with the dedicatory epistle "To the Right Honourable the Ladie *Mary*, Countess of Pembroke." This epistle is a graceful, thoroughly orthodox example of the genre worth noting because discernible in it are many important hallmarks not only of Elizabethan courtiership but also of Elizabethan habits of publication.

Daniel's first concern is to ameliorate the onus of appearing "so rawely in publique," which he attempts by various means. His creative impetus, he says, was strictly personal: "I . . . desired to keep in the private passions of my youth from the multitude, as things utterd to my selfe, and consecrated to silence." He has been the victim of venal ambush: "I was betrayed by the indiscretion of a greedie Printer, and had some of my secrets bewraide to the world, uncorrected: doubting the like of the rest, I am forced to publish that which I never ment." Finally, he takes heart in the company he is thus keeping: "This wrong was not onely doone to mee, but to him ["Astrophel," that is, Sidney] whose unmatchable lines have indured the like misfortune."

Dispelling the opprobrium of print is almost invariably an element of front matter. Also common in volumes with aristocratic pretensions is the insistent note of elitism, which, as one reads through hundreds of epistles, begins to make the snobbery of Malvolio, Holofernes, Armado, and the audience for "Pyramus and Thisby" seem scarcely exaggerated. "The multitude," Daniel implies, ought not to sully the relationship the writer is seeking to establish with his highborn dedicatee; he describes the wings of Sidney's fame as flying at "a higher pitch then the gross-sighted can discerne." Daniel sounds a little like Spenser writing of the antipoetical Blatant Beast in *The Faerie Queene* when he asks protection from "those hidious Beastes, Oblivion and Barbarisme." Balancing this hauteur toward inferiors is the Renaissance suitor's typical maneuvering into the intended patron's benevolent custody: "I desire onely to bee graced by the countenance of your protection: whome the fortune of our time hath made the happy and judiciall Patronesse of the Muses." Daniel closes with a commonplace promise of "lines heereafter better laboured" and the usual expression of "the zealous duetie of mee, who am vowed to your honour in all observancy for ever."

Daniel's epistle raises many questions that will follow us through this chapter, questions especially pertinent to the two Shakespearean dedications to Southampton. Can we credit the elaborate excuses for publication? Was Daniel "thrust out into the worlde" all unwilling? or is he here merely indulging in deceitful-ornamental *sprezzatura*? Can we believe the expressed reasons for the choice of dedicatee? Or is it more likely that, as tutor of the Countess's young son at Wilton House, Daniel's choice was unavoidable? Then there is the most interesting question (almost never answerable) that arises as one reads any dedication: What was the dedicatee's real response to the formality? Thomas Wright asserted, also in a dedication to Southampton, that "literall labours are usually offered to such personages, with whom they particularly consort" (*The Passions of the Mind*, 1604), but is this view too optimistic? Were not books regularly received (to borrow a phrase from the Princess in *Love's Labour's Lost*) "more for praise than purpose"? These are fascinating questions. Indeed, it is fair to say that the prose and poetry of front matter are intriguing vastly out of proportion to their historical or aesthetic interest.

Shakespeare's publishing career began on a snobbish note, with his choice of a couplet from Ovid's *Amores* as an epigraph for the title page of *Venus and Adonis*: "Let base-conceited wits admire vile things, / Fair Phoebus lead me to the Muses' springs" (Marlowe's translation). Such posturing is common to the front matter of volumes native to, or in some way destined for, the court—where elitism in every respect, including the aesthetic, was the norm.[7] This elitism merits consideration because it is partly responsible for front matter's very existence and customary shape.

English Renaissance life was, in every important respect, organized according to "degree, priority, and place" (TRO 1.3.86), the existence of which was constantly reaffirmed through the observation of rituals, proclamations, protocols, and etiquettes. The closer to the venues of power—Westminster, Whitehall, the Inns of Court, Guildhall, and the great houses of peers—the more elaborate and time-consuming the observation of such formalities. Front matter, as I have suggested, was a kind of formality; it is therefore possible to hypothesize a similar "priority" in printed matter of the time: The closer a volume's subject matter, intended audience, or authorship approached the apex of society, the more imperative the courtesy of front matter. Accordingly, literature associated with the ethos beyond city walls or in the Liberties needed, as it were, no introduction. Ballads spoke for themselves, and the sensational titles (to which Londoners have long been devoted) required no politeness, as evidenced by the following: *A Most wicked Work of a wretched Witch wrought on Richard Burt* (1592), *The Truth of the most wicked and secret Murdering of John Brewen* (1592), and *A true Discourse of a cruell Fact committed by a Gentlewoman* (1599).

That front matter was often modulated according to a hierarchy of printed genres is conveniently shown in two Thomas Lodge titles listed next to each other in the *Short Title Catalogue:* One is the lurid *Life and Death of William Longbeard, the most famous and witty English Traitor* (1593), for which there is no front matter; the other, *A Fig for Momus Containing Pleasant varietie, included in Satyres, Eclogues, and Epistles* (1595), was clearly intended for a more high-toned audience. For this latter volume Lodge prepared a two-page dedication to the Earl of Derby and a two-page epistle "To the Gentlemen Readers whatsoever."

Somewhat higher in the hierarchy of genres were stage plays, though allowing publication still entailed a loss of caste. In "To the Reader" for *The Rape of Lucrece* (1608), Heywood sought to dissociate himself from those who use "a double sale of their labours, first to the Stage, and after to the presse." His excuse, akin to Daniel's, should possibly be taken with salt: "Some of my playes have (unknown to me, and without any of my direction) accidentally come into the Printers handes, and therfore so corrupt and mangled . . . that I have bene as unable to know them, as ashamde to chalenge them." But for the most part, plays appear to have been deemed beneath the formality of front matter. None of Peele's plays carry any, nor do Marlowe's—except *Tamburlaine the Great's* letter from the printer. And there is only one Marston dedication (to Jonson), along with a few letters to the reader. Further, none of Shakespeare's quartos carries authorial front matter; several of Jonson's lack formalilty, while a few get the full treatment. The 1605 *Sejanus*, for example, includes a "To the Reader," ten commendatory poems, and an "Argument"—all typical inspiration for the satire of *Coryats Crudities*, in which Jonson good-humoredly took part. Finally, *The Faithfull Shepheardesse* (circa 1610) offers a touchstone of courtly dramatic taste, so it is not surprising that it is the only play with lavish front matter from the Beaumont-Fletcher canon.

When we near the apex of the publishing pyramid, the voice of elitism in front matter acquires the unmistakable tone of court contempt. It is a voice with which we are familiar, having observed Holofernes and Armado's orgy of condescension performed on the "rude multitude" and having heard Hamlet speak of an "excellent" play that proved "caviar to the general." The manifestations of this elitism, or aristocratic *noblesse oblige*, in front matter are often astonishingly insulting and almost never entirely pleasant. Barnaby Rich's *The Irish Hubbub* (1619) amusingly shows the distinctions in "priority" that one could achieve prior to page 1. The dedication to Oliver Saint John, Lord Deputy of Ireland, is presented in orotund prose (set in italics) that is attentive to auricular figures and gauded with allusions to Roman history. Rich then separately addresses the general public as two distinct classes. In his first epistle "To the Reader" (set in roman type), he expresses in prose the hope that he will not need to ape the Painter, who, "taking upon him to picture forth the forms of sundry beasts, so unperfectly performed them, that he was driven to write over their heads, *This is a lyon*. . . ." However, in his second epistle, "To the discreet Reader," Rich is more solicitous, providing (in italic type) twenty-eight lines of iambic pentameter couplets. Such an elitist distinction, of course, underlies Shakespeare's deployment of prose and poetry in his plays.

Gabriel Harvey presses the same invidious distinction on his readers with ungallant bluntness in the dedication to *The Trimming of Thomas Nashe* (1597).

To the Learned.
Eme, perlege, nec te precii poenitebit.

To the simple.
Buy mee, read me through, and thou wilt
not repente thee of thy cost.

No wonder some have found in Holofernes a satirical attack on Harvey! And on George Chapman, too, who confessed his superiority un-blushingly in a dedication "To the trulie Learned," published about the time *Love's Labour's Lost* was written: "The prophane multitude I hate, & onelie consecrate my strange Poems to these serching spirits, whom learning hath made noble" (*Ovid's Banquet of Sence*, 1595).

The rigidity of the social hierarchy to which front matter often paid egregious homage is nowhere more apparent than in the radically different styles and tones of the two usual constituents of front matter, the dedication and the address to the reader. The former derived from ages-old feudal wellsprings; the latter derived from the burgeoning vitality of the publishing trade and was therefore more democratically aimed at anyone with the price of a book in hand. Authors naturally treated these two constituencies differently, often in breathtaking and telling ways. John Taylor, for instance, dedicated his *Nipping and Snipping of Abuses* (1614) "To the Sacred Majesty of King James" with a sonnet densely populated by Phoebus, Arion, Amphion, Pan, and Apollo. He adds the closing salutation, "Your Majesties Humble Servant." The paying customer, on the other hand, is greeted more familiarly and in prose with a "Skeltonicall salutation to those that know how to read, and not marre the sense with hacking or mis-construction." Its closing salutation is a curt "I thine, if thou mine."

Salutations themselves are often indications of the degree of formality intended. Titled dedicatees typically receive something lengthy (often organized visually on the same principle of eye-examination charts, with diminishing type sizes). George Turberville's salutation for his *Epitaphes, Epigrams, Songs and Sonets* (1567) runs,

> TO THE RIGHT NOBLE AND HIS
> singular good Lady, Lady Anne,
> Countesse of Warwick, &c. George
> Turberville wisheth increase of
> Honor with all good
> Happes.

Then follows, as usual, a simple "To the Reader." This abrupt change from effusive currying of favor in dedications to the brusque, sometimes browbeating tone of addresses to the reader may seem to us stagey and exaggerated. But it reflects with some fidelity the extremities of behavior fostered in the rigid atmosphere of a Renaissance court, where one was almost always presented with the stark choice of either bending a knee to superiors or visiting *noblesse oblige* or court-contempt on inferiors, as the whim urged. After reading several thousand dedications and addresses to the reader (a task one would wish on no one else), one begins to feel that front matter not only reflects on several important aspects of courtly existence but also on those Shakespearean figures—Richard of Gloucester, Holofernes, Malvolio, Parolles, Falstaff, Iago, and Wolsey, to name but a few—whose actions rest fundamentally on the ability to shift drastically between modes of deference and condescension as occasion demands.

Front matter also vividly evokes the harried pursuit of favor and protection from potent superiors, as well as competition among erstwhile clients for the few potential patrons on the horizon. This close, tension-ridden world projected in epistles to dedicatees and readers accords in many ways with what we know about the real-life atmosphere surrounding the realm's monarch and peers. It was, in short, a "ripe-judging world . . . full of envie," as Robert Chester wrote in his dedication to Sir John Salisbury for *Love's Martyr* (1601). Seeking to avoid appearing awkward, out of fashion, or unwittingly "rude," all suitors sought for themselves what Chester sought from Salisbury: "If Absurditie like a Theefe have crept into any part of these Poems, your well-graced name will over-shadow these defaults, and

the knowne Caracter of your vertues cause the common back-biting enemies of good spirits to be silent." For the "knowne Caracter of your
vertues" one can, of course, read: the personal power of gift, prestige of
association, or access to the even more powerful.

Richard Brathwait concluded a long and stately dedication to Southampton with the assertion that "Your protection will raise it [the volume]
above it selfe" (*The Schollers Medley* 1614), and such was the goal of all suitors
at court: to rise above their station through their work. The artful cringe
was therefore a necessary part of front matter. William Bettie, for instance,
wrote in his dedication for *The History of Titana and Theseus* (1608): "I
beseech you to shrowd this imperfect Pamphlet under your Worships
patronage"; and Nashe in *The Unfortunate Traveller* (1594) addressed Southampton with the hope, "Your Lordship [be] the large spreading branch of
renown, from whence my idle leaves seeke to derive theire whole nourishing." The previous year Barnaby Barnes employed this botanical conceit in
a dedicatory sonnet to the same earl: "These worthlesse leaves, which I to
thee present / Sprong from a rude and unmanured lande: / That with your
countenance grac'de, they may withstande / Hundred ey'de envies rough
encounterment" (*Parthenophil and Parthenope* [1593]). For writers, the
achievement of titled patronage was imperative, as Thomas Dekker made
clear in his dedication for *The Wonderfull Yeare:* "The title of other mens
names is the common *Heraldry* which those laie claime too, whose crest is a
Pen-and-Inckhorne." This self-deprecatory strategy in the search for titled
favor is a prominent element of Shakespeare's Young Man sonnets, as
chapter 5 will demonstrate in full measure.

Yet another element of courtly suit is now and then reflected in front
matter: competitiveness, which charged the atmosphere in the vicinity of
powerholders. Thomas Churchyard expresses the eagerness of all persons
in this vicinity when, in a dedication to his Queen, he admits, to a
"quenchles desire . . . that encreaseth a continuall thirst to doe well."
Churchyard continues, describing an anxiety specifically authorial but
nevertheless typical of all seekers after favor in the trains of great ones:
"beholding (most redoubted Queene) a multitude of people as well des-
posed as my selfe, that are running & preasing apace before me, some with
rare inventions & some with deepe devices to the honouring of your
Majestie, I feare they have carried cleane away so much knowledge from
me, that there is left no device, nor matter to study on, such is the bounty of
our time, & forwardnes of their wittes which are learned, that all fine
inventions are smoothly reaped from my reach, & cunningly raked away
from my use or commoditie" (*A Handeful of gladsome Verses* [1592]). *Use* and
commodity—to such utilitarian ends were all the arts—be they of conversa-

tion, politics, or poetry—deployed in the royal or aristocratic presence. And on such anxieties as Churchyard expresses are founded Shakespeare's "rival poet" sonnets.

Also familiar from Shakespeare's sonnets are the psychology and language of servitude (see especially Sonnets 57, 58, 124, 125). These frequently figure in front matter, not merely in the typical closing salutation (for example, Florio to Leicester: "Your Honours most humble and bounden, during life to commaund"). Nashe's phrasing to Southampton is telling: "My reverent duetifull thoughts (even from their infancie) have been retayners to your glorie." For the most part, one can guess, the patron's approval was of a passive sort, more often presumed than forthcoming. For instance, in *The Philosopher's Satyres* (1616), Robert Anton closes a dedication to Pembroke with the candid "hope for the passive part of your noble patronage." Anything more overt from an important figure was doubtless cause for celebration, and one can imagine genuine and explicit approval going straight to the head. Nashe writes, again to Southampton, "only your Honours applauding encouragement hath power to make mee arrogant"—a sentiment from which Shakespeare spun out the comic characters of Malvolio and Falstaff.

The fortunes of authors, as for all ambitious persons attracted to London, hinged on whims of the powerful, the mercurial swings from "smiling pomp" to "thrallèd discontent" and back. Hanging on to seemingly auspicious stars in the London firmament, some of them quick-lived shooting stars, was a tense and risky business. No work from the period conveys this more eloquently than Shakespeare's Young Man sonnets, but front matter also often does so. Though Nashe's imagery may be overripe, it still expresses the client's essential dependency on his patron for his fortune: "Unreprivably perisheth that booke whatsoever to wast paper, which on the diamond rocke of your judgement disasterly chanceth to be shipwrackt."[8] The reduction of the author's work to "waste paper" can well be taken as a kind of synecdoche for the experience of all who arrived in London with upcast eyes. Few succeeded and many failed, wasting their lives, spirits, patrimonies, or honor in the process. Those who wasted mere pen, ink, and paper could be said to have gotten off lightly.

One is tempted to pause over the characteristics of Shakespeare's age reflected in front matter: the contentiousness, extravagance of expression, vociferation, even violence. Fortunately, all these qualities are on display in a passage from John Florio's epistle "To the Reader" for *A Worlde of Wordes* (1598). This highly theatrical preemptive fusillade directed at the book's potential critics will help us to turn attention from the greater world to see

what front matter can tell us of the publishing world. Florio writes of
"those notable Pirates in this our paper-sea, those sea-dogs, or lande-
Critikes, monsters of men, if not beastes rather then men; whose teeth are
Canibals, their toongs adder-forkes, their lips aspes-poyson, their eies
basiliskes, their breath the breath of a grave, their wordes like swordes of
Turkes, that strive which shall dive deepest into a Christian lying bound
before them." There are those who would argue that Florio's description of
life on the paper-sea gives a fair account of today's publishing world.
Friends and colleagues recount enough distressing tales of books comparably tortured before acceptance, while in press, or after publication to
convince one *plus ça change*. . . .

Renaissance front matter gives frequent occasion to remember that
some things have not changed: Publishers will always tell authors that high-
toned (or "scholarly") books will make no one rich. John Davies bears this
out in his epigram "To the Printer" for *The Scourge of Folly* (1611):

> *Printer* thou tellst me good Bookes will not sell,
> Most men (thou say'st) are now become so ill:
> Then heere's a Booke belike should like them well;
> For, *Foolery*, in Folio, it doth fill.
>   *Then print this same, sith* Foolery *in print*
>   *Most men approve, the World is at this stint.*[9]

There are numerous indications that volumes were, as Thomas Coryat
phrased it, "printed in huggermugger" (*Coryats Crambe*, 1611) or that the
author was the victim of "sinister dealing of some unskilfull Printer."[10] For
lack of a better venue, Nicholas Breton added this footnote to a dedication
for *The Pilgrimage* (1592): "Gentlemen there hath beene of late printed in
London by one Richarde Joanes, a printer, a booke of english verses,
entitled *Bretons bower of delights:* I protest it was donne altogether without
my consent or knowledge, & many thinges of other mens mingled with few
of mine, for except *Amoris Lachrimae* an epitaphe upon Sir Phillip Sydney,
and one or two other toyes, which I know not how he unhappily came by, I
have no part with any of them: and so I beseech yee assuredly beleeve."
Authors complained then, as they often do now, of willful interventions by
publishers with minds of their own. In the "Postscript to the Readers" for
The Shepherds Hunting (1615), George Wither sullenly complains: "If you
thinke [the book] hath not well answered the title of the *Shepheards Hunting*,
goe quarrell with the *Stationer,* who bid himselfe God-father, and imposed
the *name* according to his owne liking." And eager authors then too moaned
at the snail's pace of their publishers. In his *Epigrammes* (1599) John Weever
included the following gibe:

My Epigrams were all new ready made,
And onely on thc Printers leisure staid;
One of my friends on Sheeps greene I did meet,
Which told me one was printing in Bridge street:
And would (if so it pleasde [me] to come thither)
Print with a warrant both gainst wind & wether.
I thanked him: my Booke to Presse now goes:
But I am gulld, he printeth only hose. [B2v]

There are reminders, too, that—as always—books (at bottom, an impersonal form of communication) seldom find the "right" reader. Thomas Bradshaw made this point in his letter "To the curteous Reader" for *The Shepherds Starre* (1592): "It is peculiar to everie one, to conceive of a booke so singular, as that no most exquisit worke can satisfie the meanest expectation of his desire in reading." Or, as Thomas Bastard finely observed in his dedication to Charles Blunt for *Chrestoleros* (1598): "The greatest adventure that I knowe is to write, mens judgements arc of so many fashions."

Also distinctly *au courant* are complaints in front matter about the proliferation of titles. Lodge wrote in *Scillaes Metamorphosis* (1589): "Our wits now a daies are waxt verie fruitefull, and our Pamphleters more than prodigall; So that the postes which stoode naked . . . doo vaunt their double apparell as soone as ever the Exchequer [a booksellers' emporium] openeth; and everie corner is tooke up with some or other penilesse companion that will imitate any estate for a twopennie almes." This is enough, Lodge complains, to "disquiet the digestion of Arte." A year before, Munday made the corollary remark about the ficklc public's short attention span: "such are affections now a daies, that a booke a sennight olde is scarce worth the reading" (*Palmerin d'Oliva* [1588]). (The big national retailing chains now market books on exactly this assumption.) Barnaby Rich tolls the mournful bell in 1610: "One of the diseases of this age is the multitude of Books, that doth so overcharge the worlde, that it is not able to digest the abundance of idle matter that is every day hatched and brought into the world."[11] And thc Bishop of Winton, contributing a heavy folio of James's works in 1616, comments on "the infinite number of great Volumes wherewith the world seemes, as it were, to bee wayed downe." All these observers were expressing astonishment and an understandable sense of oppression at the Gutenberg explosion that occurred in late sixteenth-century England. But all perspectives are relative. Anyone who has enjoyed the use of a year-by-year file generated from the *Short Title Catalogue* will know that the cards for any single year from Shakespeare's life span can be held comfortably in one hand, with cards for imaginative and bellet-tristic titles seldom measuring more than an inch. One wonders with a little morbid glee what Lodge, Rich, and Bishop Winton would make of the Everest of printed matter now produced each year.

During Shakespeare's lifetime the publishing world resembled ours in another important respect: The preponderance of titles generated by authors occupying the aristocratic, ecclesiastic, legal, or governmental heights gradually gave way to a more demotic outpouring into an increasingly crowded and competitive marketplace. "Booke-writing," Bishop Winton belatedly observed in 1616, had "growen into a Trade." In 1597, for instance, the printer Robert Jones urged his usual clientele for a title such as Breton's *Arbour of Amorous Devises* ("sweete Gentlemen") to return from "this long time of vacation." This, he says, will result "in the rejoycing of all Cittizins, and specially to the comfort of all poore men of Trades." [Including stationers.] The publishing profession was giving up its stately, caparisoned canter for something like a gallop. Much dust was raised, making it difficult for scholars now either to grasp clearly the ins and outs of the trade or to determine which were saucy barks, the proud sails, and the downright pirates on the paper sea.[12]

With regard to poetical matter, the frantic atmosphere surrounding printers and authors can be suggested by comparing the poets of *Love's Labour's Lost* (leisured, for the most part titled, and spruce in their affectations) with the Poet in *Timon of Athens*—a taut, cunning, grasping fellow whose usual company (according to the Folio dramatis personae) comprised a painter, jeweler, merchant, and mercer; clearly, the poet is but another tradesman. John Day's comment on the increasingly commercial element of poetizing, made about the time of *Timon of Athens*, applied to all imaginative titles: "Verses, tho freemen borne, are bought and sold / Like slaves."[13] Authorship was becoming a way to make money, though few authors were as candid as William Fennor in admitting as much. He expressed the hope that his *Compter's Commonwealth* (1617) would "bring future benefit to my Countrey," but adds this marginal note: "And some present benefit to my selfe." Heminge and Condell hoped the 1623 Folio would make a "present worthy" of Pembroke and Montgomery; to the readers, however, they unmincingly urged: "Read and censure. Do so, but buy it first. That doth best commend a Booke, the Stationer saies . . . what ever you do, Buy."

The consequence of all this busyness and business was more vigorous attention to the means of riveting the potential buyer's interest. There were, of course, no reviews in the modern sense or non-print media by which one might advertise a new title—aside from those be-papered posts outside the Exchequer and near St. Paul's that Lodge mentions and word-of-mouth. Therefore, the main venue of what we think of now as the advertising world was confined largely to title pages and other front matter. Very few Renaissance volumes have title pages that conform to the current laconic norm, as for example:

WHAT
YOU WILL

By
John Marston

[ornament]

Imprinted at London for G. Eld for
Thomas Thorpe
1607

And there are also few dedications curt enough to match our current taste. One of the shortest—Drayton's for *The Shepheards Garland* (1593)—is still a bit long:

To the noble, and valerous
Gentleman, Master *Robert*
Dudley: Enriched with
all vertues of the
minde, and worthy
of all honorable
desert.

The necessity for engaging cleverness and puffery was one of the prime encouragements to prolixity in the design of title pages, as Nashe wittily shows in "A Private Epistle of the Author to the Printer, Wherein his full meaning and purpose (in publishing this Booke) is set foorth" for the second edition of *Pierce Pennilesse* (1592): "Now this is that I woulde have you to do in this second edition; First, cut off that long-tayld Title, and let mee not in the forefront of my Booke, make a tedious Mountebanks Oration to the Reader, when in the whole there is nothing praise-worthie." This renunciation rings amusingly hollow for an author whose book has already taken the public's fancy and is being reissued.

Nashe is high-spiritedly going against the usual grain, for title pages manifestly performed commercial functions. Considerable ingenuity was expended on them, since, during a press run, they were struck off separately for advertising purposes. Dekker's image is from his age, but the marketing concept is still with us: "The Titles of Bookes are like painted Chimnies in great Countrey-houses [that] make a shew afar off, and catch *Travellers* eyes; but comming nere them, neither cast they smoke, nor hath

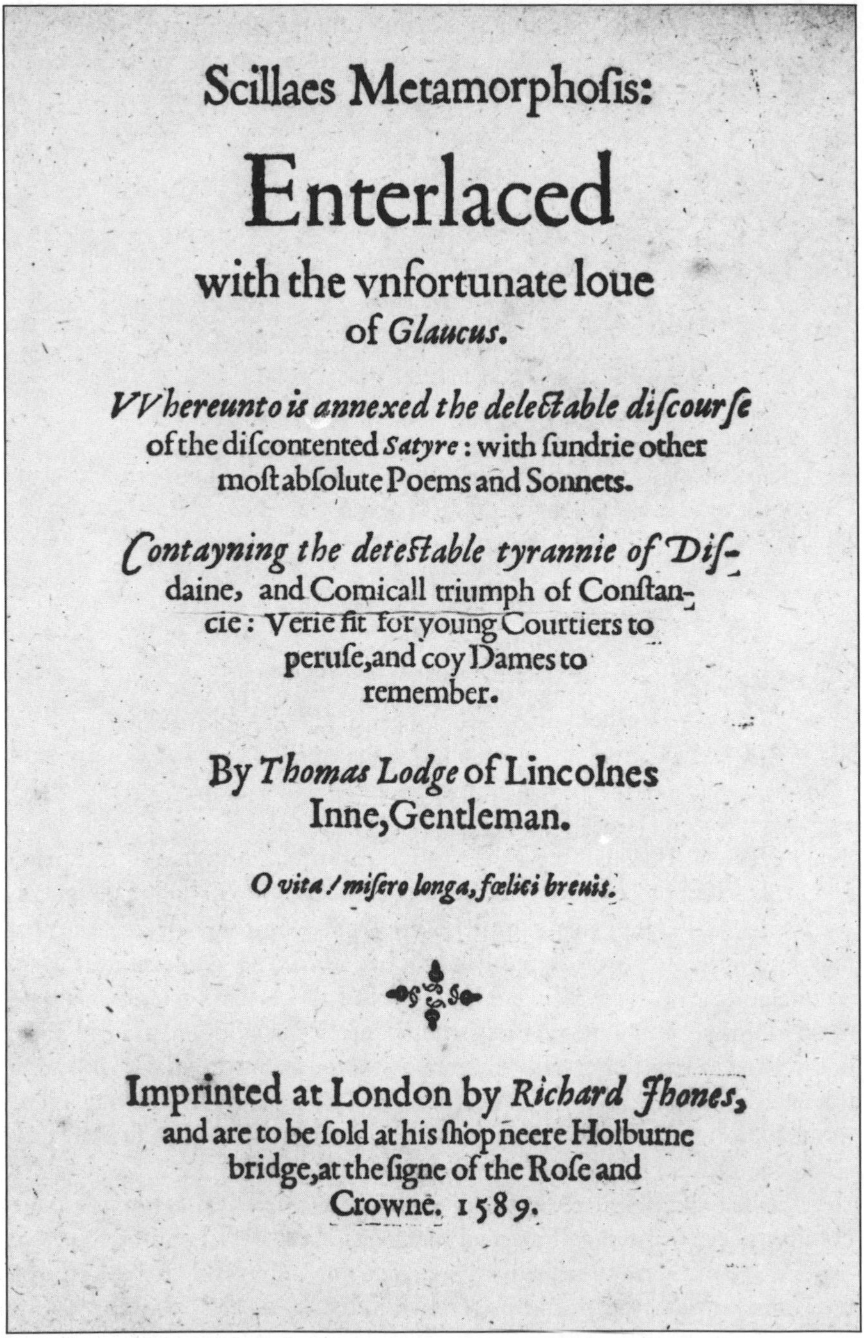

Scillaes Metamorphosis:

Enterlaced

with the vnfortunate loue
of *Glaucus.*

VVhereunto is annexed the delectable difcourfe
of the difcontented *Satyre* : with fundrie other
moft abfolute Poems and Sonnets.

Contayning the detestable tyrannie of Dif-
daine, and Comicall triumph of Conftan-
cie : Verie fit for young Courtiers to
perufe, and coy Dames to
remember.

By *Thomas Lodge* of Lincolnes
Inne, Gentleman.

O vita ! mifero longa, fœlici breuis.

Imprinted at London by *Richard Jhones,*
and are to be fold at his fhop neere Holburne
bridge, at the figne of the Rofe and
Crowne. 1589.

Fig. 1. Title page, Thomas Lodge, *Scillaes Metamorphosis*, 1589.
(Courtesy of The Huntington Library, San Marino, California)

the house the heart to make you drinke."[14] Elaborate typographical fore-
play on title pages is familiar from several Shakespearean quartos, as for
example *Romeo and Juliet's* "bad" first quarto, "An Excellent conceited
Tragedie of Romeo and Juliet, / As it hath been often (with great applause)
plaied publiquely . . . ," or the fifty-two-word title block for *Richard III*'s
first edition (which shrank to eighteen words in the Folio, where no puff
was needed). A good example of title-page formality can be found in
Lodge's *Scillaes Metamorphosis* (see figure 1), which some feel may have
inspired Shakespeare's choice of subject and stanza form for *Venus and
Adonis*. Several typefaces and sizes are employed, and the layout is
shrewdly designed to urge the eye along. Remarkably much information is
conveyed about the work, its author, the printer, the location of his shop,
and the targeted audience, along with titillating intimations and praise.

Imaginative attempts to rivet attention by upsetting the usual style of
dedications and epistles are fairly common. For instance, Marston dedicated his *Metamorphoses of Pigmalions Image* (1598) to "The Worlds Mightie
Monarch, Good Opinion," his *Scourge of Villainy* (1599) "To Detraction,"
and his *History of Antonio and Mellida* (1602) "To the onely rewarder, and
most just poiser of vertuous merits, the most honorably renowned Nobody, bountious Mecaenas of Poetry." Jonson, characteristically but also
striving for clever effect, addressed himself in *Catiline* (1611) first "To the
reader in ordinarie" ("The muses forbid, that I should restrayne your
meddling") and then "To the Reader extraordinary" ("You I would understand to be the better Man, though Places in Court go otherwise." 5:432).

The foregoing brief chronicle of the similarities of publishing habits then
and now would seem to make Shakespeare's sudden descent from England's Parnassus all the more incredible. For we have much evidence from
both periods' best-selling authors that one main highway to fame and
fortune lies in creating a distinctive style and/or formula and then reappear-
ing with it year after year. One thinks of Shakespearean contemporaries
like Greene, Lyly, and Nashe, and modern authors like James Michener,
Robert Ludlum, or Stephen King. Shakespeare could have followed his
epyllions with other successes in the same vein. But he did not, even
though his competition virtually vanished with the death of Marlowe,
thinning to the consistency of a "Water Poet" over the next decade. Because
Shakespeare changed directions, I believe we must look to the principal
difference between publishing then and publishing now to understand the
kinds of professional considerations that might have caused Shakespeare to
absent himself from verse.

We have touched on this difference as a corollary to the general opprobrium of print: the strong impression evoked by Renaissance front matter that authors perceived a hostile world beyond the stationer's shop. The year in which *Venus and Adonis* appeared, Henry Chettle wrote: "To come in print is not to seeke praise, but to crave pardon" (*Kind Harts Dreame*, 1593). This sentiment was far from uncommon, and the fear that lies beneath its surface was often expressed in vivid ways. For example, in 1595 Barnaby Barnes committed a sequence of divine sonnets "to the publique tipographicall Theatre of generall censure." The year before, Nashe complained in his usual colorful fashion about readers who "piteously torment Title pages on everie poast: never reading farther of anie Booke, than Imprinted by *Simeon* such a signe, and yet with your dudgen judgements will desperatelie presume to run up to the hard hilts through the whole bulke of it." In 1603 Dekker grimly warned that anyone who "dares hazard a pressing to death (thats to say, *To be a man in print*) must make account that he shall stand (like the old Weathercock over Powles steeple) to be beaten with all stormes." But perhaps the last and most experienced word ought to come from Rich, who wrote at the age of seventy, near the end of a lifetime of "pressing": "It is but a thriftlesse, and a thanklesse occupation, this writing of Bookes, a man were better to sit singing in a *Coblers shop*, for his pay is certaine, a penny a patch: but a Booke-writer, if hee get sometimes a few commendations of the *Judicious*, he shall be sure to reape a thousande reproaches of the *Malicious*." [15]

Authors of the time may therefore be forgiven for seeming to carry a chip on their shoulders and finding it nearly impossible to look on the bright side. For *Andromeda Liberata* (1614) Chapman devoted 250 words to "the prejudicate and peremptory Reader" but only 100 to the "ingenuous and judicious Reader." Authors often seem to become most emotional and eloquent when contemplating the worst of which readers are capable. Phrases of ridicule are thus one of the hallmarks of Renaissance front matter, invective being then a highly cultivated art. And so we encounter "wri-neck" and "narrow-eyed" critics, "cavilling Finde-faults," "lewd and viperous carpers," "malignant, ready backbiters," "squinteyed asses," and "depravers of wel-intended lines." Thomas Churchyard, in *The First Parte of Churchyardes Chippes* (1575), bastinadoes this rankling class of readers with thirteen quatrains, "To the dispisers of other mens workes that show nothing of their owne."

This well of premonitory resentment often overflows into very odd strategies that now seem perversely intended to exacerbate tensions between author and reader. What was to be gained by Matteo Aleman in beginning an epistle "To the Vulgar" with "To me it is no new thing (though perhaps it be to thee) to see (O thou vertue-hating Vulgar) the many bad friends that thou hast"?[16] In *Moriomachia* (1613), Robert Anton turns from a stately dedication to the Howard family to several lines of doggerel addressed "to the uncapable Reader." Just so, Thomas Bradshaw could not have invited a reader to good humor by addressing him thus in *The Shepherds Starre*: "Courteous Reader, I knowe no reason to moove mee to write unto you, sith I cannot remove you from your prejudiciall opinion."

Satirists of the day were sensitive to the foibles of publishing and treated this authorial aggression, as they did everything else, with mordant exaggeration. Offering some "distempered *Epigrammes*" in *A Strappado for the Divell*, Brathwait bullied: "Be honest still and thou art out of the swing of this strappado: if thou play Recreant . . . the *Author* hath vowed hee will play Arch-Pyrate with thee, tie thee like a Gallie slave to the Mast of his *Malu-Speranza*, and ferrie thee over into *Tartarie*." And in his *Abuses Stript* Wither concluded his epistle to the reader, "*I will say no more but this*, Read and Welcome, *but* Censure not, *for your Judgement is weake, and I utterly renounce it.*"

We shall never know how many would-be authors, contemplating their hostile audience, either closed their inkhorns or gave their manuscripts to the fire. We do know, however, that relatively few took the next most obvious recourse of hiding behind a pseudonym or initials. Even more rare are those who followed John Donne; in publishing *An Anatomy of the World* (1611), he excluded all clues to his identity. But there were other ways to have one's cake and eat it—publish, that is, and yet escape the stigma of print. William Percy, publishing his *Coelia* sonnet sequence in 1594, gives a typical example of the strategy of deflected responsibility for publication: "Courteous Reader, whereas I was fullie determined to have concealed my Sonnets, as thinges privie to my selfe, yet of courtesie having lent them to some, they were secretlie committed to the Presse, and almost finished, before it came to my knowledge. Wherefore making, as they say, *Vertue of necessitie*, I did deeme it most convenient to praepose mine Epistle." Convenient indeed! This—like many such ameliorations of necessity in front matter—sounds suspect, an example perhaps of *sprezzatura* in its more elaborately deceitful form. Contrary to Percy's suggestion, sonnets were not written by normal persons strictly for themselves. The timely discovery of the outrage, and the interpolation of a polite epistle begging indulgence for the poet's "toyes and amorous devises" must also strike us as altogether too fortuitous.

Demanding even more incredulity are the circumstances of another 1594 publication: *Willobie his Avisa, or the true picture of a modest Maid*, which required an (alleged?) accomplice. In an epistle, one Hadrian Dorrell related how publication came to pass. Henry Willoby, it seems, wished to "see the fashions of other countries for a time [and], at his departure, chose me amongst the rest of his friends, unto whome he reposed so much trust, that he delivered me the key of his studie, and the use of all his bookes till his returne. Amongest which (perusing them at leysure) I found many prety & witty conceites, as I suppose of his owne dooing. One among the rest I fancied so much, that I have ventered so farre upon his frendship, as to publish it without his consent." Is this conceivable? Would a trusted friend dare to presume to this unimaginable extent? Or did Willoby, before setting forth, simply say to Dorrell, I'd like to print these pieces. See what you can do, but not before I'm on the Continent; I don't want to know about it. The fact that four more editions of *Avisa* appeared over the next fifteen years, apparently without authorial apoplexy, perhaps answers these questions.

Publication by a factor is the most extreme form of deflecting responsibility for becoming "a man in print." One more example is worth our attention, since the factor in this case was extremely assiduous in the performance of his duties. The volume in question is Humphrey Gilbert's *Discourse of a discoverie of a new passage to Cataia* (1576). George Gascoigne writes that one day he was "verie bolde to demaunde of [Gilbert] howe he spente his time in this loytering vacation from martial strategemes." Gilbert "curteously tooke me up into his Studie, and there shewed me sundrie profitable and verie commendable exercises, which he had perfected painefuly with his owne penne." Among these was a manuscript on a route to Cathay. "I craved [it] at the said *S. Humphreyes* handes for two or three dayes to reade and to peruse. And hee verie friendly granted my request, but stil seming to doubt that thereby the same might, contrarie to his former determination, be Imprinted." Gascoigne liked what he read: "Wherupon I have (as you see) caused my friendes great travaile, and mine owne greater presumption to be registred in print."

This scenario must raise a smile because it is almost impossible to believe. If the stigma of print was so terrible, it is hard to reconcile Gascoigne's friendship with such presumption. More plausibly, the two friends recognized that Gascoigne, already several times an author, was just the person to see the discourse through the press. Be that as it may, our present interest lies in what Gascoigne then writes in his epistle to the reader: "But since I have thus adventured both his rebuke, and mine owne reproofe, let me thus muche alledge in both our defences." There are five points to this defense. The first appeals rather crazily to common sense: "It is but a Pamphlet & no large discourse, & therefore the more to be borne withall: since the faults (if any be) shalbe the fewer, because the volume is not great." The second and third we have already met: "It was ment by th'autour, but as a private Letter unto his Brother . . . and therefore his imperfections therein (if any were) are to be pardoned"; "it commeth foorth without his consent: So that he had neither warning nor time to examine, nor yet to amende anie thing that were worthie misliking." The fourth defense is the one that would be central today: "it treateth of a matter whereof no man hath heretofore written particularly."[17] The last defense is the most philosophical: "it is to bee considered, that of thinges uncertaine, the greatest Clerke that ever was could write but probably." For good measure Gascoigne adduces the approval of "a great learned man"—John Dee—in this enterprise. Blurbs had not yet been invented.

Gilbert's alleged reluctance to publish and Gascoigne's elaborate excuses for doing so are commonplace in Renaissance front matter. Except possibly in instances of posthumous publication, however, these qualms are usually hard to accept at face value. In every case a volume has appeared; scruples have been overmastered. These scruples, I believe, go beyond mere pessimism about finding the appreciative reader, as Brathwait expresses it: "I have ever resolved to have this Motto: *Catoni solus dormio*: But where that Cato is, there's the difficulty. Hee is too heavy for the Court, too wise for the Citty, and too precise for the Countrey" (*The Schollers Medley*, 1614). Such scruples also go beyond the strenuous task of finding a patron who could provide "a sufficient rampier to shield me from the battery of . . . venemous tongues" (Florio, *First Fruites*).

These scruples, as Florio's phrasing hints, have more to do with the sociopolitical implications of publication, which was inevitably a calling of attention to oneself and ultimately a form of ascent or aspiration. Any form of earned, or labored, rather than inherited ascent caused considerable tension along the jealously guarded lies designating "degree, priority, and place" in English society. Publication exerted pressure along these lines and naturally excited envy. The worst epithet Greene could muster for Shakespeare was "upstart," and this is the worst that Norfolk can imply about Wolsey in *Henry VIII* (1.1.58-66). Also perceived as threatening in this hierarchical system was the ability and willingness to rise without becoming "allied / To eminent assistants"—as Norfolk says Wolsey does. As regards front matter, though, the exception proves the rule: volumes with courting pretensions did not dare to omit the formalities expected by the powerful. The absence of a dedication in the 1609 edition of the Sonnets thus led the author of the *Dictionary of National Biography* essay on William Herbert, Earl of Pembroke, to reject him as their dedicatee, "Mr. W. H.": "Pembroke's rank and dignity rendered it practically impossible that he should be deprived of those customary formalities of address which formed a prominent part of all extant dedications to him." Like all forms of ascent, publishing benefited from protection, if not encouragement, from "eminent assistants." Front matter existed, that is, took the various forms in which it appears, to ease and mask with politeness the urgent search for such assistants.

London presented "a ripe-judging world . . . full of envie" not only for poets but also for all who competed for the few available patrons. In this charged atmosphere the political act of publishing a volume was, like any overtly ambitious act, bound to excite hostility. The only ways to neutralize envious backbiting was by the forms of *sprezzatura* we have been examining. For example, Thomas Bradshaw wrote that every reader possesses an "emulous and covetous minde" (*The Shepherds Starre*); he might have been describing those who danced attendance in the Tudor or Stuart court. Front matter is an extraordinarily politicized venue; the air of hostility that hangs over it can thus be taken as a reflection of the greater political world, where viperous carpers like Antonio and Sebastian in *The Tempest* were everywhere. Composers of front matter, like all courting souls, had to take great care "in this moralizing age, wherein every one seeks to shew himselfe a Politician by mis-interpreting" (Nashe, *Pierce Pennilesse*). All authors who published their work were therefore subject to the squeamishness felt in this *sprezzatura* of Alfonso Ferrabosco: "Least I fall under the *Character* of the vaine-glorious Man, in some opinions, by thrusting so much of my industrie in Print, I would all knew how little fame I hope for that way." [18]

Publishing required elaborate mediation and elicited much hand-wringing because it represented not only an ascent but a descent as well, a submission to the populace. No wonder authors were queasy about the prospect, and no wonder too that dedications and epistles to the reader often rest uncomfortably next to each other, as in the case of Edmund Bert's *Approved Treatise of Hawkes and Hawking* (1619). The dedication to the Earl of Oxford is in the usual fulsome vein; however, the address to the "friendly" paying reader makes it clear that he is an undesired interloper in what ought to have been a strictly patron-client transaction: "I did never purpose to publish in common these my labours, but to have given them privately to whom they are dedicated, and to whom I stand devoted." Submission to the marketplace is expressed more pertinently for the present study by Giles Fletcher the Elder in a dedication to Lady Molyneux dated 4 September 1593. Offering his *Licia, or Poemes of Love*, Fletcher adduces two reasons why such "trifling labor" as "Poems and Sonnets of Love" is accounted "a thing foolishly odious in this age": "one, that so many base companions are the greatest writers, the other, that our English *Genevian* puritie hath quite debarred us of honest recreation." The crisis of the aristocracy, in other words, was occurring in the economy of letters as it was everywhere else. Base companions—and a great one was just about to make his entrance with *Venus and Adonis*—were establishing themselves ever more prominently as authors and as readers. The scene was becoming, in every sense of the word, more vulgar. Authors, though happy to let slip their displeasure at the necessity, became increasingly obliged to address their commercial public and the marketplace, where their labors were "bought and sold/Like slaves."

Fletcher's second point suggests why poets were more particularly subject to embarrassment when they determined to come into print. The vast outpouring of ecclesiastical titles from the period, dwarfing the scattered volumes that now give the Elizabethan age its golden reputation, is sufficiently suggestive of the heavy pall of "*Genevian* puritie" cast over English life. Heaviness, gravity, solemnity, impassivity— one suspects that these were the more usual poses in the corridors of power. John Harington's strenuous, often eloquent, unpublished "Treatise on Playe" (*circa* 1596) suggests as much, and it was precisely his celebrated playfulness that prevented him from being taken seriously at court. The affectation of seriousness is also hinted in Elizabeth's fury at the possibility that her writing of verse might become public knowledge and sully her dignity. Though one might enjoy aureate and amorous conceits, it was safer to enjoy them condescendingly. Thus Nashe had the effrontery to admit in his prefatory essay to *Astrophil and Stella*, "my stile is somewhat heavie gated, and cannot daunce trip and goe so lively, with oh my love, ah my love, all my loves gone, as other Sheepheards that have beene fooles in the Morris time out of minde." Even Sidney required excuse from his printer in this kind: "the Argument perhaps may seeme too light for your grave viewe." Chilliness, or the affectation of chilliness, was the usual response to poetry. Thus, cool appeals to gravity were in order even when the work being presented was lighter than air. The printer of some of Spenser's poems, including *Muiopotmos*, advertised them in his epistle as "verie grave and profitable." In 1594 Percy promised, apropos of the "toyes and amorous devises" of *Coelia*: "ere long, I will impart unto the world another Poeme which shall be more fruitfull and ponderous." Similarly, Shakespeare promises in his dedication for *Venus and Adonis* "some graver labour" to follow.

Before we turn to dedicatees themselves, one further dedication deserves our attention. It is unique, remarkable, and, I believe, sheds some light on Shakespeare's abandonment of genres requiring "dedicated words."

George Wither wrote this dedication for the satirical volume of poems *Abuses Stript and Whipt* (1613), which apparently became the rage of London (four editions in that year) and, like *Venus and Adonis* for Shakespeare, gave Wither's career a flying start. Like all poets whose muse is cankered, Wither warns his reader, in a separate epistle, to expect bluntness, rather than "*Poeticall* additions or faigned *Allegories*." He also explicitly dissociates himself from the formal, aureate style of three of the period's most aristocratic poets: "Do not looke for *Spencers*, or *Daniels* wel composed numbers; or the deepe conceits of now flourishing *Johnson*: no; say Tis honest plain matter, and that's as much as I expect."

Exercising, therefore, the license of satire, Wither offered ("contrary to the worlds custome") an eight-page dedication titled "To himselfe, G.W. wisheth *all happinesse*." Wither thus renounces the usual courtesies of front matter and offers seven reasons for doing so. These constitute as piercing an anatomy of the custom of dedications as the period affords and suggest why a sensible author might well wish to throw over dedications entirely. This makes Wither something of a Montaigne among dedicators—subversive, astonishingly self-composed, and self-serving, with an air of truculence never met in dedications to aristocrats: "I will not like our *Great-ones* stand so much upon my authority as to make my *Will* my *Reason*" (One thinks of Shakespeare's supremely willful great one, Lear.) Here are Wither's reasons:

First, is this: I could not amongst all men finde any man in my opinion so fitting for this purpose, but either my *Worke* was unworthy, or too worthy his Patronage. Secondly, it is said: *Obsequium amicos veritas odium parit*: and I doubting my free speech would hardly make a *Diapason*, pleasing to the eare of a common *Mecanas*, thought it best to hold my tong. . . . Thirdly, seeing I know but what men appeare, & not what they are, I had rather indure the *Kites tyranny*, then with *Aesops* Dove make the Sparrow-hauke my *Champion*. Fourthly, if I have spoken *Truth* it is able to defend it selfe; if not, who-ere be my Patron, it is I must answere for it. Fiftly, forasmuch as I know my own mind best, I purpose if need be to become my owne *Advocate*. Sixtly, for my owne sake I first made it; and therfore certaine I am I my selfe have most right unto it. But seaventhly, & lastly . . . I have made this *Dedication* to thee poor *world-despised Self* even to put thee in mind . . . that thou take heed to thine own words. [A3v́4r]

Wither then moves into a long homiletic renunciation of the world's "vanities and presumptions."

Such dedicatory hubris is impressive and distinctive. The assumption that the patron must fit the work and not vice versa is striking, as is the notion of a *common* Maecenas (the classical Roman epitome of a generous patron). The sense of how difficult it is to discern true virtue in the appearances of the powerful and of the unwillingness to risk trusting them is daring. The notions (reason four) that truth can defend itself and that patrons could not prove useful in concealing falsehood would have struck the average Renaissance courtier as a dangerous, foolish indulgence in "neat integrity" (Donne's phrase). The last three reasons are prime expressions of a firmly centered self.

As usual for the satirist, the voice here is one of self-ostracism from the norms and customs to which the author is obligated. In this, Wither's dedication calls to mind a Shakespearean character who notoriously acts "contrary to the worlds custome" and who will appear again in subsequent chapters: Coriolanus. Wither, refusing great ones a right to his labor and announcing that he will write "to my selfe, whose disposition I am better acquainted with" is cast from the same mould as the proud Roman. For example, his "self" shares the Roman's cynicism about human nature ("Thou knowest," Wither says of his self, "mans nature to be uncertaine, and prone to forgetfulnesse") and, like Coriolanus has "made the World [his] enemy" and been exposed "to the malice thereof." The satirist's warning is pure Coriolanus: "I had a care to please my selfe as wel as others; and if the World blame me as too sawcy with her, 'tis for want of manners " And Coriolanus feels about the Roman plebes as Wither does about his readers: "I have had experience of your insufficiencie." Wither, in sum, seeks to affect exactly the pose of Coriolanus when the warrior boasts that he will "stand / As if a man were author of himself / And knew no other kin" (5.3.35-37).

In real life an author, or any suitor, who persisted in such "rough, unswayable, and free" behavior (5.6.25) would have enjoyed a brief, futile courtly career. Coriolanus's pose is unfeigned and leads toward tragedy; Wither's pose is a humorist's Mercutio-like *jeu d'esprit* that leads us toward comedy. But our present purposes require us to draw a serious conclusion from this dedication: A Renaissance poet restive at the impositions of writing courting poetry and the dedications it entailed might well have thought along the lines expressed by Wither in the passage I have quoted. Whether Shakespeare, after writing *The Rape of Lucrece*, entertained Wither's sixth reason for renouncing dedications and vowed never to write another, we shall never know. But I am tempted to think of the "blinde custome" of dedications handed to Shakespeare by "methodicall antiquitie" when I read Coriolanus's derisive

Custom calls me to't.
What custom wills, in all things should we do't,

> The dust on antique time would lie unswept,
> And mountainous error be too highly heap'd
> For truth to o'erpeer. Rather than fool it so,
> Let the high office and the honor go. [2.3.117–22]

⁂

High office and honor in Shakespeare's time were monopolized by a small, select class of Londoners. The best that suitors, especially suitors who were "base companions," could hope for was to enjoy the comfortable shade provided by important genealogical branches, to borrow an image of which dedicators were fond.[19] Competition for this shade was keen, with suitors using great ingenuity and whatever means available to pierce into the targeted presence: ladies eager to be in waiting their beauty and ancestry, merchants their accumulated wealth, artisans their skills, country gentry their patrimony—and authors their books: "O let my books be then the eloquence / And dumb presagers of my speaking breast, / Who plead for love and look for recompense" (SON 23).

The importunate attentions of authors pleading for aristocratic love and looking for various kinds of recompense were among the occupational hazards of high office or title during the Renaissance. Edward Blount, printer of a 1616 translation of Epictetus's works, wrote aptly of "this scribling age, wherein great persons are so pestered dayly with Dedications." Blount's dedicatee scarcely needed to be told this. He was William Herbert, Earl of Pembroke and then Lord Chamberlain. Aubrey accounted Herbert "the greatest Maecenas to learned men of any peer of his time or since," with more than eighty-five books dedicated to him, chief among them being the first Folio (his brother shared the honor).

Before reviewing the two Shakespearean dedications we should consider, perhaps I should say sympathize with, some of the age's more prominent dedicatees like Pembroke and attempt to imagine how it felt to be on the receiving end of so many dedications. One way to do this is by reconstructing the "dedicatory lives" of these figures, a task facilitated by recourse to Franklin Williams's *Index of Dedications and Commendatory Verse in English Books before 1641* (1962), which is based on the numbering in Pollard and Redgrave's *Short Title Catalogue*. In the process, we may also be able to assess certain generalizations about dedications of the time. One of these, noted previously, is Wright's assertion that "literall labours are usually offered to such personages, with whom they particularlie consort." Thomas Heywood makes a similarly optimistic assessment: "Elaborate Poems have ever aym'd at learned Patrons, who valued Books as your best Lapidaries praise Jewels, not by their greatnesse, but their goodnesse."[20]

Wright and Heywood are expressing an ideal, and no doubt ideal matches between subject matter and dedicatee occurred now and then. But it seems clear that more often than not dedicatees must have been indifferent, bemused, or bored by the prospect of reading the volumes carrying their names. Let us see first, though, what Williams's index can tell us.

A census of books either dedicated to "the greatest Maecenas" or carrying epistolary matter addressed to him presents a picture at once predictable and curious. Predictably, dedicators followed the fortunes of their targets, encouraging the assumption that a book's subject was not necessarily tailored specifically to the intended patron. For example, during the first three decades of Pembroke's life, dedicatory activity was desultory. Henry Parry, a future Bishop of Worcester, struck first, when Herbert was fourteen and still only earl-apparent, on the lugubrious note of *Victoria Christiana* (1594). But it was a prophetic and typical note for, in the cases we shall examine, a constant feature is the high percentage of sacred titles—a reminder of the awesome hegemony of exegetical, homiletic, and sectarian titles during this period. Of the nearly ninety titles in which Pembroke figured, almost fifty can be classified as religious. It is impossible to reconcile what we know of Pembroke's life with so much "heavenly eloquence."

Pembroke's early years present an oddly mixed bag, averaging not quite one title a year between 1595 and 1610: a study of water works, a *Theorike and practike of moderne Warres*, and Augustine's *City of God*. In 1603, in James's honor, Pembroke's former tutor Daniel presented him with a *Panegyrike Congratulatorie* that included the "Defence of Ryme." And there is some drollery here too. In 1602 when Pembroke was in disgrace in the Fleet because of the Mary Fitton liaison, his good angel John Davies of Hereford presented him with *Mirum in modum: A Glimpse of Gods Glorie and the Soules Shape;* his bad angel Francis Davison dedicated the *Poetical Rapsody* to him with a sonnet that begins by flagrantly "salving" the "amiss" as the speaker does on Shakespeare's Sonnet 35: "Great Earle, whose high and noble minde, is higher / And nobler, then thy noble high Degree: / Whose outward shape, though it most lovely bee, / Doth in faire Robes a fairer Soule attier." Aside from succeeding to the earldom in 1601, the most important promotion of Pembroke's career was his appointment as Lord Chamberlain in 1615. Dedicators scurried: in the preceding five years there had been six dedications; in 1616 alone there were ten. From then until his death in 1630, Pembroke's dedications rose markedly to about four a year.

What can be said of this long list of titles dedicated to Pembroke? While the odds favored sermons from one divine or another, it is safe to say the Earl probably never knew what would appear next on the paper flood: a history of Venice, a genealogy, a treatise on gunnery, a book of songs, a dictionary, or an *Elementa Jurisprudentiae*. On a few occasions he must have been not only flattered but interested. He was particularly concerned with foreign explorations and must have received a few geographies and Moryson's *Itinerary* with pleasure. In 1614 Pembroke became a member of the East India Company and the following year received Henri de Feynes's *Exact and curious survey of all the East Indies*. No doubt the complete works of Jonson, whose book buying Pembroke is well known to have subsidized, came to him in 1616 as no surprise.

The list of titles is indeed an impressively long one, but how substantial was his "achievement" as a dedicatee? It is difficult to deny Aubrey's high praise to the dedicatee for Jonson's *Workes* and the co-dedicatee for Shakespeare's Folio. But, taking into account Pembroke's relatively long life and high office, his dedicatory experience does not show a strikingly individual personality. For anyone familiar with the pages of the *Short Title Catalogue*, the titles Williams listed under the Earl's name reflect in a very general way the typical landscape of publishing at the time: many divine texts and then a grab bag of subjects from hither and yon, excluding, of course, titles beneath the Earl's station.[21] One might guess that Pembroke favored poets, to be sure, but it would be hard to vouch for his sophistication or taste in what we see. He garnered Davies' *Microcosmos* and Chapman's *Homer*, but many of the smaller fry are present too: William Browne with *Brittania's Pastorals*, Anton's and Wither's satires, a religious poem by Quarles, and the complete works of the "Water Poet." The overall effect is less than astonishing. One senses vigorous attentions on the part of ambitious dedicators and passivity on the part of the dedicatee. This renders the more pregnant Anton's hope, expressed to Pembroke, "onely . . . for the passive part of your noble patronage" (*Philosopher's Satyres*, 1616). No single person could have summoned genuine interest for very much in this vast array; books were received and dedications perused with greatly varying degrees of pleasure or ennui. Some no doubt made less impression than a Hallmark card does today.

Easily the most stunning dedicatory life of the period was Prince Henry's. The boy might have been forgiven if, toward the end of his short life (1594-1612), he had begun to feel a dyspeptic bibliophobia, for between 1599 and 1612 he was the object of almost a hundred dedications and epistles. He was thus perfectly situated to enjoy the satire on front matter in *Coryats Crudities*, which was dedicated to him. Though Henry achieved something of a reputation for patronizing authors, contemporary descriptions of him suggest that, unlike Prospero, he was not dedicated to closeness and his books. Charles Cornwallis, for instance, mentions several of the Prince's pastimes (see quotation on page 119); reading was not one of them. The library he accumulated in his later years was distinctly not principality large enough.

The census for Henry suggests that his experience was generally like Pembroke's. Over a third of his volumes are devoted to religious matters. Henry was not without some interest in the period's religious controversies and diplomacy, but one suspects in this interest a boy's taste for the heroic exertions these promised to entail on the Continent. Henry's career began at the age of five on the appropriate note of his father's *Basilikon Doron*. His interests were extraordinarily diverse; hence, a higher percentage of volumes demonstrably accord with what we know of him: equitation (Markham's *Cavelarice; or the English Horseman*); gunnery (de Gheyn's *Exercise of Armes for Caliures, Muskettes, and Pikes*); music (songs from Jones, Morley, and Ferrabosco); architecture (the superb Serlio translation); bibliography (a catalogue of the Thomas Bodley library); and his special naval passion (Wright's *Certaine errors in navigation*). Some other titles were practically inevitable: Robert Fletcher's *Nine Worthies* (the Prince was to be the ninth Henry), an English-Scots history, and George More's *Principles for yong Princes*.

Henry's dedications and epistles leave one startling impression perti nent to our study: Poetry and poets loom small and very peripherally in the princely entourage of books. Most notable is Chapman's translation of the *Iliad*, and there is a small volume of Horace. As for native poetry, there is Hugh Holland's *Pancharis* (1603), William Alexander's *Paraenesis to the prince* (1604), a Chapman poem called *Euthymiae raptus, or the Teares of Peace* (1609), and a reprint of the old-hat *Mirror for Magistrates*. That is all. Where, one wonders, was the legion of poets during his brief but flourishing life who sang his praises so strenuously at his death?

To Lucy, Countess of Bedford, Jonson wrote a poem to accompany "Mr. Donne's Satires." It began, "Lucy, you brightness of our sphere, who are / Life of the muses' day, their morning star! / If works (not th'authors) their own grace should look, / Whose poems would not wish to be your book!" (66). The census for Lucy reminds us that the *Index* can only tell us about patron-client relationships that issued in publication. It would not reveal Donne's devotion to her, nor would the mere dedication of *Cynthia's Revels* disclose Jonson's. Daniel's gratitude, though, is memorialized in the dedication of his *Vision of Twelve Goddesses*, and there are four dedications from Drayton. Another of Lucy's clients, Florio, dedicated both his Italian-English dictionary and the 1603 Montaigne translation to her. Also notable are a volume of Dowland songs, a treatise on chess play, and an epistle to Lucy in Chapman's 1610 edition of the *Iliad*. There is much here in which the Countess could have taken pride, but we can nevertheless observe that her long dedicatory life does not seem to have been very busy, considering she was such a well-publicized patroness: from 1595 until her death in 1627, there were only about thirty dedications and a half-dozen epistles (about one title a year). As usual, religious texts—seventeen in all—predominate. And the list of titles, though wide-ranging, must also be accounted shallow, offering no real generic focus and boasting no poetical title of the first rank. No great poems wished, in Jonson's phrase, to be her book.[22]

A figure from the preceding generation with the reputation of a patron to poets was Edward de Vere, seventeenth Earl of Oxford, who succeeded to the hereditary title of Lord High Chamberlain in 1562 at the age of twelve and lived until 1604. He flourished, of course, before the explosion of publishing at century's end, and as might be expected his census is decidedly modest, consisting of fewer than thirty dedications and epistles. Only four are religious texts; two of these are verse translations from the Bible (by Golding and Lok). Otherwise, Oxford received a bellettristic potpourri: a Latin Castiglione, Greene's *Gwydonius*, Lyly's *Euphues and his England*, Munday's translation of *Palmerin d'Oliva*, Thomas Watson's *Passionate Centurie of Love* sonnet sequence, and two John Farmer songbooks. Dwarfing these titles and a very odd miscellany of other items is the 1590 edition of *The Faerie Queene*, which appended an epistolary sonnet to Oxford (and sonnets for eight others). Oxford may have enjoyed a reputation for favoring poets (and was known to be skilled in verse), but it would require clairvoyance to prove this from the *Index*.

Most prominent figures fared roughly as (to take a random example) did Edward Russell, third Earl of Bedford. In his lifetime (1574-1627), he received fifteen dedications. Twelve were for religious texts; one, a poetical work (Drayton's *Englands Heroicall Epistles*); one, a travel book; and another, a life of the Earl's father.

We arrive now at Henry Wriothesley, third Earl of Southampton (1573-1624). Though he lived almost as long as Pembroke, his census is much more modest. He received twenty-two dedications (five shared), of which ten brought him religious works. Aside from the Shakespearean dedications, the only other noteworthy volumes represented are Florio's *Wordes* (1598), Ferrabosco's *Lessons* (1609), and Nashe's *Traveller* (1594). Those who like to imagine something of the Earl lies in Shakespeare's characterization of Adonis may find intriguing the fact that the very first dedication came with John Clapham's *Narcissus sive amoris juvenilis descriptio* (1591). Southampton was extremely lucky in his epistolary fortunes. He received ten (again, some shared), every one of them for a poetical work: Barnes's *Parthenophil and Parthenope* (1593), Lok's *Ecclesiastes in Poetrie* (1597); Markham's tragedy *Sir Richard Grinvile, Knight* (1595); the *Anagrammata T. Egertoni* (1603); Davies's *Microcosmos* (1603); Daniel's *Panegyrike* (1603), *Philotas* (1605), and *Complete Works* (1623); Chapman's *Homer* (1610); and Wither's *Abuses Stript* (1613).

Southampton's reputation for encouraging poetry may have been merely the consequence of wishful thinking among poets. If it was genuine, the published evidence is rather thin, though, as we know, patronizing activities did not necessarily result in publication. At any rate, Southampton's reputation blossomed almost overnight. In 1594, by which time only *Narcissus*, *Parthenophil*, and *Venus and Adonis* had appeared, Nashe wrote of Southampton: "A dere lover and cherisher you are, as well of the lovers of Poets, as of Poets themselves." Two decades later the reputation had assumed a graver tone, with Brathwait addressing the Earl as "Learnings best Favorite": "In these times (my honourable Lord) wee may find some Roiall Seedes of pristine Nobility (wherein we may glory) reserved, as it were, from so great ruines for the preservation of Learning, and the continuance of all vertuous Studies; amongst which your Noble Selfe, as generally reputed learned, so a profest friend to such as be studious of learning" (*The Schollers Medley*). Some years later this reputation was cemented by a large donation for the library of his Cambridge college, St. John's.

What are the effects of reading a lifetime of Southampton dedications and epistles? One is to be happy on Shakespeare's behalf that he was among the first dedicators. Perhaps the Earl had not yet tired of this dubious perquisite of being a great one; however, one fears that the boy, already twelve years an earl in 1593, was probably by then somewhat jaundiced with court contempt. Any teenager capable of writing an essay in Ciceronian Latin on the theme "All men are moved to the pursuit of virtue by the hope of reward" and sending it to his guardian Burghley, as Southampton did the year *Venus and Adonis* appeared, was presumably capable of piercing into the motives of poets in pursuit of patrons.

What is certain, however, is the tedious sameness of Southampton's front matter, where we find the typical spectacle of authors maneuvering into strange postures because they believe, as the Steward says to the Countess in *All's Well That Ends Well*, "we wound our modesty, and make foul the clearness of our deservings, when of ourselves we *publish* them" (1.3.3-5). This sense of modesty wounded by the temerity of publication is intimately related to the psychology of clientage in general and is, for instance, often strikingly apparent in the Sonnets. Virtually all dedications say, in so many words and often with very similar horticultural imagery, what the speaker of Sonnet 37 says:

> I, made lame by fortune's dearest spite,
> Take all my comfort of thy worth and truth.
> For whether beauty, birth, or wealth, or wit,
> Or any of these all, or all, or more,
> Entitled in thy parts to crownèd sit,
> I make my love engrafted to this store.[23]

The speaker of Sonnet 72 confesses, "I am shamed by that which I bring forth"; even greater the shame of publishing what one wrote. The self-deprecation of Sonnet 103 ("Alack what poverty my muse brings forth") is a nearly constant element of the Southampton dedications, as the following phrases from them suggest:

> unpolisht, rough, unsmoothed Poetry
> this phantasticall Treatise
> this handfull of leaves . . . these unpolisht leaves . . . my idle leaves
> mine aborted infant . . . maymed and corrupted
> these worthlesse leaves . . . Sprong from a rude and unmanured lande
> these blasted leaves
> this my abortive issue
> the stubborne stroke of my harsh song
> the fruit of some idle houres

The ennui of receiving dedication after dedication farced with sentiments of this sort appears to have been constant for the Earl, except for some specially egregious tactics that might have elicited real disgust. One author not very appetizingly promises a future work "seeming full of prolixitie, yet with delight avoyding satietie." Another, wisely hiding behind initials, offers a dedicatory "Catalogue of those names unto whom this work is appropriated," and then lists the King, Queen, Prince, and twenty-nine others in addition to the Earl. There is but one breath of almost-fresh air—a dedication that manages its task with poise and simplicity. This is Ferrabosco's, and the fact that it is one of the shortest of all is not its least charm:

> TO THE PERFECTION
> OF HONOUR,
> My Lord,
> *HENRY,*
> EARLE of South-hampton.

Whilst other men study your *Titles* (Honourable Lord) I doe your *Honours*; and finde it a nearer way to give actions, then words: for the talking man commonly goes about, and meetes the justice at his errours end, not to be beleev'd. Yet, if in modest actions, the circumstances of singularitie, and profession hurt not; it is true, that I made these *Compositions* solely for your Lordship, and doe here professe it. By which time, I have done all that I had in purpose, and returne to my silence:

> Where you are most honor'd
> by   *Alfonso Ferrabosco*

We shall now take a look at the front matter in Shakespeare, some of which requires little comment here. Well known and justly admired is the front matter of the Folio: the Droeshout engraving; the poised, touching dedication to Pembroke and Montgomery (though one wishes Heminge and Condell could have avoided calling the plays "these trifles," not once but twice); the address "To the great Variety of Readers," which contains the first and still best advice on how to appreciate Shakespeare ("Read him therefore; and againe, and againe"); the supreme encomiastic poem by Jonson; and Holland's "Upon the Lines and Life of the Famous Scenicke Poet." The publisher of the 1622 quarto of *The Trageody of Othello*, Thomas Walkley, prefixed an epistle, "The Stationer to the Reader," which began: "To set forth a booke without an Epistle, were like to the old English proverbe, *A blew coat without a badge*, & the Author being dead, I thought good to take that piece of worke upon mee." Why Walkley felt thus obliged is hard to fathom, since plays ordinarily came from the press without epistolary formalities.

The 1609 quarto of *The Famous Historie of Troylus and Cresseid* appeared with a one-and-a-half-page essay titled "A never writer, to an ever reader. Newes." This non-Shakespearean epistle is of present interest mainly because it is so obviously a product of the marketplace. Its purpose is to assure a return on investment, and one senses here that its author is trying to make the best of what might have been an unremunerative situation. Why, after all, buy a play never "stal'd with the Stage"?[24] Though blatant puffery, we must admit it is perfectly accurate: "This authors Commedies . . . are so fram'd to the life, that they serve for the most common Commentaries, of all the actions of our lives, shewing such a dexteritie, and power of witte, that the most displeased with Playes, are pleasd with his Commedies." The writer then turns to a harder sell—"beleeve this, that when hee is gone, and his Commedies out of sale, you will scramble for them"—and finally to a little bullying: "Take this for a warning, and at the perrill of your pleasures losses, and Judgements, refuse not."

The *Troilus* epistle is heavy (to borrow a phrase from Chapman) with "the leaden gravitie of [a] Mony-Monger."[25] But the gravity of the two Shakespearean dedications is of an entirely different kind. These, the author's sole efforts in this species, are reproduced here and deserve careful examination (see figures 2 and 3).

My principal conclusion about these dedications can be stated at the outset. Experienced against the background of hundreds of dedications from imaginative and bellettristic volumes of the period (with special attention to years bordering the appearance of *Venus and Adonis* in 1593 and *The Rape of Lucrece* in 1594), Shakespeare's two dedications are in every respect orthodox and impersonal. They might in fact be called the only thoroughly unremarkable productions we have from Shakespeare's pen were this carefully calculated orthodoxy itself not worthy of remark. We have already sampled their obsequious tone and "serviceable" posture in several contemporary dedications; what is required here is some attention to Shakespeare's diction and imagery, almost every instance of which represents a cliché among contemporary dedicators.

The identification of *Lucrece's* published form as a "pamphlet," for instance, performs several standard dedicatory functions. First, it identifies the size of the poet's labor as being small and therefore (as we learned from Gascoigne earlier) the more easily borne. In the same vein, Lyly called *Euphues* "this pamphlet," Richard Barnfield hoped that "this small Pamphlet may recreate your mindes" (*Greenes Funeralls*, 1594), and Spenser described a poem (*Daphnaïda*, 1591) about the length of *Venus and Adonis*, as "this Pamphlet." Second, *pamphlet* also probably intimated that the subject matter might be enjoyable, in counterdistinction to "tractates," "commentaries," and "treatises." The printer Robert Jones knew that "curteous Gentlemen" would provide a market for "any pleasing Pamphlet," just as stuffy John Case railed in 1592 at the appearance of "so many pamphlets . . . of wanton love and daliance."[26] Third, Shakespeare achieved a note of self-deprecation with the term *pamphlet*, then the epithet of choice for this purpose. William Webbe abhors the "infinite fardles of printed pamphlets" pestering the country, especially "such as are either mere Poeticall, or which tende in some respecte . . . to Poetry." Cornwallis was particularly hostile to the printed matter with which Shakespeare chose to associate *Lucrece*: "Pamphlets, and lying Stories, and News, and two penny Poets I would knowe them, but beware of beeing familiar with them: my custome is to read these, and presently to make use of them, for they lie in my privy, and when I come thither, and have occasion to imploy it, I read them, halfe a side at once is my ordinary, which when I have read, I use in that kind, that waste paper is most subject to, but to cleanlier profit."[27] One wonders whimsically if the fact that only one copy of the first *Venus and Adonis*

TO THE RIGHT HONORABLE
Henrie VVriothesley, Earle of Southampton,
and Baron of Titchfield.

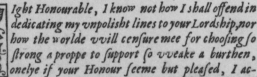 *Ight Honourable, I know not how I shall offend in dedicating my vnpolisht lines to your Lordship, nor how the worlde vvill censure mee for choosing so strong a proppe to support so vveake a burthen, onelye if your Honour seeme but pleased, I ac-count my selfe highly praised, and vowe to take aduantage of all idle houres, till I haue honoured you vvith some grauer labour. But if the first heire of my inuention proue deformed, I shall be sorie it had so noble a god-father : and neuer after eare so barren a land, for feare it yeeld me still so bad a haruest, I leaue it to your Honou-rable suruey, and your Honor to your hearts content, vvhich I wish may alvvaies ansvvere your ovvne vvish, and the vvorlds hope-full expectation.*

Your Honors in all dutie,

William Shakespeare.

Fig. 2 Dedication, *Venus and Adonis*, 1593.
(Courtesy of The Bodleian Library, *Arch G e 31(2)*, A4r)

TO THE RIGHT

HONOVRABLE, HENRY
VVriothesley, Earle of Southhampton,
and Baron of Titchfield.

 HE loue I dedicate to your Lordship is without end:wherof this Pamphlet without beginning is but a superfluous Moity. The warrant I haue of your Honourable disposition, not the worth of my vntutord Lines makes it assured of acceptance. VVhat I haue done is yours, what I haue to doe is yours, being part in all I haue, deuoted yours. VVere my worth greater, my duety would shew greater, meane time, as it is, it is bound to your Lordship; To whom I wish long life still lengthned with all happinesse.

Your Lordships in all duety.

William Shakespeare.

A 2

Fig. 3. Dedication, *The Rape of Lucrece*, 1594.
(Courtesy of The Elizabethan Club, Yale University)

edition has come down to us is attributable to such hygiene. At any rate, Shakespeare's only other use of the word *pamphlet* (1H6 3.1.2) describes a cunningly prepared document.

In many other respects Shakespeare's tactics are typical. When a poet was making his debut, it was natural for him to allude to "the first heire of [his] invention." In the same year as *Venus*, Anthony Chute presented an epyllion to Sir Edward Winkfield with a reference to "the first invention of [his] beginning Muse" (*Beautie Dishonoured*). It was also tempting, as we have seen, to presume on the continuation of the client-patron relationship by promising, as Shakespeare did, some future "labour." Daniel promises "lines heereafter better laboured" along with *Delia* (1592), and Nashe promises Southampton more rashly: "A new brain, a new wit, a new stile, a new soule will I get mee, to canonize your name to posteritie, if in this my first attempt I be not taxed of presumption" (*Traveller*).

Every author sought to convey his dependence through dedications, as Shakespeare did by "choosing so strong a proppe to support so weake a burthen" and by advertising the patron's "Honourable" disposition rather than his lines' own worth. Comparably, Lodge expressed fear that his poems would be "subject to much prejudice, except they [be] graced with some noble and worthie patron" (*A Fig for Momus*, 1595). Nashe pursued a more elaborate image in addressing Southampton: "Except these unpolisht leaves of mine have some braunch of Nobilitie whereon to depend and cleave, and with the vigorous nutriment of whose authorized commendation they may be continually fosterd and refresht, never will they grow to the worlds good liking, but forthwith fade and die on the first houre of their birth." Finally, it was established form to close as Shakespeare does with a wish for the patron's continued welfare. For a gentleman one could be reasonably mild: "desiring the continuance of your worshippes favour unto me." For an earl a little more exertion was in order: "Thus praying continuallie for the increase of your Lordships Honour, with all other things that you would wish, or God will graunt. . . ." For royalty all stops were pulled out: "Thus prostrating my selfe at your Majesties feet, incessantlie craving pardon for my bold attempt *etc.*"[28]

Nor does Shakespeare earn credit here for originality of diction. Renaissance poets commonly called their lines "unpolisht." William Barksted dedicated the "unpolish't pen" of his "maiden Muse" to the Earl of Oxford (*Hiren*, 1611), William Alexander hoped that the Countess of Argyle would "take the patronage of so unpolished lines" (*Aurora*, 1604), and Robert Pricket asked the earls of Southampton and Devonshire to "excuse my unpolish, rough, unsmoothed Poetry" (*Honors Fame*, 1604). Poets also constantly likened their works to offspring (Shakespeare's "first heire of my invention"), as when Anton "sacrific[ed] this new borne babe of his humble duty" to the Howards (*Moriomachia*). There is much neonatal anxiety in front matter of the time, and not coincidentally, it also figures often in Shakespeare's sonnets. In Sonnet 59, for instance, the speaker fears that, "lab'ring for invention [he may] bear amiss / The second burthen of a former child!"[29]

The mention of barren land and bad harvest, too, is commonplace. Turberville describes his *Epitaphes* (1567) as "a fewe Sonets, the unripe seedes of my barraine braine," and in a sonnet to Southampton from 1593 Barnes offers his collection of lyrics, "sprong from a rude and unmanured lande" (*Parthenophil*). Shakespeare's image appears in rough paraphrase in yet another address to Southampton: "If these blasted leaves be acceptable to your Lordship, when the fruites are ripe, you shall receive a fatter crop" (Wright, *The Passions of the Minde*, 1604). *Barren*, too, occurs in the Sonnets several times in the context of poetizing: "means more blessed than my barren rhyme" (SON 16), "My verse so barren of new pride" (SON 76), and "The barren tender of a poet's debt" (SON 83).

Finally, Shakespeare tells Southampton that he will take advantage "of all idle houres." It is astonishing how much literature of this busy time was produced by authors who claimed to be idle. The word has occurred several times in the preceding pages, and there are countless other instances of its invocation. Nashe refers to the "idle leaves" of his *Unfortunate Traveller*, and Giles Fletcher calls his *Licia* sequence a "trifling labor . . . of an idle subject." Spenser, in paraphrase, thinks that *Colin Clout* will show him to be "not greatly well occupied," and John Hind calls his *Lysimachus and Varrona* the "fruit of some idle houres." Robinson's *Schoole of Musicke* became his "first fruits from idlenesse," while Dickinson's *Arisbas* assumed shape as "the frute of some few idle houres." In the same vein, it is pertinent to note, Adonis on two occasions (VEN 422, 770) denounces Venus's amorous themes as "idle."

In sum, the two dedications are (except in their relative brevity) perfectly typical specimens. They touch all the usual bases very efficiently, as does Sonnet 26, which some readers have dubbed the "dedication" sonnet of the sequence and which shadows the two actual dedications in much of its diction.

✑

The foregoing pages, I hope, have served my ulterior purpose in this chapter, which was to impart some flavor of the literary scene in Shakespeare's time as it manifested itself in the printed addresses of authors to their contemporaries. A further purpose, however, has been to discover in

Shakespeare's dedications whatever evidence there might be for explaining a relatively speedy departure from the ranks of courting poets. What we have found allows some plausible though still speculative conclusions. Most obviously, the dedications show Shakespeare cleaving to tradition. They leave the impression that, preparing for his debut, he may have perused several already-published volumes to learn what was considered "good taste" in dedicatory prose and then crafted his own, pro forma. The two dedications certainly would not have raised the eyebrows of the earl or any casual reader, because they contain no unusual or particularly felicitous touches. Such careful orthodoxy tends therefore to sink this notion expressed in the *Dictionary of National Biography*: Southampton "doubtless inspired Shakespeare with genuine personal affection." The dedications are too formulaic to be convincing as expressions of genuine feeling. They were written not merely to "plead for love" but rather, however sotto voce, for "recompence" of a tangible or intangible kind.

An eloquent though brief reference in *Timon of Athens* to the custom of front matter serves to encourage this admittedly cynical conclusion. As the action of this play commences we are introduced to several clients competing for the "magic" of Timon's "bounty":

> Painter: You are rapt, sir, in some work, some dedication
> To the great lord.
> Poet: A thing slipp'd idly from me.
> Our poesy is as a gum, which oozes
> From whence 'tis nourish'd. [1.1.19-22]

This passage about artistic courtiership, like so much of the play, is brilliantly sarcastic. As Shakespeare wrote it in 1607 or 1608 did he recall his own experiences in waiting, more than a decade before? For the general features of being a poet-in-waiting at an aristocratic great house (for example, Southampton House in Holborn) could not have varied greatly from the theatrical version in *Timon of Athens*. The Painter's *rapt* is especially wicked, for he is using a term of art from the Poet's profession—the *furor poeticus*—with which the wealthy layman is conned. Also wicked is the implication that as much "rapture" is devoted to the composition of the dedication as to the poem itself. The Poet's rejoinder is a perfect blend of fatuity and complacency: He well knows that a poet to the great should function only *idly*.

After the precipitous downfall of the patron, we are reminded once more of the dead-serious transactions underlying the *politesse* of front matter. One of Timon's servants describes what happens when his "untirable and continuate goodness" suddenly ceases for lack of funds: "his poor self, / A dedicated beggar to the air, / With his disease of all-shunn'd poverty, / Walks, like contempt, alone" (4.2.12-15). Editors have not noticed that among the senses of "dedicated beggar" is the suggestion that Timon, the object of countless dedications, remains in the end a beggar. These dedications have been worth nothing, filled with "virtuous lies" rather than "niggard truth" (SON 72); they are just another form of the hypocrisy that issues from an aristocrat's entourage of "mouth-friends."

Timon of Athens, to which we shall return when we consider the institution of patronage, casts the calculation of courting poets in the worst possible light. Yet, this calculation was a dominating feature of courtly life and is nowhere more apparent than in dedications. As we shall see in chapter 4, courtly life enforced the observation of very fine lines of decorous distinction, and these too are visible everywhere in front matter: in studied variations in tone, diction, even typography. When Spenser made his poetic debut he had "E.K." urge upon Gabriel Harvey "the patronage of the new Poet" by praising "his due observing of *Decorum* everie where, in personages, in seasons, in matter, in speech, and generallie in all seemely simplicitie of handling his matters, and framing his wordes" (*The Shepheardes Calender*, 1579). Virtually all Renaissance dedications were composed by such exceptionally well-behaved authors. Churchyard might have been speaking for all of them when he explained to the Earl of Essex, "dutifull regard towards the purchasing of your L [ordship's] favor hath so sifted every word and sentence, that not one verse or line shall bee offensive to sounde judgement and good construction" (*A Musicall Consort*, 1595). But the inevitable consequences of sound judgment and good construction when practiced by legions of dedicators, however, are not felicitous: repetitiveness, tedious homogeneity in style, stiffness, and more or less appalling variations on "fair, kind, and true" (SON 105). Shakespeare's two dedications are of the same ilk.

Clearly, it is impossible for me to join J. Middleton Murry in his appreciation: "Surely, this dedication [for *Venus and Adonis*] is, in its kind, a lovely thing."[30] This and the companion dedication are not lovely at all, but rather staid and customary; writing them could hardly have given Shakespeare a frisson of creative pleasure. Lady Macbeth's "O proper stuff!" is the phrase for them. That Shakespeare could have looked with some pleasure on the prospect of never having to compose another dedication I think can be suggested in one final way: by offering one general conclusion about Renaissance front matter and another about the playwright's artistic personality.

This can be done by remarking on the obvious: *Venus and Adonis* and *The Rape of Lucrece* are addressed exclusively to the *aristos*; there is no epistle to the reader, no address to the *demos*. This fact eloquently informs us of Shakespeare's ambition, manifest in these aureate poems, to achieve success among the great ones. Churchyard tells us (*A Musicall Consort*) that "in all ages reasonable writers, that kept an orderly compass, were suffered in verse or prose" by "honorable personages," and Shakespeare's two dedications are manifestly the efforts of a writer striving to appear reasonable and of orderly compass. There were many poets in the English Renaissance (all second-rate or worse) for whom the epithets *reasonable* and *orderly* are perfectly apt. But we have the Sonnets, the plays, the testimony of Ben Jonson ("would he had blotted a thousand") and of the entire Augustan age, as well as our hindsight, to tell us that Shakespeare was neither a "reasonable" nor an "orderly" artist. He was rather, as Arthur Mizener wisely observed, "always wantoning on the verge of anarchy."[31]

That Shakespeare was bound sooner rather than later to burst the reasonable and orderly bonds of dedications—and of courting poetry altogether—can be conveniently suggested by drawing attention to an epitome of all Renaissance dedications to great ones, which is reproduced in full in the Appendix. It is addressed by John Hind to Southampton and displays all the hallmarks of dedicatory prose. It also happens to duplicate each of Shakespeare's tactical maneuvers in the *Venus and Adonis* dedication. The reader will quickly see that I have deliberately chosen an exquisitely exaggerated example of the style. I have done so in order to render more striking the contrast I wish to make here between the aristocratic ambiance of dedications and the demotic or plebeian ambiance of epistles to the reader. To this end I ask the reader to compare Hind's super-refined dedication with a similarly exaggerated epitome of the popular style: Thomas Dekker's "To the Reader" from *The Wonderfull Yeare*, reproduced in full in the Appendix.

One might, as I have done, read through countless volumes of the time in order to arrive at a sense of the discrete worlds evoked by dedications to aristocrats and epistles to common readers. Or one might simply read Hind and Dekker. In Hind's ponderous prose we have the knee-crooking world of Westminster, Whitehall, and the great houses of London's peers, which were populated by "dwellers on form and favor" (SON 125). Hind's dedication is exceedingly formal and polished to a high gloss. But it is cold, exuding nothing but the "icy precepts of respect" (TIM 4.3.258). Dekker's epistle offers a bracing contrast, as bracing perhaps as the experience of ferrying across the Thames from Whitehall steps to the boisterous Bankside in Shakespeare's day. Dekker's unruly, idiomatic, garrulous (some would say diarrhetic) spree has the distinctive flavor of the Liberties. The freewheeling satire, vivid images, and sheer vitality of language are positively Falstaffian. One might even venture that the reputation of the Elizabethan age for unsinkable spirit, ribaldry, contentiousness, and volubility is finely borne out in Dekker's rodomontade.

Shakespeare's career makes it possible to draw at least one certain conclusion from the stylistic contrast posed by Hind and Dekker: Sonnet 105 to the contrary, Shakespeare did not keep his "verse to constancy confined" in pursuit of noble patronage. His artistic horizon widened, making possible his "epistles" to the great variety of readers . . . and auditors: the plays themselves. Thomas Powell wrote, in a dedicatory poem to Southampton: "Let golden artists practice quaint imposture, / And study to a semblance of perfection" (*A Welsh Bayte* [1603]). Shakespeare was sensitive to the element of "quaint imposture" in the ministrations of "golden artists" at court, as the Sonnets and many passages in the plays suggest. Perhaps he sensed, too, the futility of studying after dutiful perfection in the mercurial atmosphere of a Renaissance court, where many mouths were uttering such "virtuous lies" as "Kind is my love today, tomorrow kind, / Still constant in a wondrous excellence" (SON 105).

Rather than fool it so, he retired from the courtly scene, let the high office (of, say, a laureate) and the honor go. For him it turned out not to be a question of exchanging one world for another, as Antony does. "The court's a learning place," says Helena (AWW 1.1.107), and Shakespeare clearly took his learning with him to the Bankside. (His court learning proved very useful when, in the Romances, he made his remarkable reentry into the courtly aesthetic.) Shakespeare's experience in the courting poet's world became a part of the "wide and universal theater" he had been, and would continue, creating as a dramatic poet. His two dedications are ornate excrescences of a formal rather than a "real" world . . . and are, to my mind, pregnant hints why Shakespeare ventured more exclusively into another literary métier. Like Antony, he left the solemn politic world of the great ones. At the same time he left the artistic world of what Dekker called "Castalian Pen-men" for more trivial pursuits, producing what Heminge and Condell were pleased to call "these trifles." But they are trifles, of course, only in the sense of Chapman's wise observation: "He that shuns trifles must shun the world." [32]

Chapter Three

Poet's Labors Lost

Patronage in Shakespeare

'Tis the iron age and vertue must have
Estredge-like concoction, or else die in an
Hospitall for want of a Patron.
                              —Robert Anton

THE IDEAL relationship between patron and individual client (the corporate clientage of players is beyond the scope of this study) is frequently invoked in the literature of the Renaissance—most often, naturally, in the "dedicated words which writers use / Of their fair subjects, blessing every book" (SON 82). William Webbe's epistle for his *Discourse of English Poesie* (1586) offers a typical example: "The wryters of all ages have sought as an undoubted Bulwarke and stedfast savegarde the patronage of Nobilitye (a shield as sure as can be to learning) wherin to shrowde and safelye place their severall inventions."[1] But this idea, like so many humanist ideals current in Tudor and Stuart England, was prodigally honored in the breach, rarely in performance. George Peele, counting himself lucky in the patronage of the "wizard" Earl of Northumberland, lamented in his "Ad Maecaenatem Prologus" of 1593 that

> other Patrons have poore Poets none,
> But Muses and the Graces to implore.
> Augustus long agoe hath left the world:
> And liberall Sidney, famous for the love
> He bare to learning and to Chivalrie,
> And vertuous Walsingham are fled to heaven.

And Peele closes with a glance at "Courts disdaine, the enemie to Arte."[2]

"Courts disdaine," of course, proved the enemy to all classes of ambitious persons who gravitated toward the center of power, wealth, and prestige: suitors, entrepreneurs, adventurers, upscale gentry, foreigners, and artisans, as well as authors and poets. The figures with whom we are here mainly concerned hoped to achieve advancement literally by their "Arte," but all who came to court were also obliged to practice the kind of calculating art referred to by Gabriel Harvey (one of those rare Renaissance admirers of Machiavelli) when he specified "three causes of Advancement" in his marginalia: "1. Art. 2. Industry without art. Experimentes of all fortunes. Great mariages. Sum egregious Act. 3. Service in warre, in peace."[3] Any person arriving at court with upcast eyes had ultimately to depend on the exercise of this cunning, this "fine counterfeasaunce" and "legier demaine" (Spenser's phrases) and (in modern terms) this "tactical flexibility."[4] Exercising this art was an exhausting, corrosive, and—because the odds against success were great—desperate business. Though the goals of their efforts may have differed, the anxieties experienced by suitors, courtiers, and poets at court must have been very similar. Virtually anyone busy trying to advance in courtly preferment could close a letter as did one of the late queen's chief servants in May 1603:

> In trouble, hurrying, feigning, suing, and
> such-like matters, I nowe reste
> Your true friende,
> R. Cecil[5]

That "Courts disdaine" was a common obstacle for all comers is also reflected in the melancholy conclusion of Sir John Harington, variously a suitor, courtier, and poet first in Elizabeth's court and then James's: "Howe my poetrie maye be relishde in tyme to come, I will not hazard to saie. Thus muche I have lived to see, and (in good soothe) feel too, that honeste prose will never better a mans purse at cowrte; and, had not my fortune been in *terra firma*, I might, even for my verses, have daunced bare foot with Clio and her school-fellowes untill I did sweat, and then have gotten nothinge to slake my thirst, but a pitcher of Helicon's well."[6] Some years earlier Harington had apostrophized in the mordant spirit of Wyatt to his own John Poins: "Now, what findeth he who loveth the 'pride of life,' the cowrtes vanitie, ambition's puff ball? In soothe, no more than emptie wordes, grinninge scoffes, watching nightes, and fawninge daies" (1:170). As his phrasing suggests, the situation of the courtier or poet seeking patronage was, as has been often remarked, very similar to that of the *amour courtois* protagonist who seeks to ameliorate the disdain of an aristocratic lady. This figure is constantly racked by profoundly conflicted feelings— "driving to desire," as Wyatt wrote, but "adread also to dare" (226). It is not surprising, therefore, that some of the master images of courtly love poetry appear frequently in descriptions of courtly life. As the author A. D. B.

observed in a description of James's court, "The Court in some sort doth represent and resemble love."[7]

One image of the lover's confusion is the maze. Wyatt writes of the lover's "long error in a blind maze chained" (78), while in another ballade the lover exclaims, "Alas, I tread an endless maze" (121). Courtly life presented a similar challenge. In *A Looking Glasse for the Court* (1575) Guevara describes the court as "a perpetuall dreame, a botomelesse whorlepole, an inchaunted phantasy, and a mase"; Thomas Churchyard, in *A pleasant Discourse of Court and Wars* (1596), writes, "Court is a maze of turnings strange, / A laborinth of working wits"; and the eminent courtier Henry Wotton explained that he preferred, in his first published work, *The Elements of Architecture* (1624), *"to deale with these plaine* compilements, *and tractable* Materials, [rather] *then with the* Laberynthes *and* Mysteries *of* Courts." The "maze" that Prospero's island presents to the shipwrecked courtiers in *The Tempest* (3.3.2; 5.1.242) is, in an important sense, the maze of courtly life.[8]

Another master image of Renaissance love poetry is that of the lover as "a galley charged with forgetfulness," driven from a happy haven by the lady's stormy hauteur. Naval imagery was also useful to those wishing to describe the unpredictable fluctuations of courtly life. The author of *The Court of . . . King James* (1619) speaks of the great men who "waded through and vanquished the various stormes and jeopardous casualties of the turbulent sea . . . of the Court," and in *The Honest Man; or, The Art to please in Court* (1632) Nicholas Faret refers to "this Art and Sea of the Court" and to those daring men who "cast themselves into the tumults wherewith great Courts (like unto great Seas) are continually tossed."[9] Donne's two verse epistles, "The Storm" and "The Calm," are a virtual allegory of the ambitious courtier's alternately frentic and idle life. And one can understand well the appeal of the marine image to a weary Robert Cecil, as in 1603 he contemplated the arrival of a new monarch: "I am pushed from the shore of comforte, and know not where the wyndes and waves of a court will bear me" (Harington, 1:345).

The most compelling and illuminating similarity in the experience of all suitors at court, however, lies in the paradoxical nature of their effort. Romeo's spate of impossibilities derives from the hoary tradition of oxymoronic Petrarchism:

> O brawling love! O loving hate!
> O any thing, of nothing first create!
> O heavy lightness, serious vanity,
> Misshapen chaos of well-seeming forms,

> Feather of lead, bright smoke, cold fire, sick health,
> Still-waking sleep, that is not what it is!
> This love I feel. . . . [1.1.176-82]

Samuel Johnson could see "neither the sense nor the occasion" for "all this toil of antithesis," but clearly it serves to convey Romeo's courting/poetical exuberance. This rhetoric of paradox, of mixed feelings and intentions, is preeminently the rhetoric of courtly existence. Daniel Javitch has written pertinently of *Il Libro del Cortegiano:* "As Castiglione portrays them, the courtiers at Urbino show little tolerance for earnest partisanship or single-mindedness of any kind, but prize, instead, flexibility and even paradox in demeanor and points of view." [10] The language of paradox was, as well, the appropriate language for the Tudor court, whose image, as Patricia Thomson has acutely observed, was "Janus-faced." Thomson isolated in Wyatt's poetry the central theme of frustration, which is so often expressed in paradoxes: as when Wyatt writes of seeking "to accord two contraries" and finding himself "Imprisoned in liberties" (121); or when Donne, in his sixth elegy, exclaims about courtiers, "Oh, let me not serve so, as those men serve / Whom honours' smokes at once fatten and starve" (101); or when Harington, licking his wounded pride in temporary rustication, gamely promised, "I will walke faire, tho a cripple" (1:339).

The more forceful rhetorical form of paradox is the oxymoron, and it is used ubiquitously to capture the nature of courtly existence. Walter Mildmay warned, "Know the Court but spend not thy life there . . . I would rather wish thee to spend the greatest part of thy life in the country than to live in this glittering misery." [11] A. D. B., the anonymous historian of James's court, shrewdly if cravenly warned his readers, "I purpose not heere to discourse of the . . . Gay-grievances of a Courtiers life" (Av) and later refers to its "glorious misery" (163). In *A Looking Glasse for the Court* we are told that the man who leaves the court "hath escaped from a fayre prison . . . from a greate sepulchre" (19r). Shakespeare's Bastard in *King John*, an astute commentator on the futility of courtly suit, describes its fashionable "dialogue of compliment" as "Sweet, sweet, sweet poison for the age's tooth" (1.1.213). And Sidney famously writes in his *Arcadia* about those happy pastoral folk who are "free of proud fears, brave begg'ry, smiling strife / Of climb-fall court." [12]

✍

The foregoing provides a preamble to some important questions: Does the vision of courtiership in Shakespeare's plays reflect on his view of the suing poet's life as well? How does Shakespeare express the relationship between the poet's and the courtier's manners of addressing the challenges at climb-fall court? What, in other words, are Shakespeare's attitudes toward the styles of patronage? And did they change as, during his active years, Stuarts succeeded Tudors and feudal aristocracy gave way to a commercial oligarchy? Did Shakespeare's attitudes also change as the source of patronage, the nobility, suffered the crisis of confidence so lavishly illustrated by Lawrence Stone? I shall venture answers to these questions by focusing on *Love's Labour's Lost* and *Timon of Athens*, but first it is necessary to ponder the beginnings of Shakespeare's London career and the avenues that lay open to him in the early 1590s. It will also be necessary to ponder the attitudes toward the writer's profession conveyed in his plays.

Richard Helgerson has suggested that, in 1570, there was only one viable path for the poetically inclined writer, that of the leisured amateur.[13] By 1590, Helgerson is able to identify three choices: One could take the aristocratic amateur path; become a publishing professional; or strive to attain the politicized, public, and formal role of laureate as Spenser, Jonson, and Milton did with various kinds of success. Before Shakespeare made his final choice (typically a "none of the above" choice), he made a feint in the direction of the professional poet with the two long poems dedicated to Southampton. "The love I dedicate to your Lordship is without end," he wrote in presenting *Lucrece*, "wherof this Pamphlet without beginning is but a superfluous Moity." One might pass *pamphlet* off as a nice self-deprecating conceit, Shakespeare exuding false modesty as he placed himself among the rabble of two-penny poets. But I wish to suggest in the following pages another view: the view that, as we can now see from hindsight, he was making a true statement. For it appears that Shakespeare never again personally displayed an itch to bestride the press.[14] This poet capable of writing *The Rape of Lucrece*, *Titus Andronicus*, and *Love's Labour's Lost*—conceivably in the very same year—was obviously keeping several avenues open and very quickly must have considered that making his way in the world as a poet suing for direct patronage of his individual talent was an unsatisfying alternative. He soon chose, instead, the indirect, corporate patronage of a well-placed nobleman for a company of players.

Even an observer less shrewd than Shakespeare might have sensed in the late 1590s what we now, because we repute it a literary golden age, find hard to imagine: poetry offered a flinty field for professional endeavor. Sidney's *Defence*, we must remind ourselves, resonates against an impressive array of ill will and cultural aspersion. The evidence for this antiliterary bias is everywhere, not just in the scattered complaints of poets like Spenser at blatant beasts who do not spare "the gentle Poets rime." In a "generall Defence of all Learning," Daniel pointedly asked, "How many

thousands never heard the name / Of *Sidney*, or of *Spencer*, or their Bookes? "
The editor of the six large volumes of *The Lisle Letters* remarks bemusedly
that only once does a correspondent take it in mind to mention such a thing
as a book, perhaps for reasons explained by Donne in his satiric *Courtier's
Library*: "The engagements natural to your life at Court leave you no leisure
for literature." A little literature apparently went a long way in a Renaissance court. The satirist who wrote *The Philosopher of the Court* wittily
described the nature of the "understanding of all Artes and liberall Sciences, whereby we become right Courtiers": "It is singular good to have
some pretie sprinckled judgement in the common places and practizes of all
the liberall sciences, chopt up in hotchpot togither."[15] Be, in other words,
something of a Polonius.

In a more earnest book on courtly etiquette, the *Galateo of Maister John
della Casa* (1576), the association of deep reading with asocial behavior is
strong: "It ill becometh a man when hee is in company, to bee sad, musing,
and full of contemplation. And albeit, it may bee suffered perchaunce in
them that have long beaten their braines in these *Mathematicall* studies,
which are called (as I take it) the *Liberall Artes*, yet without doubte it may
not be borne in other men" (27). The Lord Treasurer Burghley seconded
this view in a letter of advice to Harington in 1578: "Onlie I woulde
particulerlie warne you, that (to seeme a good fellow) you sytte not in your
studie reading, when you shoulde be in the hall hearinge" (1: 132). Too
much study—that way lay the social dysfunctions of a Jaques, Hamlet,
Cassius, or Prospero.

Certain facts bear out the low esteem of books during the Renaissance.
Lawrence Stone's appendix of references to substantial libraries between
1556 and 1642 contains only sixteen entries, some of which are tellingly
vague: Lord Hatton is said to have possessed "3 cart loads" of books; the
Duchess of Suffolk owned "a chest full." Stone's compilation supports a
conclusion made decades ago: "Another indication of the limitations of
literary interests of the day may be gathered, though but in scanty measure, from extant family account books and inventories. Surprisingly,
these contain few references to books."[16]

Surprising? Only to those who, like A. L. Rowse, prefer a roseate view
of the Tudor court: "It was also cultivated and even intellectual; there was a
radiating interest in the arts and crafts, in painting and jewelry, languages
and literature." But there are hints and vignettes enough to suggest that G.
K. Hunter's view is the more plausible one: "Anyone who approached the
Tudor court supposing that it was another Florentine Academy was liable
to a series of rude shocks."[17] Poetry and poets were a decidedly minor and
peripheral ornament at Elizabeth's court, as Harington's report of her

reaction to the purloining of one of her own poems by a lady-in-waiting might suggest: "The Queen did find out the thief, and chid her for spreading evil bruit of her writing such toyes, when other matters did so occupy her employment at this time; and was fearful of being thought too lightly of for so doing."[18] The life of John Harington—perhaps the most notable and longest-lived poet-courtier of the time—offers many sobering insights into the precarious place of the poet at the Tudor court. In October of 1601 he writes from the country: "I had a sharp message from her [Elizabeth] brought by my Lord Buckhurst, namely thus, 'Go tell that witty fellow, my godson, to get home: it is no season now to foole it here.' I liked this as little as she dothe my knighthood, so tooke to my bootes and returned to the plow in bad weather . . . the many evil plots and designs have overcome her Highness' sweet temper. She walks much in her privy chamber, and stamps with her feet at ill news, and thrusts her rusty sword at times into the arras in great rage" (*Letters*, 90). In a similar manner a few years later, the dying queen turned away some of Harington's epigrammatic trifles with these sad words: "When thou dost feel creeping time at thy gate, these fooleries will please thee less: I am past my relish for such matters."[19]

Court life provided Harington a bumpy ride, and the question How helpful was his knowledge of the liberal authors in the event? is a nice one. Perhaps the answer lies in a letter Harington wrote as he set forth once again for the country, this time in the wake of James's accession. He writes to the soon-to-be Earl of Suffolk, Thomas Howard, striking the prototypical humanist pose: "Each nighte do I spende, or muche better parte thereof, in counceil with the aunciente examples of learninge; I con over their histories, their poetrie, their instructions, and thence glean my own proper conducte in matters bothe of merrimente or discretion" (1: 338). This turns out, however, to be a mere biding of the time, for the letter ends with Harington, driven as a moth back to the flame, describing his plan of attack on the new regime: "I have made some freindes to further my suite of favour withe the Kynge, and hope you will not be slacke in forwardeing my beinge noticede in proper season." One succeeded at court, not by the "arts," but by the intercession of patrons or powerful friends, by machination, luck, attractive appearance, and the accidents of personality in the holders of power. Time was running against poor Harington. Howard wrote to him in 1611 (when Harington was fifty-years-old): "You are not young, you are not handsome, you are not finely; and yet will you come to courte, and thinke to be well favoured?" (1: 397).

The fortunes of the book or the man who wrote one were little better under James. All classes of hopeful suitors, including poets, were swept up in the initial euphoria of James's arrival, as John Chamberlain indicates in a letter of 12 April 1603: "These bountiful beginnings raise all mens spirits and put them in great hopes, insomuch that not only protestants, but papists and puritanes, and the very poets with theyre ydle pamflets promise themselves great part in his favor" (1: 192). But except for a few favorites who were scarcely lettered, these hopes were dashed, and the Stuarts settled into an even more bibliophobic slough. John Nichols compiles an extensive list of gifts given to the King—among them mares, a gold cup, hawks, ploughs, a Persian dagger, crocodiles, an umbrella, a coach (with two coachmen), a satin robe, armor, a diamond ring, a leopard, and setting dogs.[20] But no books, perhaps because, as Dekker wrote in his dedication for *The Wonderfull Yeare*, "Bookes are but poore gifts."

Indeed, Nichols's only reference to books in his vast work concerns the possibility that they were sold in the playhouses. Alan Westcott is probably exaggerating only slightly when he observes of Prince Henry's expenses: "It need not cause surprise that the payments for tennis balls were over three times as great as the sums spent in support of literature; it might be shown that the expenditures of his royal father for his 'privie buckehoundes' during any one year would have kept alive all the worthy poets in London for the same length of time."[21] Chamberlain's numerous letters show not the slightest interest in imaginative literature, aside from a testy snobbism over Latin style (Bacon's will not "abide taste or touch") and the odd Chaucerian allusion. A magnificently condescending remark from him on the Globe theater rebuilt after the 1613 fire brings us handily back to Shakespeare: "I heare much speach of this new playhouse, which is saide to be the fayrest that ever was in England, so that yf I live but seven yeares longer I may chaunce make a journey to see yt" (1: 544).

Chamberlain confides in his letters that he does not feel comfortable at court. While Elizabeth was alive he admitted: "Me thincks still I am out of my element when I am among Lords, and I am of Rabelais minde that they looke big *comme un millord d'Angleterre*" (1: 45). However, under a new monarch and with fourteen years' experience, he felt much the same: "I am a meere straunger to the court and court busines, more then by hearsay, which is as uncertain and varies as often as the severall humors and affections of the.parties I meet with" (1: 391). It is easy to imagine Shakespeare early in his career feeling the same way and deciding not to follow the path of a dedicated courting poet, choosing instead to remove to the world that Chamberlain makes seem so far away—the world of the Globe theater.

Shakespeare, it appears, chose to absent himself from competitive "justling and suing for places in the privie chamber" (Chamberlain's phrase, 1: 133) in favor of a career over which he would be able to exert more personal control. This career would surely not leave him—like Jonson—fulminating at a muse who would subject him to the whims of the ungrateful great:

> Away, and leave me, thou thing most abhorred
> That hast betrayed me to a worthless lord;
> Made me to commit most fierce idolatry
> To a great image through thy luxury.
> Be thy next master's more unlucky muse,
> And as thou hast mine, his hours, and youth abuse.
> Get him the time's long grudge, the court's ill will.[22]

Jonson tried to remain *of* the court throughout his flourishing years, and he was left a bitter, poor old man. Shakespeare, on the other hand, seems to have come early to a different stance: "I see a better state to me belongs / Than that which on thy humor doth depend" (SON 92). He turned from the rigors and uncertainties of climb-fall court and toward those of a life in a company of players. And he ended his career in a presumably restful, financially secure retirement. Rather than become a professional poet or a laureate (the choice of aristocratic amateur was closed to him), Shakespeare became an entrepreneurial writer. One might even say that he was, as a sharer in his company, a self-employed writer. His dissociation from the ethos of the idealized titled-patron/skilled-poet relationship is, I think, reflected in the uses to which he puts the vocabulary of professional authorial identity in his plays. In a variety of ways these plays also suggest how peripherally loomed the world of poets and their books in the Renaissance.

Consider, for instance, *poet* and *poetry*. The word *poet* is used six times by Jonson and Holland in the Folio's dedicatory poems, far exceeding the number of congenial appearances of the word in all the plays. The unnamed poet who appears in the fourth act of *Julius Caesar* to urge a reconciliation between Brutus and Cassius is ignominiously shuffled away: "Get you hence, sirrah; saucy fellow, hence! . . . What should the wars do with these jigging fools?" (4.3.134-37). The other poet in this play, who unfortunately bears the same name as one of the conspirators, is the only one in Shakespeare's canon willing to make a flat assertion of his profession: "I am Cinna the poet" (3.3.29). And he is dragged off by the Roman mob to an unknown fate: "Tear him for his bad verses." The poet in *Timon of Athens* is—like everything associated with the courtly ethos in that play—the focus of extreme derision. Characters who happen to praise poetry are hardly among the elite in Shakespeare's dramatis personae: Holofernes,

Pandarus, Touchstone, Fluellen, and Tranio in *The Taming of the Shrew*. However, among those who satirize it are some of Shakespeare's most charismatic figures: Theseus, Mercutio, and Henry V.

Shakespeare apparently felt no desire to second Sidney's noble defense: the word *poesy* occurs but five times in his plays, always in derogatory circumstances; *poem* occurs but a single time, when Polonius refers to a stage work that does not observe the unities; and three of the four occurrences of *poetical* come in the witty attack on poetic pretensions in *As You Like It* (3.3). The other comes in a tellingly barbed interchange from *Twelfth Night:*

> Viola: I will on with my speech in your praise, and then
>   show you the heart of my message.
> Olivia: Come to what is important in't. I forgive you the praise.
> Viola: Alas, I took great pains to study it, and 'tis poetical.
> Olivia: It is the more like to be feign'd. [1.5.189-96]

Shakespeare's associations with the word *poet* are predominantly negative: It is paired with *feign(ing)* five times. Poets inhabit a world of caprice (AYL 3.3.8), lying (TIM 1.1.220), cliché (R3 1.4.46), mere "numbering" (ANT 3.2.16), "airy nothing" (MND 5.1.16), and "barren tender" (SON 83). One must look into some obscure corners (for example, TIT 4.1.14; "The Passionate Pilgrim" 8.1) to find respectful references to poetry.

One might expect the less pretentious *verse(s)* to appear in more clement contexts, but this is not the case. The word occasionally occurs when the speaker wishes to be kind but the effect is satiric, as in the Host's description of Fenton: "He capers, he dances, he has eyes of youth; he writes verses, he speaks holiday, he smells of April and May" (WIV 3.2.67-69). The memorable instances are more harsh. Egeus accuses Lysander of writing "with faining voice verses of faining love" (MND 1.1.31), and Titania chides Oberon for his philandering:

> But I know
> When thou hast stolen away from fairy land,
> And in the shape of Corin sat all day,
> Playing on pipes of corn, and versing love,
> To amorous Phillida. [2.1.64-68]

Katharine receives from Dumain "Some thousand verses of a faithful lover. . . . A huge translation of hypocrisy" (LLL 5.2.47-49). Henry warns Kate not to set him "to verses" (H5 5.2.132), and Timon's praise of the Poet drips with sarcasm: "Thy verse swells with stuff so fine and smooth" (5.1.84).

Rhyme and *rhymer* were standard pejorative epithets for the lower rungs of the poetic profession, as witness Webbe: "I scorne and spue out the rakehelly rout of our ragged rymers" (*Discourse*, 37). In Shakespeare's canon there is one unequivocally positive occurrence, in Sonnet 55's "Not marble nor the gilded monuments / Of princes shall outlive this pow'rful rhyme." For the rest (Sidney's forensics to the contrary), rhymes are "guilty" (LLL 4.3.137). The comic butt Armado calls on some "extemporal god of rhyme" (1.2.183); Henry V berates "these fellows of infinite tongue, that can rhyme themselves into ladies' favors" (H5 5.2.155-56); Troilus foolishly boasts of "rhymes, / Full of protest, of oath and big compare" (3.2.174-75); Mercutio conjures Romeo to "speak but one rhyme" to prove he is a a madman (2.1.9); Egeus damns Lysander with "thou hast given her rhymes" (1.1.28); and Gower excuses "the lame feet of my rhyme" (PER 4.ch.48). In Shakespeare, rhymes are toys and trifles—"O rhymes are guards on wanton cupid's hose" (LLL 4.3.56)—and more likely than not defective: "bootless" (LLL 5.2.64), "rude harsh-sounding" (JN 4.2.150), "poor" (SON 107), "vild" (JC 4.3.133), "babbling" (ADO 5.2.39). As well, all fourteen appearances of *sonnet(s)(ing)* are subversive.

Other possible epithets of professional identification can be quickly noted. *Writer(s)* occurs very seldom, and then in the sense of scribe or with a derogatory edge. Hamlet sarcastically notes that the boy actors' "writers do wrong them, to make them exclaim against their own succession" (2.2.350). (The plural is sometimes used merely to suggest "authorities.") Elsewhere the implication is that writers are a sheeplike race (TGV 1.1.42; SON 82). *Writing* is almost always used to mean handwriting. References to the writer as *author* are few (LLL 4.3.308; H5 Epilogue) and derisive. Incidentally, *dramatist* and *playwright* are not in Shakespeare's vocabulary.

What, then, of the emanations of poets, the stuff that, as the Poet in *Timon of Athens* so unctuously phrases it, "is as a gum, which oozes / From whence 'tis nourished"? (1.1.21). What of the printed form of fiction (*fiction* Shakespeare employs derisively three times)? The fortunes of *book(s)* in the Shakespearean canon accord with my assertion of the peripheral importance of books in Renaissance society at large. For Shakespeare the image of the book was far more useful than the thing itself. His uses of *book* are predominantly figurative, as when Pericles describes Antiochus's daughter: "Her face the book of praises, where is read / Nothing but curious pleasures" (1.1.15-16). More famous are the book conceits of Richard II in his mirror scene (4.1) and Lady Capulet's recommendation of Paris to Juliet (1.3.81-94). Of the fifteen appearances of *volume(s)*, two are literal and thirteen figurative (for example, Hamlet's "book and volume of my brain"). In Shakespeare's dramatic world, books more often than not are bringers of trouble: to the noble Lord Say (2H6 4.7.24ff); to Henry VI, "whose bookish rule hath pulled fair England down" (2H6 1.1.259); and of course to the studious recluse Prospero.

References to books often carry a suggestion that their contents are not worth the effort of reading. They may provide mere "saws" (HAM 1.5.100), "good manners" (AYL 5.4.91), "dainties" (LLL 4.2.24), superstition (OTH 1.2.171-74), "riddles" (WIV 1.1.201), "songs and sonnets" (WIV 1.1.199), and "base authority" (LLL 1.1.87). And many memorable lines must have delighted the unlettered Globe "general": Romeo's observation that "love goes toward love as school boys from their books" (2.2.156), Berowne's image of painfully poring over books in the king's academy (LLL 1.1.74-76), and Don Pedro's warning to Claudio not to tire his fellows with a "book of words" (ADO 1.1.307).

Nor are the products of a writer's *pen* auspicious. Theseus's famous comment on the power of the "poet's pen" (MND 5.1.15) is by no means complimentary. Elsewhere the pen is the instrument of a student (SON 16) or an author "rough and all-unable" (H5 Epilogue); otherwise, it produces "quirks" (OTH 2.1.63), ballads (ADO 1.1.252), a deposition (ADO 3.5.58), or, as Armado sanguinely hopes, "whole volumes in folio" (LLL 1.2.184).

Shakespeare's book world was, in sum, a far cry from that of major Renaissance collectors such as Lord Lumley, Sir Thomas Knyvett, Baron Paget, or the Earl of Northumberland. Very seldom, only perhaps in *Hamlet* and in the crucial appearance of Ovid in *Titus Andronicus*, can one imagine that a book in a Shakespearean play is in fact one of those noble volumes defended by Sidney. When we can guess that books on the stage might be "great" ones, it is often clear that they are there merely as bourgeois ornaments (see SHR 1.1.93; 1.2.169). The books that figure far more consistently in their physical presence on Shakespeare's stage are the books of quotidian, nonliterary life: the tablet (WT 4.4.598); hornbook (LLL 5.1.46; TNK 2.3.42); copybook (2H6 4.2.90; LLL 5.2.42); muster book (2H4 3.2.135); tally book (2H6 4.7.35); notebook (JC 4.3.98; WIV 1.1.145); lawyers' books (1H6 2.4.56); schoolboys' books; books of riddles, songs, and sonnets; the prayer book and the Bible.

The target of all the preceding vocabulary of professional identity was the potential patron, as Edward Sharpham's dedication to *Cupid's Whirligig* (1607) makes all too candidly clear: "I must needs discharge two Epistles upon you, the one [to] the Readers, that should be like haile shot, that scatters and strikes the multitude, the other dedicatory, like a bullet, that aimes onely at your selfe." As we have seen, patrons feeling themselves sitting ducks for the persistent attentions of authors must have received dedications with the same relish as a bullet. Joseph Hall's image of the "grand Maecenas [who] casts a glavering eye, / On the cold present of a Poesie" is probably close to the real-life mark.[23] Shakespeare himself did not use the word *patron* in his two dedications, though he might easily have done so. Thereafter, the word appears for him to have drifted out of the patron-client arena. It is used but one time in the sense of "patron of the arts," when Cupid addresses Timon in the masque of the Amazons: "Hail to thee, worthy Timon, and to all / That of his bounties taste! The five best senses / Acknowledge thee their patron." (1.2.122-24). The dramatic context is, of course, supremely subversive of the patron-client ideal. Furthermore, Shakespeare's associations with patronage of any kind were largely negative. Aside from a few indifferent uses in synonymy with "ruler" or "partisan," the objects of a client's attentions are dupes: the Pedant in *Shrew* (4.2.114ff) and Titus, the "Patron of virtue, Rome's best champion" (1.1.65). The word *patron* can also have the rude sense of enforcing vassalage (3H6 5.1.27). Both Shakespearean instances of *patronage* are unpleasant, giving protection to "envious barking" and "theft" (1H6 3.1.48; 3.4.32). In *Love's Labour's Lost* both the client Armado and the patron King ("my . . . body's fost'ring patron" [1.1.220-21]) are fools, each in his own way. Surely the most damning occurrences of *patron* are in *King Lear*, where the collapse of the patron-client relationship, among many others, is depicted:

> Kent: Royal Lear,
>   Whom I have ever honor'd as my king,
>   Lov'd as my father, as my master follow'd,
>   As my great patron thought on in my prayers—
> Lear: The bow is bent and drawn, make from the shaft. [1.1.139-43]

Shadowing these lines is the vignette of Elizabeth stamping while brandishing her rusty sword, warning Harington to retreat to the country. The other great image of betrayal in the patron-client relationship comes when Gloucester describes the man who will later pluck out his eyes: "The noble Duke my master, / My worthy arch and patron, comes to-night" (2.1.58-59).

❦

The essence of the ideal patron-client relationship lay in stability, consistency, and loyalty. Nothing was more inimical to this ideal than radical social flux, so powerfully represented, for instance, in *King Lear*. Change and motion at court—"This jarring discord of nobility, / This shouldering of each other in the court" (1H6 4.1.188-89)— was the great enemy of ideal patronage. Elizabeth's court, assuredly not free from intramural "shouldering," was still a remarkably stable one; in many important respects, life did not change greatly while she held the scepter. Thomas Dekker concluded as much when, in the Queen's valedictory year, he wrote that in her time the English people "never understoode what that strange out-landish word *Change* signified."[24] Perhaps Shakespeare was seconding Dekker's point in one of his last Elizabethan comedies, *As You Like It*, when he had Oliver ask, "What's the new news at the new court?" and Charles respond, "There's no news at the court, sir, but the old news" (1.1.96-98).

In chapter 1 we explored, through reference to Puttenham's *Arte*, the representation in *Love's Labour's Lost* of the premises and methods of the consciously, explicitly poetical stylist. Now possessed of a general sense of Shakespeare's vocabulary of authorial identity, we can go further and consider how poet figures behaved as they pursued their aims in the lists of clientage. In other words, how is the poet's art deployed to social advantage? No play in the canon is more illuminating in this respect than *Love's Labour's Lost*, to which we must now return. At once a homage and a critique, this play presents the various styles that patronage and clientage could assume in the waning years of the Tudor dynasty and is a convenient focus for considering Shakespeare's earliest representations of the institution, just as *Timon of Athens* will be seen to reflect important aspects of Stuart patronage. Behind the "pleasant jests" and "letters full of love" in this comedy is a credible expression of dilemmas facing the poet—amateur or professional—seeking success at court.

The most historically resonant poet-patron relationship here is between the Princess and Boyet: think of them for a moment as shadows of Elizabeth and John Harington. The Princess is a type of the intelligent, percipient ruler, and this kind of queen we often find in Harington's letters: "She lovethe plaine dealinges, and I will not lie unto her" (1: 169). After her death he wrote, "I coude relate manye pleasant tales of hir Majestie's outwittinge the wittiest ones; for few knew how to aim their shaft against hir cunninge" (*Letters*, 124-25). Elizabeth was supremely aware of the ground rules of courtly transactions and the manipulation of appearances. She well recognized that, as *The Philosopher of the Court* summarizes, "to live Courtly . . . consisteth in certaine small humanities, and chiefly in outward apparances" (13). That the Princess possesses a similar dexterity and awareness is driven home often, most vividly in her crucial interchange with the forester, whom she rewards for "telling true" (4.1.18). The representation of patronage in the play pivots on her subsequent meditation on the fact that a patron's "giving hand, though foul, shall have fair praise": "And out of question so it is sometimes, / Glory grows guilty of detested crimes, / When, for fame's sake, for praise, an outward part, / We bend to that the working of the heart" (4.1.30-33). The Princess is affectingly aware that successful courtly behavior requires knowledge of the fine art of bending: It is necessary sometimes "to followe and rule our selves by others, accustoming to doe as they doe" (*Philosopher of the Court*, 110). But happily, she acts on this awareness with poise, gentleness, and wry humor.

Boyet is Shakespeare's droll essay on obsequious courtly "dwellers on form and favor" (SON 125) who grow old in complete devotion to their patrons. Boyet is, in effect, the essence of that deferential cordiality which Elyot recommended to courtiers in *The Governor:* "Affability is of a wonderful efficacy or power in procuring love. And it is . . . where a man is facile or easy to be spoken unto. It is also where a man speaketh courteously, with a sweet speech or countenance, wherewith the hearers (as it were with a delicate odour) be refreshed and allured to love him." [25] That Boyet has procured the ladies' amused "love" is clear: "Thou art an old love-monger," says Maria, "and speak'st skillfully" (2.1.254). That Shakespeare intended his "skill" to be perceived as poetic skill is also clear. In a typically Shakespearean coincidence, for instance, Armado (who aspires to the status of a Boyet) calls for the assistance of "some extemporal god of rhyme" (1.2.174), and in the very next speech Boyet makes his first appearance with twelve lines that stamp him as a genuine extemporal poet. And he truly "turns sonnet" when he describes the men's love at first sight. In order to set this poetic performance apart from the already artificial environs of the scene, Shakespeare turned this speech into lilting, dactylic hendecasyllables (2.1.234-49). The Princess rightly responds to these entertaining lines as to a feat: "Come to our pavilion: Boyet is dispos'd."

The profit of such an existence is trifling inconsequence. One becomes, as Berowne says in his skewering of Boyet the courtly silverfish, a mere "ape of form, monsieur the nice" (5.2.325). Perhaps there is a hint in the character of Boyet that, even if the path had been open to him, Shakespeare would not have found the life of an aristocratic amateur poet to his taste. Not for him the life of a Samuel Daniel, the life of "some carry-tale, some please-man, some slight zany, / Some mumble-news, some trencher-knight, some Dick, / That smiles his cheek in years, and knows the trick / To make my lady laugh when she's disposed" (5.2.463-66).

In the relationship between the Princess and Boyet, the patron's skill deftly controls the sophistic but harmless folly of the client. With the relationship between the King and Berowne, on the other hand, we find "folly (doctor-like) controlling skill" (SON 66) in more dangerous circumstances. Because of this, and because Berowne is the play's most complete avatar of the poet, more serious questions are raised. One is satisfied to conclude that Boyet's expense of wit is a mere waste of effort; Berowne's is more particularly a waste of shame. In Berowne, then, one is more aware of a queasy bending of the poetic art amid the pressures of social intercourse. As with the other attending lords, there is a clear implication that the poetic gift gives the "power to do most harm, least knowing ill" (2.1.58). Shakespeare explores here the ethical as well as artistic consequences when a client's special intellectual and poetic "grace" bends under his patron's "might."

Berowne makes his brilliant first impression by appearing to be an example of the insociable courtier, like Castiglione's Bembo or Gaspar Pallavicino—or the real-life Sir John Perrot: "They quote him for a person that loved to stand too much alone on his own legs, and of too often recesses and discontinuance from the Queen's presence, a fault which is incompatible with the ways of the court and favor."[26] Until line 111 of the first scene, it appears Berowne will ignore Philibert's satiric advice to the good courtier to be "ready to doe whatsoever it be, according to the humors and complexions of his felowship and Courtly companie, althoughe his affections are cleane contrary" (109). But after lecturing with doctor-like skill against the folly of the proposed academy, Berowne submits to the plan and puts his wit at the King's disposal.

It is out of keeping with the play's merriment to observe that Berowne's capitulation expresses the essence of Renaissance despotism. But the observation is necessary, just as it was for Daniel Javitch to notice about *The Courtier* "that most of the beautiful manners in the book are made necessary by the loss of sincerity and free expression, by the sycophancy and servitude that individuals are made to bear in a despotic political system."[27] Often the courtly poet had to be a publicist for vanity, a firm defender of the pliable, and a seemingingly virtuous special pleader for vice. Berowne is asked for "Some flattery for . . . evil" and obliges with a ravishing defense of the indefensible (4.3.286-362) that is a thoroughly "poetic" performance. And there is no small irony in the fact that his central conceit is one that Shakespeare also used in Sonnet 14 ("from thine eyes my knowledge I derive"). Impressive though Berowne's tour de force is, by the end of the play we look back on it as one of many examples of the "excellent sharpe and quick invention" and the "bright phantasie and imagination" of Puttenham's ideal poet (3: 25) corroding ethical standards of social conduct in the service of a foolish patron.

For the play's men, as for Philibert, "Vertue is a manner of lyving according to the manner of the Court" (17). Virtue thus changes according to social circumstances; virtue is relative, malleable. In order to secure their virtuous flexibility, the courtiers of Navarre resort to language that is extensively catachrestic in the sense that John Hoskyns defined the rhetorical figure in 1599: "*Catachresis* (in English, *Abuse*) is nowe growne in fashion (as most abuses are). It is somewhat more desperate then a *Metaphore*, it is the expressing of one matter by the name of another, which is incompatible with it, & sometimes cleane contrary."[28] The women prove expert at squelching the desperate catachresis of these men:

> King: The virtue of your eye must break my oath.
> Princess: You nickname virtue; vice you should have spoke. [5.2.348-49]

The similar rejection of Berownē and his hyperboles emphasizes the sordid servitude to which the courtly poet could be subjected.

Poetry is partly responsible for the unreal world the patrons here come to inhabit. "We are infected with the style of the poets," Bacon wrote in his fragment "On Fame," and the King's announcement of his purpose in establishing the academy (to gain fame) is thoroughly infected by the sonneteer's style. Mercury was, for the Renaissance, the god of eloquence (Jonson said that Shakespeare came "like Mercury to charme" his age [264]), and Berowne is nothing if not mercurial and eloquent. But Mercury was also the con artist: "Hermes, the cheater, shall not mix with us," Jonson also wrote (107). And Berowne, as Shakespeare works hard to remind us, is also a cheater.[29] Longaville asks him, "O! some authority how to proceed / Some tricks, some quillets, how to cheat the devil" (4.3.284-85). Berowne's truant and catachrestic eloquence is too much inured to making ill shapes look good, too much founded on that division criticized in *The Art to please in Court*, "the division of life into actions and words" (145).

In the end, clients of the King are called to serious judgment, chiefly Berowne because his intelligence and poetic skill are greatest. Guevara wrote in *A Looking Glasse for the Court* (1575) that at court "wit is called vertue. . . . He that is glorious gay, they name him honorable." Rosaline's splendid final speeches show that she does not accept this premise; she disabuses Berowne of the idea that "mocks . . . comparisons . . . flouts . . . wit" constitute true virtue or honor in her eyes. Virtue is virtue. Where patrons are as perceptive and sober as the Princess, those without virtue will not be able to hide the fact by recourse to what Herbert of Cherbury called "Rhetoricall Excursions."[30] This rejection of excursions expressing what the client "ought" to say rather than what he genuinely feels will recur repeatedly in subsequent Shakespearean plays, notably the last one. Cardinal Wolsey, at once an arrogant patron and a deeply hypocritical client, is brought rudely down to earth by his own patron, King Henry, in a fashion that should remind us of the denouement of *Love's Labour's Lost:*

Wolsey: Ever may your Highness yoke together
(As I will lend you cause) my doing well
With my well saying!
King: 'Tis well said again,
And 'tis a kind of good deed to say well,
And yet words are no deeds. [H8 3.2.150-54]

Like Mercutio, Berowne is the quintessence of the dexterous, hubristic aristocrat; he is the complacent insider who is completely at ease in the environs of "presence majestical." His voluble discourse has led many to see in him a shadow of Shakespeare himself. But it is also important to consider how the delightful Don Adriano de Armado fills out the play's view of Tudor patronage. Though Armado is as inept as Berowne is skillful, this description of the former still suits the latter perfectly: "A man. . . . That hath a mint of phrases in his brain; / One who the music of his own vain tongue / Doth ravish like enchanting harmony" (1.1.163-66). The utilitarian relationship between the King and Armado approximates that which Shakespeare himself might have experienced with an aristocratic patron. There is a touch of the two dedications in Armado's grandiose salutation, "Great deputy, the welkin's vice-regent, and sole dominator of Navarre, my soul's earth's God, and body's fost'ring patron" (1.1.219-21). And in keeping with the standard view of "feigning" poets, the King promises to "use" him thus: "I protest I love to hear him lie, / And I will use him for my minstrelsy" (1.1.175-76).

But class lines cut rudely across this relationship. In this respect Armado finds himself in the position Shakespeare would have confronted if he had entertained the hope of a poetic career situated in or near the court. In the London of Elizabeth's time, a young nobody from Stratford, however honey-tongued, was as unlikely to gain preferment as a fantastical Spanish traveler. Armado is the epitome of the doomed social climber. He lives in expectation of moments like this one reported by Harington: "The Queene stoode up and bade mee reache forthe my Arme to reste her theron. Oh, what sweet burden to my next songe—Petrarke shall eke out good matter for this businesse" (1: 167). One wonders whether it is boast or truth when Armado describes a similar event to Holofernes: "I must tell thee, it will please his grace, by the world, sometime to lean upon my shoulder, and with his royal finger, thus, dally with my excrement, with my mustachio" (5.1.96-99).[31] This absurd hope for social intimacy with the great is one source of Armado's (and Malvolio's) comic effect, and it is reinforced by his plebeian urge to publish: "I am sure I shall turn sonnet. Devise, wit; write, pen; for I am for whole volumes in folio" (1.2.173-75).

Of course, Armado's mind is terminally prosaic; he is never allowed to utter authentic iambic pentameter. He is well-versed only in the clichés of the courting tradition and, as the scenes with Moth show, utterly lacks the manipulative cunning necessary to advance at court.

Armado is the master of ceremonies in the King's circle, an aptly ludicrous counterpart to Boyet, who acts in a similar capacity in foiling the "Muscovites." It is Armado who is deputized by Navarre to "present some ostentation, or show, or pageant, or antic, or firework" to amuse the women. His ambitious hopes for a coup de theatre are crushed, of course, and he is obliged to see "the day of wrong through the little hole of discretion" (5.2.723). Trivial though Armado's character and trauma are, they are nonetheless suggestive of the dangers and vulnerabilities that clients suffered as they sought to rise at climb-fall court. Armado's humiliations are predictable, but then humiliation was the likely prospect for anyone who sought to rise there. Armado hilariously lacks the necessary self-consciousness and circumspection. He is incapable of following the rule laid down by Harington as he contemplated his approaches to a Stuart monarch: "Goode caution never comethe better, than when a man is climbinge; it is a pityfull thinge to sett a wronge foote, and, instead of raisinge ones heade, to falle to the grounde and showe ones baser partes" (1: 339). Shakespeare, I suspect, saw this prospect of humiliation in justling for place at the margins of courtly society and finally determined to risk his artistic "baser partes" in the public theater.

A word should be said about Holofernes, the last of the play's poetical clients. Cornwallis wrote that Montaigne "hath put Pedanticall Schollerisme out of countenance" (*Essayes*, H4v), and this was Shakespeare's primary motivation too in creating Holofernes. But the character also reflects on the client-patron relationship. He is the play's "king" of language, the ghastly consequence of continual plodding after base authority from others' books. His study is riotously overshot in the presentation of the Nine Worthies, and he, like all the poetical avatars in the play, in the end stumbles and shows his baser parts. The presentation of the Worthies provides, as well, an opportunity to show off the ideal patronizing courtly audience, as Shakespeare was to do again in *A Midsummer Night's Dream*. As soon as Costard enters as Pompey, the men, along with Boyet, lay upon the performers mercilessly. The Princess, on the contrary, is supportive and understanding. She shows herself to be the kind of courtly patron that Shakespeare would have liked to serve; the men show themselves to be sarcastic scoffers, the sort who, without much trouble, could end up sounding like waspish Antonio and Sebastian in *The Tempest*.

The implications in *Love's Labour's Lost* for courting lovers are all chastening. But the play is a comedy, and so no serious harm is done. The men may possess sharp wits "whose edge hath power to cut," but in the end that edge is rendered harmlessly blunt. As well, the action takes place in an insulated environment where the various species of youthful, academic, ethical, aesthetic, and affectional folly are exhausted without serious consequences. Though styles of clientage are satirized, the essential attractiveness of courtly life is not vitiated. Chamberlain wrote of a happy time at court: "All is there very peaceable and setled, the streame running smoothly all one way without opposition. All the talke now is of masking and feasting" (1: 487). This is the atmosphere of the play: something decidedly "settled" lies behind its lively "mockery merriment." The rules of the game are known by all, and the highest wisdom and pleasure are to know that turnabout is—to indulge in the play's master pun—*fair* play: "There's no such sport as sport by sport o'erthrown" (5.2.153).

Implications in the play for poetical clients are also uniformly chastening. The authorial attitude toward poetizing figures seems the same as that of the women: "to their penn'd speech render we no grace" (5.2.147). Poetry is here the medium of disguise, prevarication, false praise—the masking of the true inward with a meretricious outward part. Poetry is displayed as a tainted adjunct to the courtier's life, which is, as most anatomies of court and courtiers' letters suggest, one of constant dissimulation. "That which is most allowed, & embraced (for that it is more masked and disguised than the others)," wrote Philibert, "is Courtly life" (12). Or, as the *Galateo* advised, "It behoves thee, to frame and order thy manners and doings, not according to thyne owne minde and fashion: but to please those, with whome thou lyvest, and after that sort direct thy doings" (4). To such sycophantic uses is poetry put in *Love's Labour's Lost*.

The experiences of poet-clients with their patrons are finally worked out to comic effect, however, and this is because poetry is also chastised before it can do serious harm. All the masculine avatars of the poetic profession fail because their poetry cannot stand up to the women's "keen conceit." Thomas Greene writes that this play "makes game of men who are maladroit at shifting roles and disguises, and so . . . the palm goes to the quicksilver wit, the alert, the volatile, the adroit improviser, the *débrouillard*."[32] The objective correlative of the men's amatory fecklessness is the ungainly poetry of the King, Longaville, Dumain, Berowne, Armado, Holofernes, and Nathaniel—all of which unwittingly proves that "affection" (for ladies, poetry, or the "letter") is not perfect love. These rude rhymes show them not in their "presence majestical" but in their "particoated presence"—as fools (5.2.102, 766).

As poets, none of the play's characters seems to have come to the momentous point that Jonson reaches in his "Epistle to Master John Selden":

> Since being deceived, I turn a sharper eye
> Upon myself, and ask to whom, and why,
> And what I write? And vex it many days
> Before men get a verse: much less a praise;
> So that my reader is assured, I now
> Mean what I speak: and still will keep that vow. [148]

One feels that only poetry written by such a poet—far from "extemporal"—would please the ladies of *Love's Labour's Lost*. Anything less would be doomed to be quoted as "bombast and lining to the time" (5.2.781). Throughout the action the men are presented as self-deceiving, and the tasking of the women at the end is specifically intended to undeceive them and cause them as men, but also by extension as poets, to address more serious questions. The "forlorn and naked hermitage" to which the Princess urges the King foreshadows Lear's stormy heath: take physic, poetry. The play does not end like an old comedy because the ladies perceive that their suitors do not, in Jonson's phrase, mean what they speak. Poetry is at least in part responsible for this defect of character.

Shakespeare's evocation of the blithe but potentially corrupting ethos surrounding the poet-client is reflected in a passage from Harington's unpublished "Treatise on Playe" (circa 1596), probably written just after Shakespeare created *Love's Labour's Lost*. Here are included many of the play's central images and concepts, as well as the Princess's fine awareness of the compromises of integrity that social existence exacts from patrons and clients alike:

> I say in defence of . . . honest or at least harmles dissimulacion . . . that thear is almost no parte of owr lyfe in which wee doe not generally affecte and effect more dawngerows practyses of dissimulacion in matters of ernest and wayght than this that I bring in, in matter only of sport and game. Wee goe brave in apparell that wee may be taken for better men than wee bee; wee use much bumbastings and quiltings to seeme better formed, better showlderd, smaller wasted, and fuller thyght, then wee are; wee barbe and shave ofte, to seeme yownger than wee are; we use perfumes both inward and outward, to seeme sweeter then wee bee; corkt shooes, to seeme taller then wee bee; lowly obaysances to seeme humbler then wee be . . . And infynit such thinges wee may observe in ourselves, which are some of them commendable in this respect, that, by good and trew endevour to seeme to bee, we may obtayne at last the habyt and grace to become to bee such indeed, according to the excellent cownsell, *Labour to bee as you would bee thought*. Wherfore, if we allow in so many thinges seeming withowt beinge, why showld wee not bee content, in this one thing, to be lesse bowntifull. [1:209-10]

The ladies' counsel at play's end is precisely Harington's: at court true virtue lies in being as one is thought to be, perfect equivalence of inward and outward part—in language, poetry, and the man. For them, as Costard succinctly puts it, "truth is truth" (4.1.48).

We are thus brought back to Katharine's observation that Dumain "hath wit to make an ill shape good" (2.1.59). Bombasting, whether of clothing, ravishing cleverness, or metrical hypocrisy, masks the ill form underneath. For the first time in their lives, the men are apparently directed to scrutinize this disparity between oath and jest, "plain-dealing" and "glozes." All their previous labors are therefore well and truly lost.

The results of poetic effort in *Love's Labour's Lost* are unspectacular, but with the Princess—a wise, gracious Gloriana—controlling the action there is nevertheless hope. None of the poetic avatars is denied his place in the court's social economy. The vitality of the patron-client relationship lies in intelligent and graceful control, and in this respect the Princess is a fitting shadow of the woman who gave England such a stable center of power: "Hir mynde was oftime like the gentle air that comethe from the westerly pointe in a summer's morn; 'twas sweete and refreshinge to all arounde her. Her speech did winne all affections, and hir subjectes did trye to shewe all love to hir commandes. . . . Surely she did plaie well hir tables to gain obedience thus wythout constraint: again, she coude put forthe suche alteracions, when obedience was lackinge, as lefte no doubtynges whose daughter she was" (*Letters*, 122). By the time (1606) Harington came to write this nostalgic memoir, the social environment for interchange between patron and client had changed radically for the worse. The P.S. to this letter—"Send me Petrarche by my man, at his returne"—suggests how out of place Harington was at the Stuart court. Shakespeare's active career spanned this transformation in the circumstances of the courtly poet, and, by looking at *Timon of Athens*, which he wrote sometime between 1606 and 1608, we can suggest in a general way the declining fortune of the poet at court.

The client-patron relationship requires confidence on both sides, and with the exception of Dull all the characters in *Love's Labour's Lost* exude confidence. We turn to *Timon of Athens* and immediately sense a crisis of confidence. There is no confidence in Athens except for Timon's, which has metastasized into recklessness. All love is "politic"; all friendship, "bare." Indeed, as a master text for *Timon of Athens*, one might adduce a little volume by one J.M. titled *A Health to the Gentlemanly Profession of Servingmen, or, The Servingmans Comfort* (1598), which laments and tries to explain the deterioration of "service." The first sentence tells all: "In this Bursse, or Exchange of humane affayres, which consisteth (as it were) altogeather in Marchandize, bargayning, buying & selling, it is very meete and necessary that there shoulde be men of all manners, conditions, and callinges . . . [in] this Mundane market." (Br). A "money-get" society, to borrow Jonson's word, was beginning to thrive in England. Why, J.M. asks, has the "knott" of "obligation" come untied? He offers three answers: (1) the compounding of true servants' metal with "untryed dregges and drosse of lesse esteeme"; (2) "the death and decay of Liberalitie or Rewarde for well doing"; and (3) "the decay of Hospitalitie, or good House-keeping." (C3r-Dv). The author finally apostrophizes the real villain: "It is Money they minde, Golde they grope after, and Gayne they groane for: Money, I say, Money is the cause of all this mischiefe and miserie" (G3r). We are some distance from the play in which money is never asked for but freely given (the "guerdon" and "remuneration" for Costard and the forester's tip for "telling true"). We are now squarely in the world of Timon as he soliloquizes to the gold he has found in the woods. This "yellow, glittering, precious gold," he says,

> Will lug your priests and servants from your sides,
> Pluck stout men's pillows from below their heads.
> This yellow slave
> Will knit and break religions, bless th'accurs'd,
> Make the hoar leprosy ador'd, place thieves,
> And give them title, knee and approbation. [4.3.26, 32-37]

It should be obvious that we are also in the world described by Lawrence Stone in *The Crisis of the Aristocracy*. Indeed, Stone's conclusion to his massive study is called "The Crisis of Confidence," and many of the reasons he summarizes there for the aristocracy's "slump in prestige" are relevant to *Timon*'s picture of courtly life and artistic patronage. Stone speaks of "the granting of titles of honor for cash not merit," and this idea is present in the lines just quoted (see also 2.2.112-16).[33] He also speaks of an "increasing preference for extravagant living in the city instead of hospitable living in the countryside," and *Timon of Athens* might well be counted the most thoroughgoing "city" play Shakespeare ever wrote. This Athens is very much like the London of Jonson's excoriating "Epistle to a Friend, to Persuade him to the Wars."[34] Timon's life (the Folio does not call it a tragedy) is ruined precisely because of his extravagance.[35] Stone further notes a growing "psychological breach" between the decadent urban, and the more wholesome rural, attitudes toward aesthetic tastes, financial probity, and sexual morality; Shakespeare treats each of these areas in the course of his action. And, finally, Stone notes a "decline of respect for superiors in church, state, society, and family." Set against the respectfulness radiating throughout *Love's Labour's Lost*, the endemic lack of respect in *Timon of Athens* is especially chilling. In the latter play the "precepts of respect" are all "icy" (4.3.260).

But it is Stone's vision of the failed suitor at court that most appropriately sets the stage for *Timon of Athens*:

Allured by the glamor and excitement of the Court, many noblemen lived out their futile lives in a vain struggle for office and profit that left them cynical, servile, and impoverished. Few predicaments can have been as desperate as that of the ageing, unsuccessful courtier, passing his days in anxious attendance in the ante-rooms of the great, fawning and flattering with practiced hypocrisy in the hopes of some small pickings from the table of Dives, consumed with hatred and jealousy as younger and more attractive personalities fought their way to the front and elbowed him ruthlessly into the background. And yet such was the magnetic power of the Court that few could tear themselves away and retire to rustic solitude to salvage something from the wreckage before they had spent deeply of both life and fortune. [36]

Echoes of such agony resound in the books of courtiership: "O unhappy and sorowfull courtier if by chaunce he growe to be a poore man, no man will succour him." [37] Nowhere is the debilitating rat race of suit more keenly evoked than in Donne's fifth satire, titled in some manuscripts, "Of the misery of the poor suitors at Court":

> Man is a world; in which, officers
> Are the vast ravishing seas; and suitors,
> Springs; now full, now shallow, now dry; which, to
> That which drowns them, run: these self reasons do
> Prove the world a man, in which, officers
> Are the devouring stomach, and suitors
> The excrements, which they void. [171]

Timon, within the action of the play, lives to experience both sides of the humiliating minuet of suitors and the "great." He is both Dives and the cynical, impoverished victim of the conspicuous consumption to which his status drove him. For Timon, and for everyone in the play, the careening, money-mad Athenian society produces a dizzying, roller-coaster environment.

The client-patron relationship is thus subjected to particular pressure. We are told in the preface to the *Works* of James I (1616) that "Book-writing is growen into a Trade" (b2v), and in *Timon of Athens* the poet's art has become one too. The Poet is without a name, and he is listed in the Folio's dramatis personae along with a Painter, Jeweller, and a Merchant. In *Love's Labour's*

Lost the functions of the poet were various and carried no price tag; in *Timon of Athens* the Poet is attached to his patron by the taut cable of money. What incites poetical devising in the earlier play is "majesty" and "grace," but in the later play it is clear that prodigal generosity fuels poetical rapture. The Poet observes, as suitors convene: "See, / Magic of bounty, all these spirits thy power / Hath conjur'd to attend!" (1.1.5-7). The Poet has become one of the status symbols necessary to a man of Timon's station. His services are not a donation; he is perceived merely as another of Timon's purveyors, Shakespeare's testimony to Jonson's view that the Stuarts brought with them a "money-get, mechanic age" (346). In the play's first scene the Poet unctuously announces his ideal: "When we for recompense have prais'd the vild, / It stains the glory in that happy verse / Which aptly sings the good" (1.1.15-17). But this ideal Shakespeare carefully reveals in everything the Poet says and does as pure hypocrisy.

The Poet "unbolts" the fiduciary relationship between art and power, which is one focus of the play's vicious satire:

> You see how all conditions, how all minds,
> As well of glib and slipp'ry creatures as
> Of grave and austere quality, tender down
> Their services to Lord Timon: his large fortune,
> Upon his good and gracious nature hanging,
> Subdues and properties to his love and tendance
> All sorts of hearts. [1.1.53-59]

Shakespeare's brilliant verb *properties* captures the merchandizing by which the Poet himself must operate. He too proves a glib and slippery denizen of Timon's court. On Timon's side, the artists are treated with condescension: "I thank you; you shall hear from me anon. . . . I like your work, / And you shall find I like it. Wait attendance" (1.1.156-64). They are obliged, as the Poet says, to "follow his strides" and fill his lobbies "with tendance" (1.1.82). The Painter presents an image of this antechamber sycophancy in his hopeful allegory of "one man beckon'd from the rest below, / Bowing his head against the steepy mount / To climb to happiness" (1.1.76-78).

In *Love's Labour's Lost* the traditional notion of "feigning" poets is lightheartedly expressed in the King's remark about Armado, "I love to hear him lie" (1.1.174). In *Timon of Athens* the conceit takes on a darker aspect. This Poet is a true liar:

Apemantus: Art not a poet?
Poet: Yes.

Apemantus: Then thou liest. Look in thy last work, where
                        thou hast feign'd him [Timon] a worthy fellow.
Poet: That's not feign'd, he is so.
Apemantus: Yes, he is worthy of thee, and to pay for thy labor.
                        He that loves to be flattered is worthy o' th' flatterer. [1.1.219-26]

Apemantus is a curious counterpart to the Princess. Just as she leads the discourse which proves that affectation is not love, Apemantus demonstrates that politeness and sycophancy do not constitute true devotion at court: "That there should be small love amongst these sweet knaves, / And all this courtesy!" he exclaims as Timon's audience in the first scene ends. Also like the Princess, Apemantus proves his awareness of the sleights of false praisers when he urges Timon to return to court with the guise and catachrestic language of a suitor:

> Be thou a flatterer now, and seek to thrive
> By that which has undone thee. Hinge thy knee,
> And let his very breath whom thou'lt observe
> Blow off thy cap; praise his most vicious strain,
> And call it excellent. [4.3.212-16]

If it is tempting to see Elizabeth as the controlling historical figure for *Love's Labour's Lost*, then James is that figure for *Timon*. Timon, after all, is an anachronistically "royal" (1.2.172) figure in democratic Athens, and his Steward sounds very much like those chief courtiers who bore the brunt of James's prodigality. The Steward asks, as James's chamberlains and many grudging Parliamentarians must have asked in the early years, "What will this come to? / He commands us to provide, and give great gifts, / And all out of an empty coffer" (1.2.189-91). During the crucial interview between Timon and the Steward in act 2, the latter paints in vivid terms the extravagance of Timon's household. This, as it happens, is an accurate description of the early Stuart court:

Steward: So the gods bless me,
                        When all our offices have been oppress'd
                        With riotous feeders, when our vaults have wept
                        With drunken spilth of wine, when every room
                        Hath blaz'd with lights and bray'd with minstrelsy,
                        I have retir'd me to a wasteful cock
                        And set mine eyes to flow.
Timon: Prithee no more.
Steward: Heavens, have I said, the bounty of this lord!
                        How many prodigal bits have slaves and peasants
                        This night englutted . . .

Ah, when the means are gone that buy this praise,
The breath is gone whereof this praise is made.
Feast-won, fast-lost. [2.2.168-75]

Perhaps James dismissed such talk as Timon dismisses his steward: "Come, sermon me no further" (2.2.176). Feast-won, fast-lost—such were the Stuarts' roseate beginning and unhappy end.

The ethos of *Love's Labour's Lost* is one of order, sociability, and approbation. *Timon of Athens*, on the contrary, emphasizes a rupture in the courteous bonds of

Piety and fear,
Religion to the gods, peace, justice, truth,
Domestic awe, night-rest and neighborhood,
Instruction, manners, mysteries and trades,
Degrees, observances, customs and laws. [4.1.15-20]

For Timon all is "confusion," and his curse is worthy of his misanthropic shadow Apemantus: "All's obliquy; / There's nothing level in our cursed natures / But direct villainy. Therefore be abhorr'd / All feasts, societies, and throngs of men!" (4.3.18-21). The world of Navarre is one of feasts, society, and throng; that is why the Princess's banishment of the King to an "austere insociable life" exquisitely fits his crimes of perjury. Far from gaining sustenance from fellowship, the characters in *Timon of Athens* are subject to humanity more inclined, as in *Lear*, to "prey on itself / Like monsters of the deep" (LR 4.2.49-50). Cannibalism, in fact, provides one of the play's master images.

In many other respects significant for the cultural environment of the poet and his patron, *Love's Labour's Lost* and *Timon of Athens* present a radical opposition. The court of Navarre is youthful and crescent, vibrantly scented of April and May; Timon's court is wintry and entropic, one that "wears as it grows," rotting itself with motion. An air of leisure pervades Navarre; time requires "bombast and lining" to fill it out. In Athens all is "importunate business" (3.6.13). In Navarre a sense of hierarchy and its corollary "respect" assure the peace; those who assume ungallant postures toward inferiors become objects of ridicule themselves. The life of Athens is a justle for place amid the demotic confusion; with fine anachronism Shakespeare has Timon liken it to "a City feast" where food cools because no man can "agree upon the first place" (3.6.66-67). Athens shows the dark side of hierarchy, where "the greater scorns the lesser" (4.3.6). In Navarre the invisible god is courtesy. The lesson we learn there is that language cannot be trusted (though with some serious effort, individuals can perhaps learn to be worthy of trust). Athens, on the other hand, is ruled by gold, and the kiss in this society is not the polite courtly maneuver but the kiss of Judas. Of this gold, Timon says, "Thou visible god, / That sold'rest close impossibilities, / And mak'st them kiss; that speak'st with every tongue, / To every purpose!" (4.3.389-92). In *Timon* neither language nor men can be trusted.

These drastically different courtly scenes inevitably affect courtly behavior. In the comedy, the wise philosopher and erstwhile loner at court, Berowne, soon bows to peer pressure and joins the foolish fraternity. In *Timon* the "churlish Philosopher" Apemantus is ostracized: "Go, let him have a table by himself, / For he does neither affect company, / Nor is he fit for't" (1.2.30-32). The ladies of France effectively "arrest" the word of the men, and at play's end they insist on the integrity of "heavenly" and "keeping" oaths. There are no such oaths in *Timon*, as Apemantus cynically implies when he says grace: "Grant I may never prove so fond, / To trust man on his oath or bond" (1.2.64-65). His point is borne out by the Painter's cold-hearted observation, "Promising is the very air o' th' time. . . . To promise is most courtly and fashionable; performance is a kind of will or testament which argues a great sickness in his judgment that makes it" (5.1.22-29).[38]

Finally, in Navarre we find a mixture of awed respect and eagerness to serve that was so often associated with Elizabeth's "presence majestical." There is something of the comedy's humor in Chamberlain's amusing anecdote: "Our frend the sheriffe of Barkeshire was almost out of hart at the first newes of the Quenes comming into the country, because he was altogether unacquainted with courting" (1: 130). There is no genuine presence in *Timon*, but rather a kind of courtly vacuum. The play's real focus is the immediate *vicinity* of the center of power, where a swarm of parasites compete for attention. That this sort of demeaning press was a Stuart innovation is suggested in the papers of Sir Julius Caesar relating to Prince Henry's household: "It came to that passe that it was growne common for the Princes servaunts to begg a place and sell it for money to strangers whereby those that by order of his Matie serving in the Princes howse [who] were to be preferred could obteyne no advancement." In a few years the crush became shocking: "At one tyme there were 24 suying to be admitted whose names Sr T[homas] C[haloner] deliv'd to the late lo: Tre[asure]r and who by acquainting his Matie therewith gave comaundement to make a staie[,] which notwithstanding litle by litle under hand was broken by secret entries made in the Court."[39]

From such lobbies filled with "tendance," the Poet and Painter escape in the last act of *Timon* to track down their former and now apparently newly wealthy patron. Their final interview with Timon outside his cave represents a corruscating valedictory appearance of the poet in Shakespeare (aside from the choric Gower in *Pericles*). As before, the Poet's first concern is clear: "Does the rumor hold for true that he's so full of gold?" (5.1.3). Throughout the scene commercial diction underscores the nature of the transaction: "'Tis not amiss we tender our loves to him" (5.1.11). It is a "sin" against their professions to fail to "profit" merely by being laggard.

There is special irony in this scene if one comes to it from *Love's Labour's Lost*. For the Poet, as his first "piece" for Timon, proposes a "satire against the softness of prosperity, with a discovery of the infinite flatteries that follow youth and opulency" (5.1.33-35). This could stand as a nice synopsis of Shakespeare's satiric point in the earlier comedy, but *this* poet's artistic plan is purely hypocritical, as Timon's aside makes clear: "Wilt thou whip thine own faults in other men?" (5.1.37). This makes the Poet a soul brother of the men of Navarre: "Now step I forth to whip hypocrisy" (4.3.149), says the hypocritical Berowne in the sonneting scene. He, the play's master poet, is soon crushed—first by the plot, then by the ladies; likewise the Poet, crushed by Timon's withering sarcasm. His *furor poeticus* is quoted as bombast:

Poet: I am rapt, and cannot cover
                 The monstrous bulk of this ingratitude
                 With any size of words
Timon: Let it go naked, men may see't the better. [5.1.63-66]

And the "bombast" clothing image of *Love's Labour's Lost* is embedded in the few sarcastic words of praise that Timon gives the Poet as his rage begins to erupt: "Thy verse swells with stuff so fine and smooth." In short order the two are driven off, with Timon shouting after them, "Out, rascal dogs!" Ignominious end for the poet in Shakespeare. And yet, for the poet as for all suitors at court, a not unlikely end: "Have I not seen dwellers on form and favor / Lose all and more by paying too much rent / For compound sweet forgoing simple savor, / Pitiful thrivers, in their gazing spent?" (SON 125).

Pitiful thrivers. The phrase returns us to the oxymoronic nature of life at court. The First Senator says to Alcibiades, "You undergo too strict a paradox, / Striving to make an ugly deed look fair" (3.5.24-25), and his point is pertinent to the demands made on language and men at climb-fall court. The language of the men of Navarre manifests a constant "sold'ring" of impossibilities ("a wit to make an ill shape good"). Of their poeticizing the Princess concludes in her own witty paradox—"beauteous as ink"—

and the most succinct summary of this courting poetry comes in the form of Katharine's oxymoron, "profound simplicity." The ladies (and Shakespeare) scrupulously counterpose the pleasures and debilities of courtly life, and this careful equilibrium is captured in the climactic (and oxymoronic) "judgment" of the Princess: "No, no, my lord, your grace is perjur'd much, / Full of dear guiltiness." The pun is the play's most brilliant: *dear* in the senses of extreme, expensive, valuable, endearing, grievous, and cherishable. Just as the Princess moderates her feelings about the deer in act 4, so does Shakespeare with this pun moderate her reaction to the men's misconduct. And in the play as a whole, Shakespeare moderates the good and ill of courtly and poetic suit.

The paradoxical and oxymoronic expressions of *Timon* are altogether gloomier and more extreme. Gold, not language, turns experiences catachrestically, paradoxically awry: "Thus much of this [gold] will make / Black, white; foul, fair; wrong, right; / Base, noble; old, young; coward, valiant" (4.3.28-30). Gold has, in the master paradox of the play, turned "the commonwealth of Athens" into a "forest of beasts" (5.3.349-50). That men in the play are at "confounding odds" is most strikingly demonstrated in the oxymorons that Timon hurls at his guests at the "banquet" of warm water: "Live loath'd, and long, / Most smiling, smooth, detested parasites, / Courteous destroyers, affable wolves, meek bears" (3.6.89-91). The Poet, we have seen, is deeply implicated in this dark view of courtly suit. For him, unlike the poets of *Love's Labour's Lost*, self-serving hypocrisy, cynical calculation, and greed have become the true "art" of art. The ideals of honesty and "being what you are" (5.1.67) have become "sin." The Poet's labors, therefore, are well and happily lost.

The Poet is Shakespeare's last, but Timon is not his last patron: Prospero with the "vanities" of his art and Wolsey with his "fierce vanities" are yet to come. Though unfolding against a more complex panorama, the Cardinal's vainglorious folly is foreshadowed in many obvious respects by Timon's career. The concept of patronage is more subtly infused in *The Tempest*, and by way of conclusion I would like to suggest that this play reflects on the style of the most important patron during Shakespeare's last active years, aside from James: Henry Prince of Wales.

The inception of Henry's courtly style was not unlike that envisaged by Navarre: "It was the King's wish, expressed to [Henry's chamberlain] Chaloner when he first signed his [account] book, that 'the forme of the Princes howse should rather imitate a colledg then a court,' by which he must have meant that it should be given to scholarly pursuits and composed in part of students and men of culture."[40] In the first years of his father's reign Henry began to inspire extraordinary effort on the part of English authors. By 1607 he had become one of England's leading literary patrons. A census of books dedicated to father and son between 1608 and 1612 suggests very well why the Venetian ambassador might have concluded that "the King has some reasonable jealousy of the rising sun." For in those years, fifty-one books were dedicated to Henry and fifty-three to James.[41] Between 1599 and 1612 nearly a hundred books were dedicated to the Prince, among them a magnificent translation of Serlio by Peake, who placed it "under the Patronage of your powerful Name."

The Venetian ambassador observed as well that Henry "is also collecting books for a library he has built."[42] Henry purchased the large Lumley library and on specific occasions, according to Birch, acted gallantly toward authors· "He shewed great generosity on all occasions towards persons of genius and merit. A good Poet, and a very honest man, presenting to him a small Poem, the Prince received it very graciously, and desired a gentleman, who kept his privy purse, to bestow on him some mark of his favour. The gentleman asking, whether a couple of Angels would not serve? 'Fie, for shame, answered his Highness, give him at least ten Angels.'" Though Henry's entourage was specially disposed to serious literary effort, it appears that he was in no danger of making Prospero's mistake of becoming too bookish. Rather, it appears that he followed the advice of George More's *Principles for yong Princes* (1611), which was dedicated to him: "It bee not good that a Prince should be too great a scholler . . . [for] great learned men are perplexed to resolve upon affairs, making many doubts full of respects and imaginations."[43]

Everything known about this splendid bird of passage at the Stuart court suggests that his inclinations decidedly favored the vita activa:

He loved and did mightily strive to doe somewhat of every thing, and to excell in the most excellent; Hee greatly delighted in all kind of rare inventions and arts, and in all kind of Engines belonging to the Warres, both by Sea and Land: In the bravery and number of great horses; in shooting and levelling of great peeces of Ordnance; in the ordering and marshalling of Armes; in building and gardening, and in all sorts of rare musique, chiefly the trumpet and drumme; in limming and painting, carving, in all sorts of excellent and rare Pictures, which hee had brought unto him from all Countries.[44]

But no reading. Such was the popular image of the Prince. Comparison with his notoriously bookish father was inevitably invidious. As the Fool advises in *King Lear:* "Let go thy hold when a great wheel runs down a hill, lest it break thy neck with following; but the great one that goes upward, let him draw thee after" (2.4.71-74). Henry's wheel of fortune was clearly rising. Such a view no doubt led Chamberlain to urge an office seeker, after the death of Salisbury in 1612, "Yf I might advise, I wold you could rather devise how to grow in with the Prince" (1: 352).

The advice was sensible, for in the first Stuart years, Prince Henry's train grew tremendously. When Henry VIII left the throne his expenses per annum were roughly £40,000; when Elizabeth left the throne they were about £55,000. In James's first year expenses shot up to £80,000 and by 1608 were nearly £100,000. Henry's household expenses kept up with this level of inflation. In 1604 his household numbered 141 ("besides servants of these servants who had intruded themselves into the court"); in 1608 the number was 233; and by the time of *The Tempest*, 1610, his followers numbered 297 with wages and 129 without—a total of 426. Thomas Chaloner commiserated in a letter to the Lord High Treasurer: "The continual increase of new servants dayly sent hether by warrente procured without my knowledge, has brought the charge so farr out of frame, that it [is] hard to conceive a course how to lessen it, seeing the necessary increase of many moor will follow the Prince's advancement in years and dignitie."[45]

Even at his young age Prince Henry was beginning to show an ability to deploy such a courtly juggernaut to consciously political ends. At age ten he christened a twenty-five-foot boat called the *Disdain* and designed by Pett; for his elevation to the Principality of Wales he commissioned his nation's first equestrian portrait. He was, in effect, showing an increasingly dexterous ability to manipulate his public image. As J. W. Williamson has concluded, "The perceptible difference between father and son really came down to their differing abilities to inspire and then to assume mythic personation."[46]

Now imagine for a moment the "old" and the "new" Prospero, respectively, as shadows of James and Henry—the former bookish and introverted; the latter, charismatic and extroverted as well as salient. Indeed, Henry's clarity and focus of mind, as well as his public savoir faire, can be seen to have given him the appeal of an Elizabeth *redivivus*. As the Venetian ambassador noted: "Everyone is afraid of falling into disgrace with him . . . he is extremely particular that everything shall be the result of his own choice . . . he will meet no opposition, as everyone is anxious to please him." This was not only the Queen's style but also the style of any effective patron. As well, many observers hopefully thought that Henry's accession might signal a return to the more solid, moderate virtues of Elizabeth: "He expressed himself, upon occasions offered, to love and esteem most such of the nobility, as were most antiently descended."[47] So much for the influx of Scots knights.

Henry showed not only Prospero's facility of rule and what in military circles is called command voice, but also the mage's charismatic patronage of the arts. Henry, like Prospero, was capable of thinking in very grand terms. Chamberlain writes than the Prince's papers "shewed him to have many straunge and vast conceits and projects" (1: 391). He was also an eager participant in the masques and tiltings that very likely influenced Shakespeare when he came to write *The Tempest*. Particularly notable were Jonson's *Hymenaei* (5 January 1606), in which the Prince danced "wth as great perfection and as setled Ma[ty] as could be devised," *The Masque of Queenes* (2 February 1609, dedicated to him), and *Prince Henry's Barriers* (6 January 1610). Perhaps most pertinent to Henry's identity as an artistic patron is the masque *Oberon* (1 January 1611), whose elaborate scenic effects and finery (especially its fairy costumes) Shakespeare may have sought to emulate in his play. Though the royal father paid the staggering bills, the patron of the event and performer of the title role was clearly the Prince: account books repeatedly refer to *Oberon* as "the Princes Maske." *Oberon* required, among many others, ten singers, six "plaiers on the lute provided by Alphonse" Ferrabosco, thirteen boys to play fairies, as well as "Players imployed in the Maske." These last, some have imagined, may have been drawn from Shakespeare's company, or they may have been from among Henry's own retinue, which came to number fifteen musicians and fourteen comedians and players. In either event, they were very probably viewed in the same light as the "meaner fellows" and "industrious" (4.1.33-35) servants who apply themselves to making the masque on Prospero's island harmonious and charming. It is important, here, to remember that Prospero's "art" is not necessarily the specific power of creation, but rather the power to control deployment of the artwork and the circumstances under which the audience experiences it. Prospero calls the masque his "vanity" because it is a perquisite, an ornament to his "art"—art that is nothing less than a means of making visible and of celebrating his complete power on the island. Clearly, Prince Henry viewed these semipolitical entertainments in which he took such keen interest in a similar way. "He did advance his own Title and Right so farre, as with modestie he might," wrote Cornwallis of him by way of describing Jonson's *Barriers* of 1610 (10: 512), and in *Oberon* the shrewd patron's awareness of how art can be manipulated according to political purposes is also manifest.[48]

In his increasingly sophisticated understanding of "what art could do in personating a man, figuring him forth in the eyes of beholders,"[49] in his penchant for "vast conceits and projects," in his various figurative projections of power, and in his charismatic presence—in all of these Henry presented a most majestic princely vision. It was a vision, placed against the feckless reality of his father's style of government, charmingly harmonious with the high hopes the English people placed in him. Among his several successful public personations was that of the perfect patron. He was (as Prospero is) an astute, firm, rewarding patron. Prospero plays many roles too, among them the role of artistic patron in the style of the young prince. Considering Henry's well-known interests in ships, sailing, colonization, and masquing, one is tempted to think that *The Tempest* might be the one Shakespearean play written more with him rather than James in mind . . . if he had Stuarts in mind at all.

But what of the poet? This play, which follows in the Folio a few pages after Jonson and Holland repeatedly refer to Shakespeare the poet, is no poet's valediction. It is, appropriately, a palinode for the producer of theatrical visions. *Projector* is perhaps the most precise word for him. Authorship is *not* among the many impressive powers that Prospero abjures in the last scene. In the surrogate courtly environment of the island, the poet is apparently numbered among the "meaner fellows." If he labored on the lovely lines of the nuptial masque with a view to fame and a respected place in the surrogate courtly culture of the island, then his labors too were lost. For neither Prospero nor the masque's delighted audience of two see fit to mention the poet's name. They praise neither his work nor his profession and do not even allude to his existence. The masque is billed as a vanity of the patron's—Prospero's—art, not the poet's, and this is how an audience is bound to remember it.

It was precisely so in real life with *Oberon*. William Trumbull the Elder left a full description of the performance and titled it "A Short Account of the Masque Made *by* the Prince of Wales" (emphasis added).[50] Nowhere does the name of Ben Jonson appear.

Chapter Four

"Chameleon Muse"

The Poet's Life in Shakespeare's Courts

I can add colors to the chameleon,
Change shapes with Proteus for advantages,
And set the murtherous Machevil to school.
—Richard of Gloucester, *3 Henry VI*

THE IMAGE of the chameleon was a natural one for describing the behavior of an evil Renaissance courtier. Not coincidentally, the image could also be useful in capturing the spirit of the Petrarchan love-object— or of the Renaissance poet himself:

Love her that list! I am content
  For that cameleon-like she changeth,
Yielding such mists as may prevent
  My sight to view her when she rangeth.
    [Robert Jones, *First Booke of Songes*]

Yet *Astrophell* might one for all suffize,
Whose supple Muse Camelion-like doth change
Into all formes of excellent devise.
    [John Davies, *Orchestra*]

The courtier, poet, and *amour courtois* protagonist each, in his own way, faced the challenge of a fluctuating, surreally disorienting world. This world, court-centered and ruled by what the Bastard in *King John* calls "That smooth-fac'd gentleman, tickling commodity, / Commodity, the bias of the world" (2.1.573-74), was at once alluring and forbidding. The ascent to favor could be spectacularly rewarding, but the possibilities for humiliating failure, not to mention financial devastation, lay everywhere. "The great weapon" for those who aimed at political, artistic, or poetical-amatory success in this world was, as Thomas Greene has written, "tactical flexibility." This was a "horizontal flexibility, the capacity to change one's style, one's strategy, one's mode of procedure, with the flux of events." To underline his point Greene cites Machiavelli: "If one could change one's nature with time and circumstances, fortune would never change."[1]

Seeking to express the tactical advantages of situational resourcefulness, the authors of these three contemporary quotations recur to the reptilian epitome of this gift. Gloucester's boast is not an idle one, as the iniquitous panoply of *Richard III* shows in full measure. Jones's song text finds the lover, rather like the crestfallen speaker in Wyatt's "Whoso list to hunt," confronting his failure to match his elusive mistress's tactical flexibility. And Davies' praise of Sidney aptly conveys the courtier-poet's ability to adapt his pen to several literary vocations and genres.[2]

The chameleon image offers a fitting prologue to the following discussion, the purpose of which will be to understand better the nature of the poet's life and the consequences of poetizing as they are reflected in Shakespeare's presentation of various kinds of courts and courtiers. There is more shared experience than one might at first suppose behind the similarly chameleonic dexterity of Richard in his vice and Sidney in his virtue. The Renaissance courtier and Renaissance poet trod similar paths up the "steepy mount" of court, used language to similar ends, and indulged in similar "making" and "re-making" of their selves as events demanded. Often, with but slight mental adjustment, the shadow of one emerges and takes on a life of its own as one reads a description of the other. The courtly chameleon is nearby, for instance, when Puttenham observes that "our maker or Poet is to play many parts and not one alone" (3:25). Nor is Davies' chameleon muse far away in this advice on courtiership from Chapman: "tis boldnes, boldnes does the deed in the Court: and as your Camelion varries all cullours a'the Rainebow both white and red, so must your true Courtier be able to varrie his countenance through all humors: State, Strangnes, Scorne, Mirth, Melanchollie, Flatterie, and so foorth."[3]

Chapman's phrasing offers two alternatives. The admonition that the courtier "varrie his countenance," for instance, might lead us to explore the specifically courtly implications of the commonplace that the world is a stage. Thespian virtuosity and courtly dexterity were in the Renaissance perceived as intimately related, and no one was better at this chameleonic role-playing to ulterior purpose than the Queen: "I have seen her smile, soothe with great semblance of good likinge to all arounde, and cause everie one to open his moste inwarde thought to her; when, on a sudden, she woud ponder in pryvate on what had passed, write down all their opinions, draw them out as occasion required, and sometyme disprove to their faces what had been delivered a month before. Hence she knew every one's parte and by thus *fishinge*, as Hatton sayed, she caught many poor fish, who little knew what snare was laid for them."[4] These are precisely the methods of Iago, who smiles and smiles while laying the snares for his victims ("the net / That shall enmesh them all . . ." [2.3.362]). Nor are they far removed from those of Hamlet, whose skill in manipulating his interlocutors comes in part from haunting plays at Wittenberg.

The association of acting with courtiership was likewise a Renaissance commonplace. Sidney, for instance, in the *Arcadia* describes the evil courtier Clinias (imagine a combination of Berowne and Iago): "Clinias in his youth had been a scholar so far as to learn rather words than manners, and of words rather plenty than order; and oft had used to be an actor in tragedies, where he learned (besides a slidingness of language) acquaintance with many passions and to frame his face to bear the figure of them" (387). This "slidingness" of language, the power of impersonation (as we say, sliding into a role), made the court a genuine stage for real-life "makers" and spawned such assertions as this by Donne: "Believe me Sir, in my youth's giddiest days, / When to be like the Court, was a play's praise, / Plays were not so like Courts, as Courts are like plays" (213).[5] Chapman wrote: "Why, sir, the Court's as twere the stage: and they that have a good suite of parts and qualities, ought to presse hither to grace them."[6] And Jonson has Crites point out courtly denizens in *Cynthia's Revels* in theatrical terms:

> There stands a *Neophyte* . . . [who] repeates
> (Like an unperfect *prologue*, at third musike)
> His part of speeches, and confederate jests,
> In passion to himselfe. Another sweares
> His *Scene* of courtship over . . .
> A fourth, he onely comes in for a *mute:*
> Divides the *act* with a dumbe shew, and *exit.* [4: 91]

The court was habituated to what might be called theatrical license, as well as license of many other kinds. Masks, disguises, and roles were a part of the courtly scene, and for some a far from disagreeable part. There is a lovely passage in Castiglione in which Federico Fregoso warns the courtier not to dance the unseemly "double-footinges" and "Barletta" openly, "unlesse he were in a maske." And he adds, "to be in a maske bringeth with it a certaine libertie and licence" (99).

In Shakespeare, however, the courtier-as-actor is a dangerous or deeply conflicted personage. Richard of Gloucester speaks like another Clinias when he vaunts his actor's talent: "Why, I can smile, and murther whiles I smile, / And cry "Content" to that which grieves my heart, / And wet my cheeks with artificial tears, / And frame my face to all occasions" (3H6

3.2.182-85). His cohort in the next play of the tetralogy, Buckingham, shows that he too can set Machiavelli to acting school:

> Tut, I can counterfeit the deep tragedian,
> Speak and look back, and pry on every side,
> Tremble and start at wagging of a straw;
> Intending deep suspicion, ghastly looks
> Are at my service, like enforced smiles;
> And both are ready in their offices
> At any time to grace my stratagems. [R3 3.5.5-11]

The world of the actor is one of seeming. To the extent that the habitual assumption of guises creates a disparity between appearance and reality, it is usually deplored in Shakespeare's plays. The ideal is rather the mind that "suits" with its "fair and outward character." "Disguise," says Viola-Cesario in *Twelfth Night*, "I see thou art a wickedness" (1.2.51; 2.2.27).

Donne wrote of the court that "there, things that seem, exceed substantial," and it is this pervasive seeming all around him that Hamlet, master observer of acting style, rejects at Elsinore: "Seems, madam? nay, it is. I know not 'seems'" (1.2.76). And then he sarcastically derides the too-obviously theatrical signs that fool the court into thinking he is sad merely because "all that lives must die": "These indeed seem, / For they are actions that a man might play; / But I have that within which passes show, / These but the trappings and the suits of woe." Not the least cause of Hamlet's distemper is his sense of what a dull-witted audience the court at Elsinore provides him. His performance is caviar to this general. The subject of the courtier-as-actor is a large one, and it could scarcely be exhausted without examining carefully his other notable Shakespearean incarnations: Prince Hal, Coriolanus, and Prospero.

Chapman's suggestion that the chameleon courtier "varrie his countenance" has taken us in the direction of the courtier-as-actor, but he is a well-known and well-studied figure, especially among recent explorers of Shakespearean metadrama and Renaissance self-fashioning, for example, James Calderwood and Stephen Greenblatt. As I have suggested, there is a second way of looking at the chameleon courtier, which derives from Chapman's remark that "your Camelion varries all cullours." This phrase, referring as it does to the domain of the poet and to his deployment of the colors of rhetoric, draws our attention more directly tò the poet-as-courtier.

We know much about the poet-as-courtier's alter ego, the courtier-as-poet, simply because so many of the significant poets of the English Renaissance—Wyatt, Surrey, Sidney, Spenser, Greville, Raleigh—were courtiers. It has been an axiom of recent criticism that their "state of consciousness" as courtiers helped to shape the tension and dynamic of their finest verse. In a chapter on "The Psychology of a Courtier," for instance, Raymond Southall writes of Wyatt: "Through the convention of *amour courtois* . . . his own poetry expresses the doubts, anxieties, trials and tribulations of an unusually sensitive mind confronting a perplexng and dangerously insecure world."[7] I propose in the following pages to reverse this critical approach and explore the possibility of learning about the Renaissance poet's life by searching for the shadows, surrogates, and avatars of the poet's vocation and styles among Shakespeare's imagined courts and courtiers. Helena says in *All's Well That Ends Well*, "the court's a learning place" (1.1.177), and I believe it is especially so for those interested in learning more about the Renaissance poet's motivations and fears.

The poet-as-courtier is ubiquitous in Shakespeare's plays, and by way of showing what I mean by such an assertion and returning briefly to the image of the chameleon, let me draw attention to a minor Shakespearean character. The mythological equivalent of the chameleon was Proteus; there is no surprise in their appearance together in my epigraph. The connection was not an uncommon one. Michael Drayton, for example, wrote in "Peirs Gaveston": "*Camelion*-like, the world thus turns her hue, / And like *Proteus* puts on sundry shapes."[8] The figure of Proteus was also apt for conveying the strange transformations in style and behavior induced by courtly experience. Jonson thus included him among the typical dramatis personae at court:

> With him there meets some subtle PROTEUS, one
> Can change, and varie with all formes he sees;
> Be any thing but honest; serves the time;
> Hovers betwixt two factions, and explores
> The drifts of both; which (with crosse face) he beares
> To the divided heads, and is receiv'd
> With mutuall grace of either. (4: 90)

Consider, then, Proteus, the gentleman of Verona whose acquaintance we made in chapter 1 in a different context.

One of the many "lives" of the Renaissance poet was that of *amour courtois* stylist and this is what Proteus represents. We first meet him as we first meet Romeo: "I leave myself, my friends, and all, for love. / Thou, Julia, thou hast metamorphis'd me . . . " (TGV 1.1.65-66). Also like Romeo, Proteus is able to vent the rhetoric of Petrarch with gay abandon: "Sweet love, sweet lines, sweet life!" (1.3.45 *etc.*). But, unlike Romeo, Proteus does not remain "dully sluggardiz'd" in his native town; he is sent off by his father to attend "the Emperor in his royal court" (1.3.38). The transit of Proteus—who in the page Speed's words epitomizes "the chameleon Love" (2.1.172)—from Verona to the imperial court results almost immediately in a terrible ethical metamorphosis. This is demonstrated in the play's most important speech: Proteus's soliloquy (2.6.1-43), which shows him, once in Milan, springing into a full-fledged Machiavel, vowing "three-fold perjury," and seeking (in a manner similar to Berowne) through language to "excuse it" and show how "vows may heedfully be broken."

Proteus's speech is a minor-league premonition of the vicious soliloquies of Richard III and Iago. While these two invoke hatred in their cause, Proteus calls on "love": "Love, send me wings to make my purpose swift, / As thou hast lent me wit to plot this drift" (2.6.42). Proteus, in other words, represents in a compressed, melodramatic way the corruption of a Petrarchan stylist-suitor who comes to court. His false and hyperbolic aesthetic quickly falls to the disposal of "treachery" and the plotting of "some sly trick" (2.6.41,32). In a short time he is using the poet's "lovebook" on which he formerly prayed (1.1.19) as a means of duping a loverival:

> But you, Sir Thurio, are not sharp enough:
> You must lay lime to tangle her desires
> By wailful sonnets, whose composed rhymes
> Should be full-fraught with serviceable vows . . .
> Say that upon the altar of her beauty
> You sacrifice your tears, your sighs, your heart;
> Write till your ink be dry, and with your tears
> Moist it again, and frame some feeling line
> That may discover such integrity. [3.2.67-76]

Though Shakespeare deals with Proteus crudely as a pawn in his loosely-crafted plot, he does stand among the playwright's many surrogates for the poet-at-court. The Duke of Milan admires his "discipline" in courtship (3.2.87), but the effect of Shakespeare's manipulation is to make us suspicious of the uses to which the love-poet's discipline is bent at "the royal court." With this appropriately disconcerting figure of the protean or chameleonic poet in mind, we can turn to a broader canvass of Shakespearean shadows of the poet at court.

Before commencing, though, we must consider briefly the constitution and central characteristics of the court itself. In *Coriolanus*, Menenius calls the court the "heart" of the Roman body politic (1.1.136). Like so much of the political science of Shakespeare's Greek and Roman plays, the statement carries distinctly contemporary implications. Often blithely anachronistic, he presented courts and courtly existence in a way more closely bound to his own notion (that is, a Londoner's notion) of "the royal court" than to the location of his action, be it Sicily, legendary Britain, Vienna, or Athens. It is well, therefore, to pause for a moment over the demography of the English court.

Consider, first, the pyramid of English society. The overwhelming majority of the turn-of-the-century population of over 4 million—including farmers, laborers, menial servants, apprentices, the jobless, itinerant, and dregs—made up the lowest echelon. Above these was a class comprising an estimated 160,000-260,000 individuals who in some way were privileged by landhold, rent, accumulated assets, or domicile. Next above this class were the approximately 16,000 persons who constituted the lesser country gentry, followed by the still more affluent class comprising 1,000-2,500 members of the greater country gentry (wealthy, established families and holders of knighthoods, deputy lieutenancies, commissions of the peace, and shrieval offices) and the most powerful commercial and professional figures in London. Above them towered the sixty or so peers of the realm and, at the apex, the royal family.[9]

One does not arrive at the English court, however, merely by truncating the pyramid somewhere near its apex; that procedure would give us the English aristocracy. The court itself was a kind of miniature version of the entire pyramid. "The court," as Wallace MacCaffrey has summarized, "comprehended the chamber, the household, the gentlemen pensioners, and the yeoman guards, and accounted for at least a thousand persons. It was divided, on the one hand, into an elite of peers, knights, ladies and gentlemen, and, on the other, into a mass of household servants, guards, hunting or stable attendants, and artificers. The line of division between the two was a sharp one, and advancement across it uncommon in Elizabeth's time."[10] MacCaffrey estimates that, in 1567, the elite consisted of perhaps 175 men and a dozen women, and it is doubtful that the figure grew very much under Queen Elizabeth. The court in the Shakespearean canon is approximately faithful to the social conflux that MacCaffrey describes. Within the close confines of the royal chambers and household it was natural and inevitable that the likes of a Moth, Stephano, Duke of Buckingham, Parolles, Duchess of Gloucester, Angelo, Cloten, Bushy, Sir Walter Blunt, Osric, Wolsey, Malvolio, Sir John Falstaff and others would rub shoulders in the daily course of events.

Successfully breaching the verge of the English court, let alone succeeding thereafter, was a trying and sordid task. Francis Bacon wrote as positively about this task as one might in his essay "Of Nobility": "There is rarely any rising but by a commixture of good and evil arts." More typical, one feels, is Thomas Churchyard's admission in a letter to Sir Christopher Hatton: "I know it is miserable to crave, servitude to receive, and beggarly to want; which three afflictions my betters are visited with, and my inferiors cannot avoid." The courtier's life was essentially that of a suitor, and virtually all the contemporary descriptions of this life, both historical and fictional, suggest that it was a nerve-racking one. Donald Friedman has written that the "lifelong subject" of Wyatt's poetry was "the mind's quest for a serene integrity," and this was not least because the courtier's life conduced neither to serenity nor to easy conservation of one's integrity. John Hussee, one of the principal correspondents in *The Lisle Letters*, described the Tudor court as presenting a "wily world" where there was "nothing but every man for himself." [11] It was a world in which Iagos and Richards ("I am myself alone" 3H6 5.6.83) could move freely and often with devastating efficiency. It was also a world in which those possessed of what Machiavelli called "culpable innocence" were extremely vulnerable. Such was the doom of Lisle himself—destroyed by two men who, as Byrne wrote, "loved the man" after their fashion—and the pious Henry VI of Shakespeare's first tetralogy and too trusting Othello. Culpable innocence nearly ruins Prospero too.

Shakespeare's presentation of the suitor at court is, like Donne's in his fifth satire, harshly mocking. The playwright had a keen ear for "court-contempt" (WT 4.4.734), and his histories are rife with displays of this arrogance. Suffolk, for example, bids a lieutenant remember "How in our voiding lobby hast thou stood / And duly waited for my coming forth" (2H6 4.1.61-62). At least four other plays rest fundamentally on the effects of court contempt and the "servile fearfulness" (JC 1.1.75) it engenders: *Julius Caesar* (Caesar surrounded by "sweet words / Low-crooked curtesies, and base spaniel fawning" [3.1.43]); *Hamlet* (the prince imagines the skull is a courtier's, "which could say, 'Good morrow, sweet lord! How dost thou, sweet lord!'" [5.1.83]); *King Lear* (the supreme effect of the first scene must be Lear's reckless court contempt); and *Timon of Athens* (Apemantus derides those who suffer the "willing misery" and "most wretched being" of courtly suit [4.3.242, 246]).

Glancing allusions to qualities of the suitor's life are scattered throughout the plays. First, there is the importance of "connections." Dr. Caius will make Anne Page a good husband because he is "well money'd, and his friends / Potent at court" (4.4.89), and Shallow tells Davy with good reason that "A friend i' th' court is better than a penny in purse" (5.1.31). Autolycus boasts, "I am a courtier cap-a-pe, and one that will either push on or pluck back thy business there" (4.4.737). This was indeed the Tudor court's primary means of doing business. Everyone, including the monarch, was in some degree subjected to a throng of "glib and slipp'ry creatures" importunately pressing their "love and tendance" in exchange for favor and favors.[12]

This frenetic tedium of so many persons eagerly "smelling out a suit" (ROM 1.4.78) lay at the center of the courtly rat race. Shakespeare often caught the ultimate triviality and idleness of the "ruffle" at court (LC 58) or in a "palace full of tongues, of eyes, and ears" (TIT 2.1.127). Hal and Falstaff joke about the boredom of "waiting in the court" for the "obtaining of suits" (1H4 1.2.70-72), and *As You Like It* hints at the folly of hoping for "new" news at a court where nothing much ever essentially changes. In the same vein Coriolanus ridicules those who

> sit by th' fire, and presume to know
> What's done i' th' Capitol; who's like to rise,
> Who thrives, and who declines; side factions, and give out
> Conjectural marriages, making parties strong,
> And feebling such as stand not in their liking. [1.1.191-95]

Lear proposes a similar pastime to Cordelia: "So we'll . . . hear poor rogues / Talk of court news; and we'll talk with them too— / Who loses and who wins; who's in, who's out" (5.3.11-15). Such was the ambiance in the environs of Whitehall and Westminster.

The usual experience of the Renaissance courtier was one of futility. Guevara summed up his own at the end of his *Looking Glasse for the Court:* "The recompence is this, that I have gotten there a graye heade, feete full of goute, mouth without teeth, raynes full of gravel, my goodes layde to pledge, my body charged with thought, and my soule litle clensed from sinne" (66). Such was the experience of those who came to court (both the great and the nameless) in Shakespeare's time, a point that can be made by turning to his last presentation of the courtier's drama, *Henry VIII*. Wolsey inscribes the fall-of-princes story clearly enough and eloquently; he is a type of those pitiful thrivers who "trod the ways of glory, / And sounded all the depths and shoals of honor" (3.2.435-36). More telling to my mind, and splendidly typifying Shakespeare's habit of giving deeply resonant expressions to nameless characters, are the words of an old lady attending the suddenly ascendant Anne Bullen:

> Why, this it is! see, see,
> I have been begging sixteen years in court
> (Am yet a courtier beggarly) nor could
> Come pat betwixt too early and too late

> For any suit of pounds; and you, O fate!
> A very fresh fish here—fie, fie, fie upon
> This compell'd fortune!—have your mouth fill'd up
> Before you open it. [H8 2.3.81-87][13]

The number of persons of consequence and inconsequence who came to court and left it with similar bitter words must have been large indeed. Poets were subject to such feelings, too. Jonson sounds just the Old Lady's note of rancor when he denounces his "mean mistress," poetry: "She doth emulate the judicious but preposterous bounty of the time's grandees: who accumulate all they can upon the parasite, or freshman in their friendship; but think an old client, or honest servant, bound by his place to write, and starve" (393).

In general, the path to success at court, for political and artistic suitors alike, did not lie in the personally undertaken frontal attack. A figure like Jonson, for example, who depended proudly on his own centered self rather than on well-placed intermediaries, astute bribery, and a willingness to assume various social disguises, would have been almost bound to fail. Horace's advice, adapted by Webbe in his *Discourse of English Poesie*, was particularly apt to life in the Tudor court: "Let a Poet first take uppon him, as though he were to play but an Actors part." The poet is advised further to "exercise the part of gesturer" in order to achieve a careful *sprezzatura*, with the ultimate objective of masking personal ambition. The Janus faces of courtly life—one Castiglione's, the other Machiavelli's—thus come into clear focus: "For so to hyde ones cunning, that nothing should seeme to bee laborsome or exquisite, when notwithstanding, every part is pollished with care and studie, is a speciall gyft which *Aristotle* calleth κρηψν"—a word that provides the root for *cryptic*.[14] Though Shakespeare turned his back on the courting poet's life early in his career, he did not, I believe, desist from the poet's cunning indulgence of Aristotle's gift for concealment. The lyric poet is present in most of his plays—seldom in his own person, but ubiquitously in roles that show him playing in one way or another "an Actors part." The following survey of a half-dozen shadow roles of the poet at court will provide us another view of his life in the Renaissance.

One point should be clarified at the outset. This survey is not intended to typecast several minor and major characters in the canon as poets. Identifying various styles, vices, and goals of poetry and then labeling as poets any characters exhibiting these would, in almost every case, arbitrarily diminish the fullness of their existence within their respective dramatic worlds. My purpose, therefore, is to draw attention to occasions in which the playwright seems to have consciously affected or, to use the Baconian verb, *in*fected his characters with the style of the courting poet. In other words, the focal point of this survey is the "poetical" color purple—in which Shakespeare was deep-dyed early in his life—and how it became but one color on the dramatic poet's full palette. In plays of the middle and later period, which are the primary focus of this chapter, the lyric poet's eye can be seen to roll in a fine frenzy on increasingly calculated dramatic occasions, while explicit references to poetizing are often deployed with a hostile edge and always as a poignant element of characterization. This survey of several plays written after the flow of Shakespearean honey became less copious will, I hope, further illuminate Shakespeare's perceptions about himself as a poet and about his early years in the galley of rhymers. That this survey will convey something of contemporary perceptions about poetry and poets I am more confident.

In Shakespeare's Elizabethan plays, the poet, as might be expected, most frequently assumes the guise of a courting lover. He appears, as Henry V says, as one of "these fellows of infinite tongue, that can rhyme themselves into ladies' favors" (5.2.155-57). Disconcertingly, though, the language of only unreflecting, foolish, or hypocritical lovers assumes an exaggerated, often parodic "poetical" style. This role of "false" suitor is, like most of the poet's roles in Shakespeare, a suspect one. Thomas Elyot called poets and orators "artificial speakers (named in Greek *Logodedali*)," and false suitors in the plays are, as the etymology hints, creators of verbal mazes, either for themselves or for the objects of their desire.[15]

Venus and Adonis, a poem often admired for its dramatic qualities, provides a perfect opening example of this type. The discussion in chapter 1 suggested to what extent the continuously replayed scene of the suitor pestering for favor lies behind the poem. Venus's urge to undress Adonis is reflected, for instance, in James's rebuke to Raleigh: "You will never let me alone. I would to God you had first my doublet and then my shirt and when I were naked I think you would give me leave to be quiet."[16] Even more to the point for the playwright's career, the poem's comedy reflects the courtly arena in which striving, upstart poets competed for the attention of powerful patrons. The "beauteous combat, willful and unwilling" (365) is a parable of this sordid competition, and Venus's anxiety is in the end like that of the Old Lady in *Henry VIII*, who never comes pat to "any suit of pounds": "worse than Tantalus' is her annoy, / To clip Elizium and to lack her joy" (599-600). Venus thus stands as her creator's first pessimistic reflection on poetical suit.

If the status of "A Lover's Complaint" were more firmly canonical, it might serve to make many of the same points. For this poem, published along with the Sonnets in 1609, is in effect about an Adonis (the complaining young woman) who has given in to the "craft of will" of a Venus (a young poet-orator who is obviously one of Elyot's *logodedali*). The young man's predation is aided by clearly poetic abilities: He is an extemporal virtuoso ("He had the dialect and different skill, / Catching all passions" [ll.125-26]); he is acquainted with the world of "deep-brain'd sonnets" [l.209]; and he thinks "characters [that is, written speech] and words" are merely the playthings of art. His passion—like Venus's—is "but an art of craft" (l.295). His combination of verbal dexterity, handsomeness, and hypocrisy is especially reminiscent of Berowne's, just as the pervasive distrust of the poetic style reflects the central issue of *Love's Labour's Lost*. But in the poem the poet-lover's labor is not lost: like Tarquin in *Lucrece* he achieves his carnal triumph.

The poet as false suitor in Shakespeare usually smells of April and May. Youth was the age of man for courting as well as for poetry, as Jaques observes: " . . . the lover / Sighing like furnace with a woeful ballad / Made to his mistress' eyebrow" (AYL 2.7.147-49). But youth was also the age for courtiership: Naunton wrote of Fulke Greville, "He came to the Court in his youth and prime . . . that is the time or never."[17] In fact, one might well introduce Shakespeare's young "fellows of infinite tongue" by reference to the jejune Petrarchism of the first three dozen poems in Greville's *Caelica* sequence (toward its end he becomes a dour Calvinist). The overwrought and too self-conscious conceit of these *Caelica* poems— "Ah silly *Cupid*, do you make it coy" (Sonnet 19) and so forth—clearly reflects their author's lack of genuine engagement, and it is just this effect that Shakespeare strove for in some of the youthful-suitor characters of his early years. Proteus, we have seen, is a small, but pristine, example of the type; *Love's Labour's Lost* provides several more examples. The experiences of these individuals show that poetry is false suit ("A huge translation of hypocrisy" [5.2.51]) and that the poetical suitor himself is likely to prove false.

Variations on this pejorative conclusion occur in more familiar Shakespearean contexts. In order to prepare the distinction (noted by Friar Lawrence) between Romeo's "doting" on the divine Rosaline and his "loving" Juliet, Shakespeare gives the boy exaggerated Petrarchan postures in act 1. But he wisely quotes briefly from the "lover's book of words" to achieve his effect (1.1.171-82, 228-37). A little Petrarchism goes a long way on stage, and Shakespeare manages, instead, to rivet attention through Mercutio's witty attacks on poet-suitors. With similar economy, he establishes the volatile, untested love of Hermia and Lysander at the beginning of *A Midsummer Night's Dream*, where he gives them an interchange of richly conceited rhymed couplets (1.1.169-223). The balloon of ornate poetic style is punctured by the plain-style pin in Viola-Cesario's first encounter with Olivia in *Twelfth Night* (1.5.169ff). The effect of her poetical ostentation is prosaic; indeed, Shakespeare does not shift from prose into iambic pentameter until Viola drops her "well penn'd" stuff (1.5.250) and speaks from the heart.

This last bright comedy of manners from Shakespeare's pen—like his first, *Love's Labour's Lost*—offers many satiric glances at the poet's profession. The steamy, self-indulgent ambiance surrounding Duke Orsino is roughly that of Theseus's lunatic-lover-poet. His tastes explicitly hark back (the play was written in about 1601) to a time when the "gaudy blossoms" of Petrarch were still thick on the bush. He asks for a song and explains, "it is silly sooth, / And dallies with the innocence of love, / Like the old age" (2.4.46-48). Olivia turns back a second attempt by Cesario at courteous periphrasis with words that the Princess of *Love's Labour's Lost* might have uttered: "'Twas never merry world / Since lowly feigning was call'd compliment" (3.1.97-98). As in the earlier comedy, the "licence of ink" (3.2.44) brings licentiousness rather than humane liberality. Even Viola, her pretenses as a poetical false suitor dropped in the Clown's presence, voices the critique of the poets' "lowly feigning" that lies behind so many Shakespearean actions: "They that dally nicely with words may quickly make them wanton" (3.1.14).

The conclusions of the two plays tell us something about the poet in Shakespeare. In *Love's Labour's Lost*, the twain of rhyme and emotional sincerity do not meet and mate; for us, if not for the men, this denouement is peculiarly apt and satisfying. In *Twelfth Night* the avatars of rhyme (the Duke) and emotional sincerity (Viola) do meet and mate, as in an "old play." Many critics have found this ending neither satisfying nor attractive, and I suggest that this is partly because the unreconstructed poet-as-suitor Duke is too mercurial a creature for a world-without-end bargain—a point with which Anne Hathaway Shakespeare, alone in Stratford, might have been privately inclined to agree.

Shakespeare's poets-as-false-suitors mentioned thus far all appear in comic contexts. It is now necessary to pause over the dark shadow of this type who, like the harmless Longaville, possesses "a sharp wit match'd with too blunt a will, / Whose edge hath power to cut, whose will still wills / It should none spare that come within his power" (2.1.49-51). This description fits as a glove Shakespeare's most reckless villain, Richard of Gloucester, who boasts (among many other skills) the power to slip into the role of the honey-tongued Petrarchan: "I'll make my heaven in a lady's lap, / And deck my body in gay ornaments, / And witch sweet ladies with my words and looks" (3H6 3.2.148-50). This boast looks forward to the most daringly implausible scene in the canon, in which the "lump of foul deformity" sues for the hand of Lady Anne (R3 1.2.33-268). The scene represents a hideous perversion of the Petrarchan style. One of Richard's speeches imparts the flavor: "These eyes could not endure that beauty's wrack; / You should not blemish it, if I stood by: / As all the world is cheered by the sun, / So I by that; it is my day, my life" (1.2.127-30). Anne's "basilisk" eyes kill Richard "with a living death" (152), and he bluffs outrageously with a speech purloined, one might imagine, from the *Arcadia* or any other popular lover's book of words:

> Teach not thy lip such scorn; for it was made
> For kissing, lady, not for such contempt.
> If thy revengeful heart cannot forgive,
> Lo here I lend thee this sharp-pointed sword,
> Which if thou please to hide in this true breast,
> And let the soul forth that adoreth thee,
> I lay it naked . . . . [1.2.171-77]

This ornate style has its effect and Anne weakens, but Shakespeare knew his audience would perceive the dissembler's manipulation of poetical conceits. Among the many tricks of this figure of infinitely evil tongue is the trick of the poet.

The poet-as-false-suitor gradually vanished as Shakespeare matured in his art, leaving childish things and themes behind, and as his own experience as a poet receded into the past. Two midcareer plays testify to the disappearance of the type. For instance, there is a symbolic significance in his decision to cast the courtship of Henry V and Katharine—the warm obverse of Richard's and Anne's—in prose rather than in iambic pentameter. The royal suitor, assuredly one of his most eloquent characters, is made to reject emphatically and at length the skills of the *logodedali* ("I have no cunning in protestation" [H5 5.2.144]) and the poet ("a rhyme [is] but a ballad" [5.2.158]). The point is clear: the King is a *true* suitor. He is unwilling to stoop his considerable forensic skills to the backstairs world of "courtship, pleasant jest, and courtesy" (LLL 5.2.771). He thus presents himself as "a fellow of plain and uncoin'd constancy," a positively anti-poetical type of courtier that, in Shakespeare's succeeding plays, will become more and more important (for example, Horatio, Kent, Enobarbus, Belarius, and Camillo). The rejection of poetry at this climax of the great historical tetralogy is nearly as affecting as Hal's rejection of Falstaff on the steps of Westminster Abbey.

A similar distancing from Shakespeare's artistic origins is apparent in *Troilus and Cressida*, where we have one of the last noteworthy outcroppings of the lyric style of "the old age." As he did with Romeo, Shakespeare prepares Troilus for his love-trauma by casting his first-act speeches in the ornate style:

> when my heart,
> As wedged with a sigh, would rive in twain,
> Lest Hector or my father should perceive me,
> I have (as when the sun doth light a-scorn)
> Buried this sigh in wrinkle of a smile,
> But sorrow that is couch'd in seeming gladness
> Is like that mirth fate turns to sudden sadness. [1.1.34-40; cf. 50-108]

Troilus's galley is charged with many conceits—and a foolish self-conceit. His verbal style mirrors his folly in love, and when this folly reaches its ecstatic climax, in his oath-plighting duet with Cressida, Shakespeare refers explicitly to the "false compare" (SON 130) of poets:

> True swains in love shall in the world to come
> Approve their truth by Troilus. When their rhymes,
> Full of protest, of oath and big compare,
> Wants similes, truth tir'd with iteration,
> As true as steel, as plantage to the moon,
> As sun to day, as turtle to her mate,
> As iron to adamant, as earth to th' centre,
> Yet after all comparisons of truth
> (As truth's authentic author to be cited)
> "As true as Troilus" shall crown up the verse,
> And sanctify the numbers. [3.2.173-83]

Troilus's "What's aught but as 'tis valued?" has been urged as the central question of the play, and virtually every object on which Shakespeare casts his eye suffers a severe devaluation, poetry included. Pandarus delivers a last love letter from Cressida to Troilus. He reads it and, as he tears it apart, echoes the critique of poetical love suit that Shakespeare expressed on many other occasions: "Words, words, mere words, no matter from the heart" (5.3.108).

Shakespeare's last quotations from the poet's book of words occur in a theatrical context at once poignant and chilling. They are spoken by Jachimo, the "slight thing of Italy" who in *Cymbeline* wagers with Posthumus on the fidelity of Imogen. The "poisonous tongu'd" libertine opens his offensive with several inflatedly poetical lust conceits (highly reminiscent of Sonnet 129) that naturally boggle Imogen:

> Jachimo: The cloyed will—
> That satiate yet unsatisfied desire, that tub
> Both fill'd and running—ravening first the lamb,
> Longs after for the garbage.
> Imogen: What, dear sir,
> Thus raps you? Are you well? [1.6.47-51]

(One is tempted to dig for a submerged pun on the *raptus poeticus* in her *raps*.) Jachimo's rhetorical finesse and chameleonic changes of attack—he is a miniature Richard of Gloucester—are displayed in the remainder of the scene. But it is in the prurient atmosphere of the bedchamber, with Jachimo's speech over the sleeping Imogen, that Shakespeare places his epitaph on the poetic style of the old age, Petrarchism, now but another "slight thing of Italy":

>   Cytherea,
> How bravely thou becom'st thy bed! fresh lily,
> And whiter than the sheets! That I might touch!
> But kiss, one kiss! Rubies unparagon'd,
> How dearly they do't! 'Tis her breathing that
> Perfumes the chamber thus. The flame o' th' taper
> Bows toward her, and would under-peep her lids,
> To see th' enclosed lights, now canopied
> Under these windows, white and azure lac'd
> With blue of heaven's own tinct. [2.2.14-23]

Even at this late date, one must amazedly conclude, his genius for this style of his youth was still not wholly lost.

A second shadow of the poet at court seeks love of a more general, sociable kind. His suit is for approbation, and his main chance lies in projecting that affability which is the essence of the gatherings described by Castiglione and is praised by Elyot for its "wonderful efficacy or power in procuring love" (107). The poet as elegant stylist is a fastidiously self-abnegating expert in the "dialogue of compliment." His usual modes are flattery, retreat from conflict, and clever circumlocution. These were, of course, methods with which the Renaissance poet was very familiar. Puttenham's discussion of the figure in which "words tend to flattery, or soothing, or excusing" *(paradiastole)* is particularly relevant. Puttenham dubs this "the Curry-favell, as when we make the best of a bad thing" (3: 17) and prescribes its use for "moderating and abating the force of the matter by craft, and for a pleasing purpose." He then adverts to some verses that teach "in what cases it may commendably be used by Courtiers." The curry-favell, the "quick conceit" *(synecdoche)*, the "drie mock" *(ironia)*, the "merry scoffe" *(asteismus)*, the "fleering frumpe" *(micterismus)*, and the "privy nippe" *(charientismus)*—these and other such figures lay at the disposal of the Renaissance poet and, in real life, the Renaissance courtier (3: 18).

These same figures are also at the disposal of the courtly stylist in Shakespeare's plays, who must usually make the best of a demeaning if not a bad thing. The stylist's historical exemplar was John Harington, ever ready in Elizabeth's privy chambers with his "holiday and lady terms." And like Harington, the poet-as-favor-currier in Shakespeare is inevitably a peripheral figure whose most perfect incarnation, we have seen, is the "old love-monger" Boyet. His witty deflection of the Princess's serious meditation on the "crimes" we commit for the sake of praise captures the courtly stylist's inertial complacency and triviality of mind. Parodic apprentices in Boyet's art are the same play's Armado and Parolles in *All's Well That Ends Well*. And the stilted, conceitful language of Aeneas when he first visits the Greek camp in *Troilus* immediately labels him, to Agamemnon's ear, as one of Troy's "ceremonious courtiers": "I ask, that I might waken reverence, / And bid the cheek be ready with a blush / Modest as morning when she coldly eyes / The youthful Phoebus" (1.3.227-30). Aeneas's language, like the archaic offer of a single combat, smells of the poetry of the old age. A similar collision of muscle-bound masculinity with courtly effeminacy occurs on the battlefield of Holmedon when "a certain lord, neat, and trimly dress'd" (1H4 1.3.33) confronts a blood-spattered Hotspur; it is easy to imagine that this "certain lord" speaks in the style of Boyet or Aeneas.

Nowhere does the deployment of the poet-as-courtly stylist contribute more cunningly to characterization than in *Richard II*. The central interest of this play lies in watching how events "undeck the pompous body of a king," and it is the play's most striking stylistic effect that, as it proceeds, Richard is increasingly decked out in Puttenham's "pompious speech" ("using such bombasted wordes, as seeme altogether farced full of winde," 3: 22). Many have observed very generally how Shakespeare "transform'd and weak'ned" Richard's "shape and mind" (5.1.27, 26) by associating him with poetry's strong tricks of imagination, but several very specific ties to Shakespeare's non-dramatic poetry—and, hence, to the world of the professional poet—deserve reappraisal.

As Richard moves from the lean speeches of the first act to the exargastic ones of acts 4 and 5, excrescences of the lyric poet's style usher him on his way at several telling points. Poetry, it should first be noted, is a part of the "gay apparel" of Richard's court. Much is made in the play of what Holinshed called his "youthfull outrage" and the "disordered spring" (3.4.48) of his reign, and, as we have seen, Shakespeare was inclined to associate poetry with skipping youth. We are thus not surprised at York observing that the King's ear "is stopp'd with other flattering sounds, / As praises, of whose taste the wise are fond, / Lascivious metres, to whose venom sound / The open ear of youth doth always listen" (2.1.17-20). When Richard returns from Ireland he is remarkably transformed from a figure of command into a distinctly poetical suitor; the irony of his earlier "We were not born to sue" (1.1.196) begins to deepen. Once the increasingly reticent Bullenbrook takes control, Richard assumes the recessive para-diastolic style, making his conceited best of a bad situation and trying to "court" with richly figured language both his rival and his destiny.

Thus Richard becomes very like Venus. His speeches are shot through with her fantastic wishful thinking, her hyperbole (the Irish foray becomes "wand'ring with the Antipodes" [3.2.49]), her knack for periphrasis ("the searching eye of heaven . . . this terrestrial ball" [3.2.41]), her prolixity, her bathos. When Richard absorbs his first bad news from Salisbury, he replies not only with her conceit but also in a perfect *Venus and Adonis* rhymed sestet:

> But now the blood of twenty thousand men
> Did triumph in my face, and they are fled;
> And till so much blood thither come again,
> Have I not reason to look pale and dead?
> All souls that will be safe, fly from my side,
> For time hath set a blot upon my pride. [3.2.76-81]

Like Venus too, Richard resorts under pressure to formal poetic postures. His "Let's talk of graves, of worms, and epitaphs, / Make dust our paper, and with rainy eyes / Write sorrow on the bosom of the earth" (3.2.145-47) is reminiscent of Venus "insinuating" with Death: "With Death she humbly doth insinuate; / Tells him of trophies, statues, tombs, and stories / His victories, his triumphs and his glories" (1012-14).

Many of Venus's set pieces are comically subverted ("Her song was tedious") and so are Richard's. After his "antic" Death speech, Carlisle reproves, "wise men ne'er sit and wail their woes" (3.2.178). Idleness, we have noted, was a poetical trait. Shakespeare promised Southampton to occupy "all idle houres," and Venus's theme is "idle over-handled," and that phrase applies to several of Richard's ornate conceits. He exacerbates a tear image, but then observes, "Well, well, I see / I talk but idly, and you laugh at me" (3.3.170-71), and the Gardener is soon accusing him of a "waste of idle hours" (3.4.66).

My present purpose tempts me to see a pun in Bullenbrook's remark about Richard: "The rage be his, whilst on the earth I rain" (3.3.59). For in the later stages of the play it is precisely Richard's "rage," or *furor poeticus*, that allows Bullenbrook to ascend the throne. Just after this sarcastic remark, Bullenbrook makes withering fun of his "poetical" rival by mocking the aubade stuff of the lyric tradition (which Shakespeare had so recently trotted out a half-dozen times in *Romeo and Juliet*):

> See, see, King Richard doth himself appear,
> As doth the blushing discontented sun
> From out the fiery portal of the east,
> When he perceives the envious clouds are bent
> To dim his glory and to stain the track
> Of his bright passage to the occident. [3.3.62-67]

This antipoetical satire acts as a prologue to Richard's "performance" of dejection, which Bullenbrook in perfect silence shrewdly allows him to play out over two hundred lines. Bullenbrook knows the exargastic style must fall of its own weight. The "mirror" scene is similarly indulged. The "O flatt'ring glass" speech shows Richard hopelessly immured in the Sonnets' lyric style: "Look in thy glass and tell the face thou viewest" runs Sonnet 3 (see also Sonnets 22, 62, 77, and 103 for variations on the conceit).

Cunning deployment of the overtly poetic style helps Shakespeare establish that Richard's "intellect" is "depos'd" (5.1.27-28), his "tired majesty" infected with poetry's isolating fantasies. In his last scene he completes the transit from king to courtly stylist ("I have been studying how I may compare") and effeminate introvert ("Yet I'll hammer it out. / My brain I'll prove the female to my soul"). Alone, he must be his own currier of favor.

Perhaps in the end Shakespeare succeeded too well in his identification of Richard with the "light" vanities of lyric poetry. For in act 5, by which point Shakespeare's artistic interest seems to have waned, Richard becomes too obviously typecast by the hoary clichés of lovelorn Petrarchans: the "fair rose" withered, dewy "true-love tears," the self-indulgent "sighs, and tears, and groans" of the "lamentable tale of me." He becomes, to borrow Berowne's description of Cupid, the "anointed sovereign of sighs and groans" rather than a genuinely tragic figure from English history.

∽

A third shadow of the lyric stylist at court is that of the entertaining servant: the clown, or jester. It was a demeaning role. Jonson has a courtly poet introduce himself in the masque *Neptune's Triumph* thus: "The most unprofitable of his [majesty's] servants, I, sir, the *Poet*. A kind of a *Christmas* Ingine; one that is used, at least once a yeare, for a trifling instrument of wit" (7: 682-83). Being a trifling instrument of wit was not easy; it is hard to be amusing at a moment's notice and to an unpredictable audience. Harington, who came closest to being Elizabeth's poet-jester, described in colorful terms the mercurial atmosphere in which he had to operate: "When she smiled, it was a pure sun-shine, that every one did chuse to baske in, if they could; but anon came a storm from a sudden gathering of clouds, and the thunder fell in wondrous manner on all alike" (*Letters*, 125).

Struggles to accommodate this kind of court volatility occur frequently in Shakespeare, in famous as well as out-of-the-way circumstances. In *The Comedy of Errors*, Antipholus of Syracuse beats his bondman Dromio for a jest, and the latter asks why. Renaissance jesters—and, in their own way, Renaissance poets—had to live with the answer given to Dromio:

> Because that I familiarly sometimes
> Do use you for my fool, and chat with you,
> Your sauciness will jest upon my love,
> And make a common of my serious hours.
> When the sun shines, let foolish gnats make sport,
> But creep in crannies, when he hides his beams:
> If you will jest with me, know my aspect,
> And fashion your demeanor to my looks,
> Or I will beat this method in your sconce. [2.2.26-34]

It is not so far from this bullying to Lear's threat to another jester, "Take heed, sirrah—the whip." Better known but in the same vein is Viola's analysis of the jester's art:

> He must observe their mood on whom he jests,
> The quality of persons, and the time;
> And like the haggard, check at every feather
> That comes before his eye. This is a practice
> As full of labor as a wise man's art. [TN 3.1.62-66]

Though Shakespeare's fools and jesters speak predominantly in prose, their art is still intimately related to that of the poets. It was the skill of both to "dally nicely with words" (3.1.14). Touchstone is thus naturally able to speak knowingly to the country folk both on courtiership (AYL 3.2) and on the meaning of *poetical* (3.3).

There is another important poet-jester connection: the quality of the fool's life, like that of the courtly poet, depended on the stability of the socio-political atmosphere in which he served. Touchstone thrives in rustic exile under the benign Duke Senior, as do Feste in the well-ordered household of Olivia and the Countess of Rossillion's clown in *All's Well That Ends Well*. Conversely, the Fool's security vanishes at the beginning of *King Lear*; he quite naturally vanishes when his court collapses after the abdication. Foul-mouthed Thersites must pass for a jester in the ghastly world of *Troilus and Cressida*; while the Clown in *Othello*, Shakespeare's flimsiest, is worthy of a shaky, newly established "court" poised on Cyprus at the edge of civilization. Something is rotten in Denmark, and this is perhaps why there is no successor to poor Yorick, the former king's jester at Elsinore. Nor is there one in the volatile, humorless political world of *Henry VIII*, even though history offered a real-life one named Patch.

The fourth guise a poet-at-court might assume carried more respect, though his functions were similar to those of a jester. This was the life-of-the-party or witty cohort—the time killer who blossoms especially in plays where much leisure is entertained. This was another role that Harington tried, with variable success, to play under Elizabeth. However, under James he apparently hit the mark, for Howard wrote in 1611 that the king had taken to referring to him as that "merry blade" (1: 391). Such affable fellows, adept at what Sidney called "tongue-delight," are particularly prominent in Shakespeare's Elizabethan plays. (Gonzalo, who tries to "minister occasion" for merriment in *The Tempest*, is a later example of the type.) Salerio, one of Antonio's entourage in *The Merchant of Venice*, is a comprimario example of the ebullient companion. One can tell from his first speech that his knack for tongue delight is a poet's knack:

> Your mind is tossing on the ocean,
> There where your argosies with portly sail
> Like signiors and rich burghers on the flood,
> Or as it were the pageants of the sea,
> Do overpeer the petty traffickers
> That cur'sy to them, do them reverence,
> As they fly by them with their woven wings. [1.1.8-14]

Boyet, we have noted, is such a figure, and there is special irony in Berowne describing him with the same epithet—"honey-tongued" (5.2.334)—that Meres used in 1598 to praise a new poet on the London scene: "mellifluous & honey-tongued Shakespeare."

Berowne himself is surely the most lavishly achieved of Shakespeare's witty fellows. Rosaline says of him, "His eye begets occasion for his wit, / For every object that the one doth catch / The other turns to a mirth-moving jest" (2.1.69-71). And no more need be said here about his identification as a poet. Benedick in *Much Ado About Nothing*, as many have noted, is a charismatic variation of Berowne. By a few well-placed allusions to poetizing in this play, Shakespeare implicates the exargastic style in the folly of any person who "dedicates his behaviors to love" (2.3.9). Love renders one foolish-poetical, as Benedick himself observes of Claudio: "He was wont to speak plain and to the purpose (like an honest man and a soldier), and now is he turn'd ortography—his words are a very fantastical banquet, just so many strange dishes" (2.3.18-21). Which is to say, love causes him to join the erstwhile poetical party of Armado and Holofernes. When love finally comes to Benedick, it turns this predominantly prose-speaking man into a producer of his own "paper bullets of the brain" (2.3.240). When Margaret asks him for "a sonnet in praise of [her] beauty" in exchange for her go-between services, he promises one "in so high a style . . . that no man living shall come over it" (5.2.4-6). And, though he boasts he was "not born under a rhyming planet" (5.2.40), we are not in the least surprised when we learn that he, like the men in *Love's Labour's Lost*, has secretly fashioned for his mistress "A halting sonnet of his own pure brain" (5.4.87). Mercutio is yet another variation of the witty cohort and, like Berowne, holds in his play a position of intellectual first among equals. His extemporal Queen Mab scherzo demonstrates this just as vividly as Berowne's battle oration for "affection's men-at-arms." It should be noted, though, that this attractive role for the poet-at-court, that of already-arrived aristocratic amateur, was precisely the one that was closed to Shakespeare himself.

The rough-and-tumble of courtly competition provided yet another guise for the poet-at-court, that of social climber-parasite: Jonson's "mushrompe gentlemen, / That shoot up in a night to place, and worship" (3: 449). The type in Shakespeare is usually comic, but its most spectacular exemplar in the canon is the hubristic Wolsey in *Henry VIII*. Wolsey, like any ungently born poet in the Renaissance, is "not propp'd by ancestry whose grace / Chalks successors their way" (1.1.59-60). Also poetlike, "the honey of his language" (3.2.22) allows Wolsey to cast his "spell" on the court. Wolsey is a self-made man, and the very image that Norfolk uses to describe this fact applies to the poet's creative process: "Spider-like / Out of his self-drawing web, he gives us note / The force of his own merit makes his way" (1.1.62-64).

It was much easier, and surely more commonplace, to find occasion for laughter at inept social climbing. When this happens in Shakespeare, the poet's art is usually close at hand. The puritanical Malvolio, suffering delusions of elevation, wobbles in with his yellow cross-garters and is soon quoting a "very true sonnet" (3.4.23). Similarly risible is Sir Andrew Aguecheek, taking dictation of Cesario's poetical speech ("That's a rare courtier— 'rain odors'" [3.1.86]). Armado too satirizes the notion that an ability to "turn sonnet" and write "whole volumes in folio" will somehow catapult one to social heights. He is an Iberian Aguecheek—the upstart crow at Navarre's court. Or perhaps Philibert's ornithological image is more apt: "skillesse minions . . . Counterfaite Courtiers whiche simper it in outwarde shewe, making pretie mouthes, & marching with a stalking pace like Cranes" (16).

No figure shares in the ludicrousness of the upstart poet-at-court more vividly than Parolles. The very first thing we learn about him has a poetical flavor: "I love him for his sake, / And yet I know him a notorious liar, / Think him a great way fool" (AWW 1.1.99-101). Parolles follows Bertram to the royal court and promises Helena, "I will return perfect courtier." Like Wolsey, his origins are humble: "You are more saucy with lords and honorable personages," says Lafew, "than the commission of your birth and virtue gives you heraldry" (2.3.260-62). Parolles has only dexterity of tongue to recommend him. Like Armado and Aguecheek, he is obsessed with the fashionable surfaces of courtly life. "The soul of this man is in his clothes. Trust him not in matter of heavy consequence" (2.5.43-45). Nor can one trust his language, which is much aided by the devices of the poet: "I spake but by a metaphor," Parolles informs the Clown (5.2.11). He is, as his name tells us, a man of mere words, no matter from the heart.

There is, it happens, a most appropriate rhetorical figure for Parolles in Puttenham. It is one of the figures of "false semblant" and describes precisely the method by which Parolles hopes to succeed at court: "*Hip-erbole*, or the Over reacher, otherwise called the loud lyer" (3: 18). Parolles' experience is, in this respect, something of a parable for the upstart poet at court, who was by professional definition a figure of "false semblant"; his stock in trade, after all, was "rhymes, / Full of protest, oath, and big compare." Loud poetical lying was a manifestly suspicious enterprise and inevitably excited proprietary defensiveness in established courtiers (such as Shakespeare's Norfolk and Lafew), who were eager to reduce all artistic servants to the demeaning ranks of minstrelsy. Few if any upstart poets of the time were successful. Sooner or later they had to relinquish their hopes, rather as Parolles does at his end: "Simply the thing I am / Shall make me live" (4.3.333). The sentiment is oddly but pertinently reminiscent of that disgruntled poet of the centered self, the bricklayer's stepson Ben Jonson.

୭ଡ଼ଉ

The last, and in many ways most fascinating, of the possible roles a poet could play at court was that of satirist. The player of this role had no easy time, paying homage as he did to a cankered and insociable muse. This tightrope role urged one to assume introspective, sick-thoughted postures on a highly sociable, unphilosophical stage. Placability, which Elyot placed next to affability among the qualities of "gentleness," was the courtly rule. Hence Fregoso's advice in Castiglione: "Our Courtier," he says, shall not "vexe and stirre men like flies and . . . contrarie every man spitefully without respect." Of those courtiers who act only according to their own "brains" Philibert urges, "Wee must sende them to *Tymon Misantrope*, that enemie of mankinde, and exclude them cleane from our companie." Samuel Daniel, a courtly poet eminently placable, advised all writers to be sociable and conforming:

> For not discreetly to compose our partes
>   Unto the frame of men (which we must be)
>   Is to put off our selves, and make our Artes
>   Rebels to Nature and Societies;
>   Whereby we come to bury our desarts,
>   In th'obscure grave of Singularitie.[18]

Sharing this view, Puttenham thus criticized the "sharpe Satirist" John Skelton for "more rayling and scoffery then became a Poet Lawreat" (1:31).

But as always, it is the courtier, poet, or dramatist who chooses to rebel against nature and society that, by his striking exception, proves the rule; the Marlowes of the world will always steal the scene from the Daniels. Attention naturally focuses on courtly figures like John Perrot (see p. 104) who take pains in their "Singularitie." Erasmus, himself a fine example of the type, praised Sir Thomas More for this quality: "Your extraordinarily keen intelligence places you worlds apart from the common herd." Two notable instances of singularity in Castiglione are Bembo, in his neo-Platonic ecstasy in book 4, and Pallavicino, in his exuberant rejection of the "deceit" of *sprezzatura*. Gabriel Harvey thought it Aretino's "glory" that he had the courage simply "to be himself: to speak, & write like himself: to imitate none, but him selfe & ever to maintaine his owne singularity." And Harvey described Socrates, the archetype of the satirical "alien" insider, as a "continual Ironist." The phrase is pregnant. For the fascination of all the above figures lies not only in a willingness and energy to fashion a self separate and apart from the self that society recommends but also in the ironic distance between them and their surroundings.[19] These continual ironists feel uncomfortable at society's center stage; they tend to gravitate toward the proscenium or the rear of the stage.

The Renaissance poet who was by nature a "continual Ironist" was likewise uncomfortable at center stage. After all, Tudor-Stuart decorum, if not despotism, made the role of Juvenalian poet-at-court virtually impossible to perform. The wormwood stuff of the 1590s had in short order elicited a formal ban on satire, and *Dr.* John Donne sensibly left "Jack" Donne and his five satires behind and unpublished as he rose to London eminence. Only Jonson of the major poets displayed the nerve and occasional recklessness to test continually the limits of becoming satirical mirth, and his end was fittingly marked by the melancholy, bitter isolation that formed one element of the satirist's persona. The image of the satirist is one of reclusiveness, as Donne's opening lines of the fifth satire suggest: "Away thou fondling motley humourist, / Leave me, and in this standing wooden chest, / Consorted with these few books, let me lie / In prison, and here be coffined, when I die" (155). Avatars of the satirist in Shakespeare's plays display a similar cast of mind, and one avenue of approach to them is brief consideration of a class of characters who experience a particularly drastic form of isolation: Shakespeare's bastards. Though Shakespeare does not explicitly implicate poetry in their bastardy, these figures still reveal the effects—and limitations—of satire at court.

Bastards in the Renaissance were an unfortunate race, pariahs without rights and at the mercy of those who begot them. Baseness and bastardy were, as Edmund is keenly aware, congenital. Shakespearean occurrences of the word are telling. The scurrilous and deformed Thersites describes himself as a "bastard begot, bastard instructed, bastard in mind, bastard in valor, in every thing illegitimate" (5.7.16-18). This is a fairly accurate sketch of Caliban: "He's a bastard one" (5.1.273), says Prospero. The three principal bastards in Shakespeare's canon exhibit a sophisticated awareness of the alienated personality and, by extension, the alienated artist. Don John, in *Much Ado About Nothing*, offers a fine example of the alienated courtier who refuses to please or even address his peers. In company he says little ("I am not of many words"), but when alone with a cohort he divulges his Juvenalian credo: "I cannot hide what I am: I must be sad when I have cause, and smile at no man's jest; eat when I have stomach, and wait for no man's leisure; sleep when I am drowsy, and tend on no man's business" (1.3.13-17). Don John—the perfect antithesis of Berowne, who charms all—renounces both affability and the notion of fashioning himself to ingratiate others: "It better fits my blood to be disdain'd of all than to fashion a carriage to rob love from any." "Let me be that I am," concludes this asocial creature, "and seek not to alter me" (1.3.28-37). From this to the royal hunchback's "I am myself alone" is but a small step.

Don John, however, is a figure of alienation without the poetical bent. We come closer to the métier of the satirist when we turn to the two bastards who appear in more fully developed and sordid courtly environ- ments: Edmund in *King Lear* and Philip the Bastard in *King John*. Both are continual ironists, so perhaps this is the moment to suggest that the governing poetical figure for these characters (as for avatars of the satirist- at-court) is irony. Puttenham describes it among the figures of "false semblant or dissimulation" in these terms: "Ye doe likewise dissemble, when ye speake in derision or mockerie, and that may be many waies: as sometime in sport, sometime in earnest, and privily, and apertly, and pleasantly, and bitterly: but first by the figure *Ironia*, which we call the *drye mock*" (3: 18).

Such in sum is the verbal style of Edmund (who is, incidentally, called the Bastard throughout the quartos). He, like Don John, begins his career as a man of few words, but once his true nature is divulged in the soliloquy "Thou, nature, art, my goddess," his style becomes that of the ironist's dry mockery. This helps to account for the streak of gallows humor in his character that disconcerts some readers. Giuseppe Verdi described this streak well in a letter to the librettist with whom he was preparing a *Lear* opera: "He is not a repulsive villain . . . but rather one who laughs and jokes all the time and commits the most atrocious crimes with utter indifference."[20] Edmund thrives as the poet does: by his "invention" (1.2.20) and by his satirist's anatomy of "the excellent foppery of the world" (1.2.118). His "cue is villainous melancholy" (1.2.135), the same cue as that of the cut-and-thrust Renaissance satirist.

Even more to the point is Philip in *King John*. He is that play's most psychologically complex character, as well as its most rhetorically virtuosic (his twenty-five-line period in act 2 sets the Shakespearean record). He alone indulges in the image of alienation, the soliloquy; indeed, his two solo speeches are the play's finest. His verbal style, as Herschel Baker describes it, closely approximates that of the successful satirist's riveting persona: "He is sometimes witty, saucy, and detached, sometimes blunt and crude, but we cannot resist his candor" (Riverside 767). Indeed, Philip functions in the play precisely as the satirist does at court, perforce uttering his criticism either under his breath or when out of earshot. Nothing in the satires of Hall, Donne, or Jonson surpasses the bitter eloquence of Philip's attack on courtly time-serving and expediency at the end of act 2. This bastard is a perfect, if relatively small-scale, epitome of the courtly satirist:

He is a loner, his typical tone is one of Puttenham's dry mockery, and his conclusions are broadly subversive: "Mad world, mad kings, mad composition!" (2.1.561).

We can now turn to more prominent Shakespearean avatars of the standoffish satirist at court. These avatars come into special prominence where courts or their fictional surrogates are distressed. Caesar's court is one such, and Cassius of the lean-and-hungry look, who thinks too much, is its cynical observer. Caesar's description of his behavior reminds us of Donne's asocial bibliophile of the fifth satire:

> He reads much,
> He is a great observer, and he looks
> Quite through the deeds of men. He loves no plays,
> As thou dost, Antony; he hears no music;
> Seldom he smiles, and smiles in such a sort
> As if he mock'd himself, and scorn'd his spirit. [1.2.201-206]

This is the spirit of dry mockery. Apemantus is transparently the satirist in his play. He attacks the "wretched" courtier's existence, the flattery of the poet, and the conspicuous consumption of courtly pastimes: "What needs these feasts, pomps, and vainglories?" (1.2.242). His last two words in the play are about mankind and constitute the satirist's motto: "abhor them." *Timon of Athens'* "forest of beasts" gives Apemantus's dry mockery a full run. Similarly, Mercutio's task as a character is simply to "quote deformities"—be they in lawyers, soldiers, courtiers, factious Veronese families, lovers (who "berhyme" their mistresses), or love poetry ("the numbers that Petrarch flowed in").

Three other characters, however, help us even more than Cassius, Apemantus, or Mercutio in fixing the identity of the satiric poet at court. One is Jaques, a lord attending the banished Duke Senior. Advance publicity identifies him as "the melancholy Jaques," whose disposition is born of a supercritical sensibility. We also learn of his poetical style; indeed, it appears that Senior indulges him on this account. The Duke hears that Jaques has seen a wounded stag and asks: "But what said Jaques? / Did he not moralize this spectacle?" A lord answers, "O yes, into a thousand similes" (2.1.45). His first substantial speech displays his gift for the disagreeably reductive simile ("I can suck melancholy out of a song, as a weasel sucks eggs" [2.5.13]), and we soon hear his acid view of courtly life. Jaques compares courtly "compliment" to "th'encounter of two dog-apes" and echoes Don John's demand for freedom—satiric license, rather—from the bonds of social decorum: "I must have liberty / Withal, as large a charter as the wind, / To blow on whom I please" (2.7.47-49). He also echoes the constitutional cynicism of the satirist when he rebuts Duke Senior's sanguine "we are not all alone unhappy" with the derisory "seven ages" speech. Finally, he echoes very precisely the credo of the Juvenalian satirist when he boasts, "Give me leave / To speak my mind, and I will through and through / Cleanse the foul body of th'infected world, / If they will patiently receive my medicine" (2.7.58-61). Ministering such bitter medicine was a thankless task that risked the abrupt dismissal Apemantus in fact receives from Timon: "You begin to rail on society once, I am sworn not to give regard to you. Farewell, and come with better music" (1.2.244-46). But, then, Jaques requires no thanks, and his exit speech at the end conveys the satirist's eagerness to leave the "wide and universal theater" of human folly: "To see no pastime I. What you would have I'll stay to know at your abandon'd cave" (5.4.195-96).

A second shadow of the solitary poet is Hamlet, who so famously prefers to stand on his own legs and distance himself from courtly orthodoxies. In a chapter on "musing" in Guevara's *Galateo* we are told: "It ill becomes a man when hee is in company, to bee sad, musing, and full of contemplation" (27). The speaker in *Astrophil and Stella* Sonnet 27 behaved this way "because [he] oft in darke abstracted guise / Seeme[d] most alone in greatest companie, / With dearth of words, or answers quite awrie"— and therefore sought to dispel the rumor of his "bubbling pride" that had resulted from assuming such a Hamlet-like posture. But the courtly satirist's persona included such a menacing aloofness, and it is illuminating to view Hamlet as—among his other roles—a courtly satirist, a tragic soul-twin to Jaques. Hamlet's slings and arrows are typical of the satiric genre: rejection of the polite self-fashioning of the court ("I know not 'seems'"), the sweet poison of etiquette ("No, let the candied tongue lick absurd pomp / And crook the pregnant hinges of the knee" [3.2.60-61]), and the orotund style of courtly diction, which he apes (5.2.112-23). Everything at Elsinore is subjected to Hamlet's refrigerating wit; he is a Berowne who smells much of January and February. His tongue is as sharp as Berowne's ("You are keen, my lord, you are keen" says Ophelia), but it has more to do in a court where charming Boyet has inflated into the gaseous Polonius and where Dumain and Longaville have shrunk into the infinitesimal Osric (who is called "A Courtier" in the good quarto).

Hamlet is, to borrow from Duke Senior, "all alone unhappy" in Elsinore; hence, the flow of eloquence when he is alone. As a satirist at court, however, Hamlet goes further than the other surrogate satirists we have considered. Whereas Jaques at play's end remains a valued and entertaining if reclusive member of the Duke's entourage, Hamlet presses constantly against the limits of satiric mirth. His wit is above and beyond his audience at Elsinore. It is a more emphatically self-delighting wit; Polonius, Claudius, Gertrude, Rosencrantz and the rest must grasp what scraps of it they can manage. Hamlet, in short, examplifies a satirist-at-court on the verge of losing control of his tone and alienating his audience. One of the play's sources of tension is our observation of a highly skilled artist recklessly testing the bounds of his auditors' patience; this is exactly the métier of all verse and stage satirists.

Hostile though Hamlet's satire on Elsinore is, he nevertheless manages to remain just barely within its verge. His sense of filial duty and perhaps a certain morbidity preclude acknowledgment that there is a world else-where. Coriolanus does utter these words (3.3.135), and I believe we can profitably view him for a moment as Shakespeare's embodiment of the courtly satirist in extremis. His distincton as such is inversely proportional to his defects as a Roman. He is incapable of affability among his peers, refuses to be "supple and courteous to the people," and rejects all forms of *sprezzatura*. Indeed, he is the negative image of Castiglione's ideal. As Aufidius aptly summarizes, Coriolanus is "rough, unswayable, and free [that is, frank]" (5.6.25). In this he embraces the satirist's style, which Puttenham calls "rough and bitter" (1: 11).

Like all of the other satirical avatars, Coriolanus refuses to do what "custom" calls him to, as for instance when his mother Volumnia advises: "I would dissemble with my nature where / My fortunes and my friends at stake requir'd" (3.2.62-63). Her advice is precisely that of Puttenham to his poet, who must "behave himselfe as he may worthily retaine the credit of his place, and profession of a very Courtier, which is in plaine termes, cunningly to be able to dissemble" (3: 25). However, Coriolanus prefers to remain committed to his own identity:

> Would you have me
> False to my nature? Rather say, I play
> The man I am. [3.2.14-16]

> I'll never
> Be such a gosling to obey instinct, but stand
> As if a man were author of himself
> And knew no other kin. [5.3.34-37]

This is the essential pose of Renaissance satirists: unwilling to indulge in soothing flattery or "counterfeit the bewitchment of some popular man" (2.3.101-102). Coriolanus's refusal to submit to the *demos* or public and perform for it on the imperial Roman stage is also reflected in Jonson's bitter self-admonition not to serve "that strumpet the stage," but rather to "sing high and aloof" ("Ode. To Himself," 161).

The "falling fabric" of Roman society, like that of Shakespeare's London, offers the cankered muse much room to roam, and Coriolanus's views rehearse the main topoi of contemporary satire: the ascent to power requires a "harlot's spirit"; courtiers must worry about "who's like to rise, / Who thrives, who declines"; "courts and cities" are "made all of false-fac'd soothing" and "slipp'ry turns." Coriolanus, however, unlike such satirists as Davies, Donne, and Jonson, accepts the logical consequence of his criticism and opts for a world elsewhere. He banishes himself, as did the stage satirist John Marston, who retired to become a rural ecclesiast. (This view of Coriolanus as satirist is perhaps supported by Bernard Shaw's sly assertion that "*Coriolanus* is the greatest of Shakespeare's comedies."[21])

Coriolanus's act, of course, is fatal. However, there is no record of a poet whose centered self urged him to produce fatal verse, though occasionally an ear or finger may have been judicially severed. Coriolanus can nevertheless stand as a figure symbolic of the poet at or near the court whose proud nature made it impossible for him to become a "changeling" in his art when the pressures of historical events, particular personalities, or the specific prohibitions of censors or royal proclamations began to impinge. The Renaissance poet's courtly audience was as impatient with "singularity" as Coriolanus's Roman one.

Shadow lives of the poet in Shakespeare's courts, as the preceding discussion has suggested, are rife with tactical dilemmas, pressures toward unpleasant compromise or hypocrisy, and possibilities for humiliation. This canvass leaves a strong impression that poetry offered a false staff to those who chose to labor in this vocation at court. This impression can be ramified if we pause to consider briefly two Shakespearean courtiers— Falstaff and Iago—whose chameleonic and protean capabilities allow them to assume, as circumstances require, every one of the half-dozen disguises of the poet-at-court we have considered.

The reader may quickly object that Falstaff is neither at court nor a poet. But the Prince of Wales carries his own "court" with him, and it is a chief mark of its depravity that Falstaff looms as his chief courtier and, to use a term for Boyet, "please-man." Sir John's nature as a supremely false courtier is made apparent, in part, by his dexterous employment of several styles that we have associated with our shadow poets. And though his speeches do not, as Webbe puts it, "run uppon the olde Iambicke stroake," Falstaff is a most extravagantly poetical personage. "A good wit," he boasts, "will make use of any thing" (2H4 1.2.247), and the thing he uses most brilliantly to turn his diseases to commodity is language itself. His stock-in-trade consists of the pun, the simile, and various auricular figures. It is both apt and amusing to fill out a description of Falstaff's character from Puttenham's charming translations of Greek rhetorical jargon, especially of epithets for "vices and deformities in speech": the *straggler* (digression), the *overlabor*, the *abaser*, the *false impersonation*, the *disabler* (extenuation), the *mingle-mangle*, the *fond affectation*, the *abuser*, and preeminently the *loud liar*. Falstaff is quite literally a figure of poetic invention: no man, he says, is "able to invent any thing that intends to laughter more than I invent" (2H4 1.2.8-9). Though to be sure, Falstaff's poetical purposes are seriously out of Horatian balance; his interest is delight, not teaching, and ears that listen to him are likely to become "truant," as they do with Berowne.

Falstaff, to approach his poetical identity another way, is a comically superannuated example of Ascham's "quickest wits" at court, who "commonly may prove the best poets, but not the wisest orators." Like these wits, Falstaff is solely devoted to "easy and pleasant studies," "light to promise anything, ready to forget everything," and "ever over light and merry" (see full quotation in n. 36 on page 211). And the end that Shakespeare contrives for Falstaff in *Henry V*, "He was full of jests, and gipes, and knaveries, and mocks—I have forgot his name" (4.7.40-42), is such as Ascham predicts for those few poetical wits who "come to any great age": "few be found, in the end, either very fortunate for themselves or very profitable to serve the commonwealth, but decay and vanish, men know not which way."[22] Just as Falstaff encompasses every continent of the sinful globe, so does he show his good wit in virtually every one of the poetic roles we have examined. He is a false suitor in multiple extensions of the phrase. His primary suit is for the "love" of England's future king, behind whose back he is, however, outrageously unfaithful. Falstaff is as cunningly a false suitor on the behalf of Justice Shallow, as he is to the "most sweet wench" who runs the Boar's Head tavern. Shakespeare depended principally on this poetic role when he resurrected Falstaff in *The Merry Wives of Windsor*, where the amatory cozener turns his eye on Mistress Ford and Mistress Page: "She is a region in Guiana, all gold and bounty" (1.3.69). "I will be cheaters to them both," he exults, "and they shall be exchequers to me" (1.3.70). Then, when he enters the lists it is with a (misquoted) line from *Astrophil and Stella* and the same "serviceable vows" recommended by Proteus in *Two Gentlemen*: "I see how thine eye would emulate the diamond *etc.*" (3.3.55).

Falstaff also exemplifies the poet as courtly stylist. The ladies in *Love's Labour's Lost* quote the men's favors and letters merely as "bombast," and

Falstaff is, as Hal declares, a similarly "sweet creature of bombast" (1H4 2.4.327). Like the courtiers of Navarre, he is skillful at the witty, careless, and idling passage of time. His ruling figure in this guise is thus the leisurely "ambage," or *periphrasis* ("Let us be Diana's foresters, gentlemen of the shade, minions of the moon" [1.2.25]). Falstaff is a Boyet pushed to extreme recklessness . . . and girth.

Falstaff's most famous role is that of poet-as-jester. The Lord Chief Justice calls him, purely pejoratively, "a great fool," but students of comedy praise him thus as a highly successful entertainer. It is mainly as such that Hal finally rejects him: "How ill white hairs becomes a fool and jester!" Shortly afterward, Falstaff's attempt to speak is squelched: "Reply not to me with a fool-born jest" (5.5.48,55). The Hal-Falstaff relationship begins with a dialogue that has the same feel as many Shakespearean sets of thrust-and-parry that take place between an adroit master and his witty jester, and many moments in Falstaff's career are reminiscent of the professional jester's life. His "What, shall we be merry, shall we have a play extempore?" (1H4 2.4.279-80) is a clever deflection of attention from his cowardice at Gadshill. Further, the "play" itself gives him fine scope for mirthful impersonation. His tavern audience loves to hear him lie. So, when his audience proves icy, as it notably does with the Chief Justice, he reacts with a comedian's nervous desperation, starting for one witty mouse hole after another. For him, the worst audience is Prince John of Lancaster: "This same young sober-blooded boy doth not love me, nor a man cannot make him laugh" (4.3.87-88).

The distinction between poet-as-jester and poet-as-witty-cohort is perhaps a fine one in Falstaff's case, but one worth making, if only to remember that he does enjoy the high status of knighthood. Grotesquely fat and old, he is one of Shakespeare's several pleasant companions whose charisma, however self-aggrandizing, is hard to resist. Falstaff is, in short, a Berowne, Mercutio, or Benedick who has survived the ravages of time with their blithe insouciance. The effect is not entirely pleasant, to be sure. His tours de force, for all their dexterity, offer various kinds of "salve for perjury." And in the way Falstaff gathers his comic material in Gloucestershire, there is also an element of the arrogant aristocrat's eagerness to visit court contempt on his inferiors: "I will devise matter enough out of this Shallow to keep Prince Henry in continual laughter the wearing out of six fashions."

Falstaff's greatness as a character derives from the sociable muse of comedy, but he also now and then reminds us of the two more isolated poets at court, the parasitical upstart and the satirist. Falstaff is, to borrow an epithet that Hal uses to describe him (1H4 1.2.11), a "superfluous" person in the world he inhabits. He is all-consuming, yet produces nothing. He (like Parolles) lives by the words he utters, and his gaze (like Armado's) is cast up with a view to parity with his superiors. But Shakespeare takes care to show that a Falstaff far from the cozy, sleazy environs of the Boar's Head tavern is out of his element. For instance, when he presumes to offer one line of opinion at a council of war prior to Shrewsbury, Hal thrusts him rudely into his place: "Peace, chewet, peace!" (1H4 5.1.29). Falstaff's hopes of ascent at court, like Malvolio's, are ludicrously inflated, and he is crushed by the plot. But these hopes are the same hopes that any courtier seeing the ship-of-royal-favor nearing port would have felt. Falstaff learns of the death of Henry IV and immediately turns to Shallow to make the great promise of Tudor political life: "Choose what office thou wilt in the land, 'tis thine" (5.3.123).

The excrescences of the satirist are more subtly and seldom cast through Falstaff's role. He boasts ironically, "I was as virtuously given as a gentleman need to be, virtuous enough: swore little, dic'd not above seven times—a week, went to a bawdy-house not above once in a quarter—of an hour, paid money that I borrow'd—three or four times" (1H4 3.3.12-15). And at the end of 1 Henry IV, he promises with tongue in cheek: "I'll purge and leave sack, and live cleanly as a nobleman should do" (5.4.164-65). But satire is not Falstaff's usual style. After all, he presents precisely the globe of sinful continents that Renaissance satirists were themselves so acidulous in exploring. It is rather Hal who takes the part of satirist and harries Falstaff with "damnable iteration" whenever they are together.

In the end, Falstaff's actions as a completely dissolute courtier are rendered comically harmless; not so the actions of the great courtly villain Iago. Some may feel it is straining to view an ensign who has supposedly known only military service as a courtier, but it is a central irony of *Othello* that the Moor confronts his challenges on Cyprus as if they were military, when they are in fact the essence of oblique machinations at court. Iago professes that he lacks courtly skills, but this, like many of his protestations, is exquisitely false. The view of Iago as a courtier is also urged by Edwin Booth in his advice on playing the part: "To portray Iago properly you must seem to be what all the characters think you to be; try to win even them by your sincerity. Don't *act* the villain, don't *look* it or *speak* it . . . but think it all the time. Be genial, sometimes jovial, always gentlemanly. . . . A certain bluffness (which my temperament does not afford) should be added to preserve the military flavour of the character; in this particular I fail utterly, my Iago lacks the soldierly quality. My consolation is that we know him *more as a courtier than as a soldier.*"[23] In this view, Iago is a kind of worst-case embodiment of the dissembling courtier of Castiglione. It is but a small step to view him also as a worst-case representation of Puttenham's courtly poet, who is advised to "dissemble not onely his countenances and conceits, but also all his ordinary actions of behaviour, or the most part of them, whereby the better to winne his purposes and good advantages" (3: 25).

Pursuing his far-from-good advantages, Iago has occasion to assume, if only briefly, several of the shadow roles of the poet-at-court. He is preeminently and variously a false suitor. For instance, the play opens with the presentation of his failed suit for higher rank, which Robert Heilman has convincingly demonstrated is but one of Iago's many false disguisings of his "peculiar end."[24] Thereafter, Iago is a false mediator in the suits of Roderigo, Cassio, and finally Desdemona: "weep not; all shall be well" (42.170-71). Most striking and grotesque is Iago's false suit for the "love" of Othello himself. Though he boasts at the outset, "not I for love and duty," we eventually observe him oozing mellifluously the "love and duty" (3.3.194) he bears Othello. It scarcely needs saying that in this seduction scene Iago employs every rhetorical weapon in the poet's arsenal. He has earlier said, with his usual fraudulent *sprezzatura*, that his muse must labor for invention, but here she performs with complete ease and skill.

Beyond his role as false suitor, Iago also displays the deft touch of the elegant courtly stylist. When his purposes require, he can assume that affability of Elyot's which has such a "wonderful efficacy or power in procuring love." There is not a little of Boyet, whom Berowne calls an "ape of form, monsieur the nice" (5.2.325), in Iago, and this may help to explain Shakespeare's intentions in a scene often lamented by critics and abridged in performance: the Desdemona-Iago interview just before Othello arrives at Cyprus (2.1.100-164). For this scene fixes in the mind Iago's identity as a courtly ape—monster, rather—of form. He performs here precisely as Boyet performs for the ladies in *Love's Labour's Lost*, helping to pass time amusingly.

The scene is a brilliant stroke, for it pits a typically idling set of wit against Desdemona's preoccupation with the storm-beset arrival of her husband. Shakespeare renders this set of wit archly, unpleasantly "poetical," beginning with Iago's false admission that he is far from being an extemporal performer: "I am about it, but indeed my invention / Comes from my pate as birdlime does from frieze, / It plucks out brains and all. But my Muse labors, / And thus she is deliver'd." The subject, as usual in the *amour courtois* tradition, is paradiastolic: "What wouldst write of me, if thou shouldst praise me?" Iago's responses are cast in the rhyming couplets that, by the time of *Othello*, Shakespeare was wont to use only for sarcastic or subversive purposes. Iago is a master of many figures, chief among them Puttenham's Paradiastole or favor-currier.

Less obvious but significant are the ways Iago apes the form of the Shakespearean jester. (Robert Armin, premier comedian for the latter half of the playwright's career, is thought by some to have played the part.) The very weakness of Othello's attending Clown may be partly ascribed to the protean villain's encroachment on his role. Something of this recognition lies behind Edwin Booth's emphasis on his joviality as well as behind the special success of actors whose Iago comes, as the Princess says of Boyet, with "mirth in his face" (5.2.79). Playing the fool craves a special perspicuity: think of Touchstone, Feste, and Lear's Fool. Iago, unfortunately, is the only figure of this description in *Othello:* He "knows all qualities, with a learned spirit / Of human dealings" (3.3.259-60). Iago, though, is a terrible exception to the other fools in Shakespeare. Unlike them he uses his knowledge of the ideals by which other men live, not for comic material but as a net with which to "enmesh them all." Far from comic, Iago's subversions are violent and fatal. In a curious way, he represents the revenge of all Renaissance jesters who felt the "curse of service" and who were professionally obliged "to faune on them that froune on us, to currie favour with them that disdaine us, to bee glad to please them that care not how they offende us."[25]

Iago should also be seen, along with the inexpert Parolles and highly expert Wolsey, playing the role of poet-as-upstart. The very image of Wolsey making his way "spider-like / Out of his self-drawing web" is specially apt for Iago. Much of his energy, as his first scene with Roderigo shows, is that of the proud inferior seeking to burst from the oppression of "obsequious bondage"—the same energy that drives Malvolio to comic, and Wolsey to tragic, heights. This pure lust for power is the real identity of Iago's "peculiar end," and to disguise this lust, he trims himself not only in the "forms and visages of duty" but also in the forms and visages of the poet's art. In exercising his lust for control—whether over Roderigo's purse (a demeaningly easy task) or over Othello's life and soul (the great challenge)—Iago, the lowly ensign, becomes the image of Puttenham's courtier-poet: He is able to "dissemble his conceits as well as his countenances, so as he never speake as he thinkes, or thinke as he speaks" (3: 25).

Iago's assumption of the satirist's role at court needs little elaboration. Is there a better instance in Shakespeare of Davies' "Rebels to Nature and Societies"? Like avatars of the satirist already observed, Iago is reckless in his singularity, a continual ironist whose brain attends upon the weaknesses in human nature and whose heart, as he boasts, attends only upon itself. Like them also, Iago is a perfect figure of alienation, as his soliloquies make clear: They all occur before the central seduction scene, when there is still a society from which to stand apart. After act 3 scene 3, Cypriot "civilization" begins to decline, and the need to stand apart and soliloquize vanishes. So Iago plays the satirist's role with the best dry mockery. (Arrigo Boito, Verdi's librettist, admonished in the *Otello* production book: "Iago is a *critic* . . . a mean and spiteful critic" *Disposizione*, 4.) But as usual, Iago plays the role with a fatal twist. He does not come bearing the satirist's usual, painful, ultimately therapeutic emetics, but rather poison itself: "I'll pour this pestilence into his ear"; "The Moor already changes with my poison"; "Work on, / My medicine, work!"

Falstaff and Iago. It is dismal to suggest, as I feel obliged to do, that these two spectacularly dissolute avatars of the poet-at-court—confidence men—come first to mind as one peruses Puttenham's warmly sanguine peroration of his *Arte*, addressed to Queen Elizabeth. For his suggestion that "our maker or Poet is to play many parts and not one alone" (3: 25) applies more readily to them than to any Shakespearean character whose career one might adduce as an ornament to the poet's profession. Indeed, there are no attractive shadows of the poet from the playwright's pen who successfully perform as does the ideal personage offered by Puttenham to Gloriana: "[I have pulled] him first from the carte to the schoole, and from thence to the Court, and preferred him to your Majesties service, in that place of great honour and magnificence to give enterteinment to Princes, Ladies of honour, Gentlewomen and Gentlemen, and by his many moodes of skill, to serve the many humors of men thither haunting and resorting, some by way of solace, some of serious advise, and in matters aswell profitable as pleasant and honest" (3: 25).

The most obvious explanation for this is that Shakespeare's bent was for describing the real, rather than an ideal, world. The Tudor-Stuart court was a corrupting place: "Aretine's pictures have made few chaste," Donne soberly observed, "no more can princes' Courts" (166). The poet was unlikely to learn at court to be such a chaste poet as Puttenham has in view. The best wisdom one could hope for under the circumstances was perhaps the easy bending that the Guevara's *Galateo* advises under the "vaine" ceremonies of court: "Because it is not our fault, but the fault of our tyme, wee are bounde to followe it: but yet wee must discreetly do it" (44). Be, in Shakespeare's more mordant phrase, "a hovering temporizer, that / Canst with thine eyes at once see good and evil, / Inclining to them both" (WT 1.2.302-4).

The courtier's life was one of ceaseless balancing on very fine lines of distinction. For Puttenham it was one of remaining an "honest man and not . . . an hypocrite" (3: 25) while always artfully dissembling (recall that Greek *hypokritēs* = actor). For Jonson courtiership meant simultaneously commanding the courtly virtues of *Euphantaste* ("a well conceited Wittinesse") and *Apheleia* ("Simplicitie" [4: 166]), while for Castiglione it required the delicate task of assuring that *sprezzatura* not devolve from "ornament" into "deceite" (132). For Sidney the courtier's life entailed acting "according to art, though not by art" (*Defence*, 139). For Wyatt it meant "cloak[ing his] care but under sport and play" (76), and for Harington it meant trying to "walke faire, tho' a cripple" (1: 339). In sum, the courtier's life was a life lived most intelligently by compromise, obliquity, indirection, and the intervention of mediaries—by travel along "by-paths and indirect crook'd ways" (2H4 4.5.184) rather than via the straight and narrow highway.[26] "This is no world," said Chamberlain of courtly politics, "to thrive in by plaine dealing" (1: 564).

"By indignities," wrote Bacon in his essay "Of great place," "we come to dignities. The standing is slippery." We seldom encounter courtiers or poets who achieved great place at the Renaissance court while managing to retain their integrity as men or artists. They are certainly seldom met in Shakespeare's courts. Figures who eschew the easy path of the favor-currier tend to drift to the periphery: Archidamus, for example, in *The Winter's Tale* ("I speak as my understanding instructs me, and as mine honesty puts it to utterance" [1.1.19-20]). Or, if they are prominent, they may suffer greatly for their pains: "Be Kent unmannerly / When Lear is mad." It is shocking to think that the most affectingly described ideal courtier in the entire canon, Bertram's father in *All's Well That Ends Well*, is dead before the action begins. Of him the King of France reminisces:

> So like a courtier, contempt nor bitterness
> Were in his pride or sharpness; if they were,
> His equal had awak'd them, and his honor,
> Clock to itself, knew the true minute when
> Exception bid him speak, and at this time
> His tongue obey'd his hand. Who were below him
> He us'd as creatures of another place,
> And bow'd his eminent top to their low ranks,
> Making them proud of his humility,
> In their poor praise he humbled. Such a man
> Might be a copy to these younger times. [1.2.36-46]

The ideal Renaissance courtier, for humanists such as Elyot and Castiglione, was like Bertram's father: a figure who might provide a virtuous "copy" for posterity (Bertram would have horrified his father). The ideal courtier joined virtue "with great possessions or dignity" and, through his enticing example, urged his prince in the same direction.[27]

This ideal is memorably phrased by Lord Octavian Fregoso in Castiglione, when he shows how the courtier can "by litle and litle distil into his [prince's] mind goodnesse, and teach him continencie, stoutness of courage, justice, temperance" (265). Fregoso then resorts to a fine image: "In this wise may hee leade him through the rough way of vertue (as it were) decking it aboute with boughes to shadow it, and strowing it over with sightlye flowers, to ease the griefe of the painefull jorney in him that is but of a weake force." Sidney, the most eloquent defender of poetry in Shakespeare's time, himself the epoch's most famous courtier, chose a nearly identical image to describe the ideal poet: "He doth not only show the way [to the good], but giveth so sweet a prospect into the way, as will entice any man to enter into it. Nay, he doth, as if your journey should lie through a fair vineyard, at the very first give you a cluster of grapes, that full of that taste, you may long to pass further" (*Defence*, 113).

"Rare words!" Falstaff would say, "brave world!" The sad truth is that Spenser's lines about the evil courtier in "Mother Hubberd's Tale"— "Thereto he could fine loving verses frame, / And play the Poet oft" (ll. 908-10)—are more to the historical point of the present chapter. We learn more about the realities of the Renaissance poet's life from Falstaff, Iago, and their ubiquitous, less-versatile Shakespearean kin at court than we do from either the gallant dutifulness of Puttenham or the exhilarating oratory of Sidney.

"Fearful Meditation"

The Young Man and the Poet's Life

Dulcis inexpertis cultura potentis amici:
expertus metuit.

—Horace[1]

SAMUEL TAYLOR COLERIDGE wrote that he found the "promise of genius" in Shakespeare's early narrative poems because "the choice of subjects [was] very remote from the private interests and circumstances of the writer himself." This is a species of the genus of critical opinion that praises Shakespeare for the power and consistency of his self-abnegation, for subduing his nature ungrudgingly to what it worked in, "like the dyer's hand" (SON 111). Praising the poet's "utter *aloofness*" from his own feelings, Coleridge adds, "I have found that where the subject is taken immediately from the author's personal sensations and experiences, the excellence of a particular poem is but an equivocal mark, and often a fallacious pledge, of genuine poetic power."[2] Coleridge thus placed Shakespeare firmly in the first of the two categories of artistic creators formulated by his Romantic kinsman Schiller in *Über naive und sentimentalische Dichtung* (1796).

Venus and Adonis in particular might tempt one to view Shakespeare as Schiller did: as a type of the naive artist exuberantly unconscious of any disparity between himself and his artistic milieu. About the naive artist's heart, Schiller wrote that it "does not lie like a tawdry alloy immediately beneath the surface, but like gold waits to be sought in the depths . . . *he* is the work and the work is *he*."[3] The poet who created what Mark Twain (in one of his most unlooked-for *obiter dicta*) called "that graceful and polished and flawless and beautiful poem" might well be thought an exemplary Schillerian naïf: an artist "happily married to his Muse . . . [who] takes rules and conventions for granted, used them freely and harmoniously."[4] As Schiller also observed, however, the naive artist risks the appearance of emotional poverty: "The dry truth with which he deals with the object seems not infrequently like insensitivity." And many critics, like C. S. Lewis and Douglas Bush, have in just this fashion dismissed *Venus and Adonis* as little more than a Sevres porcelain in its cold, exquisite style.[5]

This view of Coleridge and other critics, as I urged in my first chapter, is naive in the un-Schillerian sense of the word. *Venus and Adonis* does betray in and between its lines an agon between a poet and his muse; it questions the motives of the professional poet and of the delicate minuets between poet-suitors and patron-heirs. Far from standing aloof from his creation, Shakespeare questions the motives of eloquence itself. Beneath the highly burnished aureate surface there are intimations that, as a budding professional poet, he was consorting turbulently with his muse in the manner of Schiller's sentimental artist, whose "mind cannot tolerate any impression without at once observing its own activity and reflection. . . . We never learn of his condition directly and at first hand, but rather how he has reflected in his own mind what he had thought about it as an observer of himself" (129-30). Shakespeare's poetry thus produces very complex and not easily reconcilable responses. They are, as Stephen Booth has succinctly said of the Sonnets, "hard to think about." And their effect is often like that of Schiller's sentimental artist, as Sir Isaiah Berlin phrases it: "not joy and peace, but tension, conflict with nature or society, insatiable craving" (4). The music of Shakespeare's poems, in other words, is not like that of Bach, Handel, or Haydn, which brings the mind to a fine repose, but rather is ambiguous, equivocal, and restless (Mozartean or Wagnerian?)—music that leaves one questioning, rather than contemplating.

It is therefore puzzling that Berlin would assent to the usual view of Shakespeare as a naive artist. He writes, "Among composers of genius, Verdi is perhaps the last complete, self-fulfilled creator . . . a man who dissolved everything in his art, with no more personal residue than Shakespeare or Tintoretto" (4-5). This, as has been often suggested, may be the time-honored Shakespeare of the plays, but it is not the Shakespeare of the narrative poems and Sonnets. The incontrovertible facts of his career suggest that if he had indeed felt "complete" and "self-fulfilled" as a nondramatic poet, he would scarcely have opted for an arduous, disreputable life on the south bank of the Thames. More important (and the subject of the present chapter) is the "personal residue" discernible in the verse Shakespeare wrote.

What personal residue from this most notoriously subdued of authors? the reader will quickly ask. It is observed in *Wit's Commonwealth* (1598) that "poetry, dividing a man from himselfe, maketh him worthily his owne admirer" (51v). Separating himself from his work as a courting poet was inevitably forced to do, Shakespeare appears to have found little basis for self-admiration. Rather, this distancing gave him the sentimental artist's powers of oblique, ironic (self-)observation. His Sonnets, consequently, are perhaps the most compelling subversive commentary we have, if not on his own life, certainly on the generic courting poet's quality of life. What, if not a "personal residue," could have made this possible? "I have looked on truth / Askance and strangely," the speaker admits in Sonnet 110. A true sentimental artist in Schiller's sense, Shakespeare looked askance on the humanists' idealizations of the poet's and the courtier's lives with estranged eyes. In the Sonnets especially, we view through a dark glass the "strained touches" and "gross paintings" (SON 82) of the aesthetic, the rhetoric, and the ethic of Renaissance court life.

The resulting picture is sobering . . . and in several respects like the picture that emerged from our exploration of avatars of the poet in Shakespeare's fictional courts. What follows, indeed, is a converse search for the avatar of the courting suitor in Shakespeare's lyric poems. A consideration of the Sonnets from this perspective will help us better understand why poets and poetizing fared so poorly in Shakespeare's succeeding dramatic worlds, perhaps will even suggest to us why he might have desired, like Robert Pricket, to be "freed from a Poet's name."

Before setting out on this admittedly tendentious exploration of the Sonnets as a kind of "generic" biography of a Renaissance courtier, it is worth remembering that they—like most enduring poems—have lived many lives, have experienced reincarnations in every form of exegesis imaginable (and a few quite unimaginable). Side by side on the many shelves of Sonnets criticism stand numerous compelling, convincing, and yet mutually incompatible understandings of these poems.[6] Any highly focused look at the Sonnets, such as the present one, will necessarily rest uncomfortably beside some readings, more comfortably beside others. For instance, readers will, I hope, find provocative the ways in which the following discussion challenges Alvin Kernan's presentation of Shakespeare's relationship to his lyric muse. Kernan concludes that Shakespeare preferred the risk-taking excitement of the theatrical muse of the Dark Lady to the tedious life of the aristocratic, lyric muse of the Young Man, and thus eventually devoted himself exclusively to playwriting. This theory is tempting, perhaps too tempting. The Sonnets themselves display considerable evidence, to which we shall shortly turn, that the poet's life was by no means as "open, clear, [and] idealized" as Kernan's dichotomy suggests.[7] As we have seen, the realities of being a Tudor poet were, more often than not, harsh and debilitating.

On the other hand, the conclusions I draw from the Sonnets often coincide in gratifying ways with conclusions made by other readers in quite different contexts. G. Wilson Knight, for example, writes apropos of Sonnet 118: "Behind the Sonnets lies what is called a 'perverted' love, a non-sexual, yet sexually impregnated, adoration for a boy." The difficulty for the speaker lies in trying to achieve what Knight calls the "supersexual" integration of the feeling that one's attraction is perverse, thereby attaining a "dynamic wholeness."[8] A Renaissance courtier might have recognized in this situation his own struggles to maintain, in Friedman's phrase, a "serene integrity" while suing to an unwilling, ungenerous, or unappreciative patron. The passage from Barnaby Rich's *Farewell to Militarie Profession* (1581), which gave Shakespeare the text for his comedy about true love, *Twelfth Night*, addresses Knight's distinction between real and perverse love in terms applicable to both amorous and politic lovers: "If a question might bee asked, what is the ground in deede of reasonable love. . . . I thinke those that be wise woulde answere: Desert . . . desert must then be (of force) the grounde of reasonable love." *Un*reasonable love is then described: "to followe them that flie from us, to faune on them that froune on us, to currie favour with them that disdaine us . . . who will not confesse this to be an erronious love" (sig.G). The erroneous, or perverted, love to which Knight refers thus also reflects on the social realities of courtiership, which entailed so much fawning, frowning, following, and fleeing. Knight's "pattern of integration," in other words, offers not only a psycho-sexual but also a social and political paradigm.

Joel Fineman's *Shakespeare's Perjured Eye* (1986), which appeared after I formulated my views about the Sonnets, approaches the sequence from a Derridan perspective. However, he corroborates my dark view of its ethos on several striking occasions. Fineman believes the Sonnets display "a poetics of a double tongue rather than a language of true vision" (15). The Young Man sonnets, he asserts, betray a "genuinely darker side" (69) and a "special melancholy" (140); they "characteristically imply that the poetics of praise they explicitly employ is somehow old-fashioned and exhausted" (187-88). Indeed, Fineman's conclusion that the poetry of the Young Man sonnets "only sees its visionary ideality in rueful retrospect" (140) is virtually paraphrased by my Horatian epigraph. Thomas Greene corroborates this entropic view of the Young Man sonnets when he writes of their "essential vulnerability" in an essay titled "Pitiful Thrivers: Failed Husbandry in the Sonnets."[9]

One other critical statement pertinent to my approach to the Young Man sonnets comes from J. W. Lever, who suggests that the speaker's "zealous pilgrimage" in dream-time to the Young Man's presence in Sonnet 27 figures forth "a journey of the mind." This journey, he observes, is distinguished from numerous others in Renaissance literature because "it is the projection of an alert and heightened sensibility."[10] Lever calls Sonnet 27 a crucial one in the sequence, and for my purposes it certainly is. For Lever's "journey of the mind" can also be viewed in the context of the journey of an aspiring courtier-suitor—a journey imagined by an extraordinarily alert observer of the courtier's existence. The Young Man sequence, I shall be arguing, presents a synoptic version of such a journey: It begins with a spirited, dexterous display of the proper etiquette and agilities (the elegant theme-and-variations on procreation, SON 1-14). It continues with increasingly intrusive intimations of doubt, betrayal, and self-corruption (notably SON 35, 40-42), then a slowly heightening awareness of the competitive atmosphere near the centers of power (SON 61, 67, 69, 76, 79, 80, 82), and afterward a growing desire—as the courtly rat race wears the speaker down—to quit the arena (SON 100, 101, 103-105). The journey finally ends in increasingly reckless expressions of self-loathing (SON 114, 115), plain speaking (SON 121), impossible boast (SON 124, 125), and, at the last, poignant resignation (SON 126), the speaker acknowledging that the "love" of the boy-heir is not everything. There is a world elsewhere.

Shakespeare's sonnet sequence is the only one we have that gives a sense of the Renaissance suitor's life that stands up to the evidence of contemporary memoirs, letters, documents, other imaginative literature, and subsequent historical investigations. Perhaps it is no coincidence that his sequence is the only one from the English Renaissance written by an author who turned actor and playwright. Indeed, one is tempted to see here eloquent corroboration for Stephen Greenblatt's assertion that the Renaissance "conceived of poetry as a performing art."[11] For courtiers and poets, as Castiglione and Puttenham testify, were nothing if not cunning dissemblers of their real natures and thoughts. Their lives intersected in other respects as well. Courtiers and poets depended on mediation of the same stars in the aristocratic firmament. "A Poet's life is most unfortunate," wrote William Fennor, "Govern'd by Starres of high malignant fate": so was the life of the courtier.[12] Many had occasion to feel ostracized, as Shakespeare's speaker does, from those "in favor with their stars," unable to boast of "public honor" or "proud titles" (SON 25), or helplessly subjected to "whatsoever star that guides" their "moving" (SON 26). Their ultimate objectives coincided, too; as Lord Burghley advised his son, "Be sure to keep some great man thy friend."[13] Great friends were indispensable to those who wished to rise at court, so rife was this world with the ruinous "aid" of "back-friends" and desperate attempts to leap rigid hierarchical barriers, usually by recourse to devices considerably more sordid than yellow cross-garters. This, I believe, is the world of the Young Man sonnets, and we can now turn to them to discover first the ways they evoke the essential geography of the Tudor courtly landscape and several significant aspects of the suitor's life there.

⁓

In a chapter titled "The Face of Violence" in *The Crisis of the Aristocracy*, Lawrence Stone comments on how "exceedingly irritable" men of the sixteenth century were. "Their nerves seem to have been perpetually on edge," possibly, he speculates, because they were often ill.[14] If such men were suing for favor, though, long periods of vain attendance in outer chambers punctuated by whimsical shifts of attention among the great might also explain the irritability of courtiers. Disappointment was the rule, and hence there was far more need for a "rhetoric of disappointment" than for a rhetoric of success at court.[15] In this, as in other respects, the courtly suitor's life displayed strong affinities with that of the Petrarchan protagonist. One need merely substitute the courtier for the lover in the following random titles from Tottel's miscellany to achieve the gist of most Renaissance satire directed at the court: "Of the lovers unquiet state," "The lover not regarded in earnest sute," "The changeable state of lovers," or "The complaint of a hot wooer, delayed with doubtful cold answers." Who would not be irascible and edgy under such circumstances?

The central cause of this unquiet state of the courtier, as for Wyatt's speaker in "They flee from me," was "continual change" or court volatility. And no one was more expertly volatile than the Queen herself who, we have seen, could fill the court with "a pure sun-shine" or a "sudden gathering of clouds" as her mood urged. The amusingly long synopsis for a mere 140-word poem by Francis Davison (eldest son of a royal secretary of state) captures just such a scene in thinly disguised allegory:

Strephon, upon some unkindenes conceived, having made shew to leave *Urania*, and make love to another Nymph, was at the next solemne assembly of shepheards, not onely frowned upon by *Urania*, but commanded with great bitternesse out of her presence: Whereuppon, sory for his offence, and desirous to regaine her grace whom he never had forsaken, but in shew, upon his knees he in this Song humbly craves pardon: and *Urania* finding his true penitence, and unwilling to lose so worthy a servant, receives him againe into greater grace and favour than before.[16]

Such tempests, caused for uncertain reasons ("some unkindenes conceived") and complicated by role-playing ("having made shew . . . but in shew"), appear to have been common at Elizabeth's court, and we can be sure that they did not all end with Davison's happy fantasy. The fact that Hyder Rollins imagines contemporary readers would have seen veiled references here to Elizabeth and Essex underscores the real-life authenticity of the scene Davison creates.

This court volatility is powerfully conveyed in many of Shakespeare's sonnets, though (as with Davison's poem) charm or eloquence of expression sometimes masks the sordid reality of life spent gazing on the great. Consider Sonnet 33, which—following my hypothetical allegory of the courting suitor's life span in the Young Man sequence—finds the speaker already aware of the mercurial rhythms at court and yet not oppressed by them. Indeed, the speaker is determined to make the favor currier's "best of a bad thing," which Puttenham specially recommends to the courtier. This sonnet about "unexpected inconstancy" (Booth) has as an important subtext the transactions that took place in the Tudor royal, or aristocratic, presence. It also happens to reflect the meteorological metaphor of sunlight and storm with which Harington described his queen (and, one might add, the great "Digby" portrait of Elizabeth, with storm clouds at her back):

> Full many a glorious morning have I seen
> Flatter the mountain tops with sovereign eye,
> Kissing with golden face the meadows green,
> Gilding pale streams with heav'nly alchemy,
> Anon permit the basest clouds to ride
> With ugly rack on his celestial face,
> And from the forlorn world his visage hide,
> Stealing unseen to west with his disgrace.

The morning (a usual time for audiences) is made glorious by the sovereign's flattering attention to the assembly ("mountain tops") and by the emblematic sign of affection (the kiss). Through these signs of approbation he radiates the power at his disposal, his gold gilding others and simultaneously banishing "pale" fear—fear in those who, perhaps, worry that they may not participate in the royal "alchemy" that translates silver ("pale streams") into gold. Suddenly, however, the royal face turns "ugly," though the poet's image gracefully evades the implication that the royal physiognomy itself could be ugly. The court turns chilly. Shakespeare is forced by his solar image to have the sovereign steal away, but the logic of the eight lines (and their ambiguous, disjunctive syntax, on which Booth comments at length) makes clear that it is rather the "basest" elements of the courtly assembly who must, like Davison's Strephon, steal into disgraced rustication.

The octave of Sonnet 33, then, gives the generic version of a "forlorn" courtier's sudden disappointment. The following sestet focuses on a single such experience of the speaker:

> Ev'n so my sun one early morn did shine
> With all triumphant splendor on my brow;
> But out alack, he was but one hour mine,
> The region cloud hath masked him from me now.
> Yet him for this my love no whit disdaineth;
> Suns of the world may stain when heav'n's sun staineth.

The situation described here was, for the Renaissance reader, eminently quotidian: the suitor has basked for an hour's time in the young aristocrat's presence, until the "region cloud" of courtly etiquette and the busily leisured life of the titled leaves him once again idling in an outer chamber. Shakespeare drops from the ornate height of Sonnet 33 to make the same meteorological point in the plainer style of Sonnet 34: "Why didst thou promise such a beauteous day / And make me travel forth without my cloak, / To let base clouds o'er take me . . . ?" Two lines from Sonnet 75 describe the same situation in a different way: "Sometime all full with feasting on your sight, / And by and by clean starved for a look."

The shot-silk changeability of fortune at court is reiterated often in the Young Man sonnets. The quick movement of the eyes, for instance, commonly conveyed the Petrarchan lover's doom, and the aristocrat's mercurial eye often conveys the suitor's doom in the Sonnets:

> Great princes' favorites their fair leaves spread,
> But as the marigold at the sun's eye,
> And in themselves their pride lies buried,
> For at a frown they in their glory die. [SON 25]

> Against that time when thou shalt strangely pass,
> And scarcely greet me with that sun thine eye . . . [SON 49]

> Bring me within the level of your frown,
> But shoot not at me in your wakened hate. [SON 117][17]

Waiting to learn whether the patron would frown on the courtier's "defects" (SON 49) or point graciously at him "with fair aspect" (SON 26) was made doubly nerve-racking because the process of evaluation depended on so many variables outside the client's control, not least the patron's emotions. The courtier, as the speaker says in Sonnet 88, was thus always subject to fear of the time, "when thou shalt be disposed to set me light, / And place my merit in the eye of scorn." It must have been a "fearful meditation" (SON 65) indeed, planning one's strategies and protecting one's rearward at court under these circumstances—a meditation that must have allowed few moments of contented repose.

Such moments of repose occur seldom in the Sonnets, but when they do, a suspiciously forced, protesting-too-much air is often evinced, notably in Sonnets 116 and 124. At the end of Sonnet 25 the speaker announces with magnificent sureness: "Then happy I that love and am beloved / Where I may not remove, nor be removed." But that last phrase, which no Renaissance suitor would have dared to utter, stands only to be mocked by many of the succeeding sonnets. In Sonnet 49, for example, the speaker, striking a momentary Jonsonian posture, proudly says he will "ensconce" himself "Within the knowledge of mine own desert." But a few lines later he is "poor me" again.

A second important aspect of courtiership—that it operated on the principle of deference—is also registered in many of the Young Man sonnets. For many readers the Sonnets have been about "The perfect ceremony of love's rite" (SON 23) . . . about Great Love, or *agape*, which refuses to bend with the remover to remove. But they are also about the "perfect ceremony" of courtiership, which was based on a "love" thoroughly mixed with the adulterating "seconds" (SON 125) of ulterior motives and self-service. Thus, the poet-speaker in Sonnet 23 exhorts: "O let my books be then the eloquence / And dumb presagers of my speaking breast, / Who plead for love and look for recompense." No one doubted that the "loving" courtier was looking for recompense in some form, be it mere public display of affection, a leasehold, an office, a monopoly, or similar favor for someone from the client's own entourage of suitors.

Sonnet 29, for instance, in its effusive expression of vulnerability, can be viewed as typifying a client's meditation upon his patron and the main chance. The diction (*disgrace, outcast, scope*) and the objects of desire (riches, good looks, friends, social mobility) in this sonnet are more public and social than private. The importance of the speaker's deference to the Young Man is emphasized by the multiple political connotations of *state* in the second, tenth, and fourteenth lines. *State* suggests state of mind and social status, but it also carries suggestions of fortune, estate, high rank, royal prerogative, and the "large effects that troop with majesty." And the thirteenth line—"For thy sweet love rememb'red such wealth brings"—is one of many in the Young Man sequence that shock us momentarily into a recognition of how brazenly Shakespeare sometimes captures the psychology of the courtier, here a lowly one ("myself almost despising") contemplating changing his state, if not with kings, at least with those just above him. Sonnet 29 is more about ambition than love, and the speaker's not entirely successful effort to disguise this with the well-known bird image may account for Yvor Winters' dyspeptic "we have more lark than understanding in these lines."[18]

There is no comfortable place for the self-made man in a deference society. Hence the Duke of Norfolk's antipathy toward Wolsey, who lets the court know that "the force of his own merit makes his way." The speaker of the Young Man sonnets never makes Wolsey's hubristic mistake. His deference is expertly and elaborately phrased, at least before the "crisis" of Sonnets 100-105. Sonnet 78, for example, employs terms from the literary profession to vividly express an essential fact of Tudor life: Ascent to power necessitates the "fair assistance" of the already powerful. One could "fly" (as courtly suitor or artist) only with a superior's eye of approval. Once indebted, the client was then obliged to express such elaborate deference as the poet-speaker indulges in Sonnet 78: "Yet be most proud of that which I compile, / Whose influence is thine, and born of thee." The self-deprecation in the first line is clever, with the play on the Latin *compilare* = to steal. The deference of the next line is unminced: for clients, such "dialogue of compliment" was a necessary part of the ceremony of courtiership.

The patron aided the fortunate client not only by guiding him "aloft to fly" but also by shielding him from the slings and arrows of backstairs envy. Sonnet 112 fulsomely acknowledges the importance of having a powerful patron when standing either justly or unjustly accused of "vulgar scandal." When one's patron was kindly disposed and sufficiently powerful, it was easy to outface all challenges: "For what care I who calls me well or ill, / So you o'ergreen my bad, my good allow?" No Shakespearean sonnet conveys more powerfully than Sonnet 112 the concentration in Tudor court life on *Realpolitik*, rather than on "principles." The implications are startling: one assesses "shames and praises" only from the patron's tongue, throwing all "steeled sense" of right and wrong into the "profound abysm" of clientage. Feeling certain of the patron's "Love and pity," a client could turn a deaf ear to the voices of both critics and flatterers. Costard's notion that "truth is truth" would be considered absurdly naive in this social context. The potential for moral corrosion in a deference society, Sonnet 112 suggests, was considerable. It is a natural passage from this poem's pragmatic amorality to the harshly anti-social Sonnet 121 ("'Tis better to be vile than vile esteemed").

Indeed, a third significant aspect of life at a Renaissance court was the corruption and, more important, self-corruption to which the ambitious were invited by the sheer effort of competition. These are the words of Raleigh to Cecil, but they paraphrase the complaints of the Old Lady in *Henry VIII* (see p. 131) and many a Renaissance suitor: "It greves mee to find with what difficulty and torment to my sealf I obtayne the smalest favor." [19] Temptations to corruption lay in the path of all such desperate creatures. Those who sought to partake of "courts' hot ambitions" by honest and direct approach Donne consigned ruefully to the slaughter: "If they stand armed with silly honesty, / With wishing prayers, and neat integrity, / Like Indian 'gainst Spanish hosts they be."[20]

A common image for this effortful life lay in the high seas. Donne described court officers as "the vast ravishing seas" in which the poor suitor "drowns" (171), and Francis Markham wrote that at court, "Bribes come like Spring-tides, with great Billowes, and full Seas."[21] It was natural, therefore, to liken the loss of a generous patron to shipwreck. Thus, servants of the declining Timon of Athens lament: "Leak'd is our bark, / And we, poor mates, stand on the dying deck, / Hearing the surges threat" (4.2.19-21). The great goal in this parlous world was to find and attach oneself to a patron upon whose "broad main" one could safely sail, a patron whose worth was "wide as the ocean" (SON 80). This was the exception. The rule is evoked in Sonnet 64, a climax of the sequence that addresses time's ravages. On one level, the sonnet's lines can be read as describing the wearing confrontation of hungry suitors with those wielding the powers of gift:

> When I have seen the hungry ocean gain
> Advantage on the kingdom of the shore,
> And the firm soil win of the watery main,
> Increasing store with loss, and loss with store,
> When I have seen such interchange of state,
> Or state itself confounded to decay,
> Ruin hath taught me thus to ruminate,
> That time will come and take my love away.

As in Sonnets 29 and 124, the political connotations of *state* heighten the courtly allusion in these lines. The "ruin" here is partly that of courtly busy-ness, where figures of "state" are ceaselessly thriving or decaying in their fortunes. Court life encouraged rumination like that in Sonnet 64 on the evanescence of courtly "love" and the "interchange of state." In this life, time was the natural enemy because little remained stationary amid the treacherous riptides of factional strife and the unpredictable currents of favor. The sameness of ceaseless change can perhaps also be discerned in another, more famous image of eroding time: "Like as the waves make towards the pebbled shore, / So do our minutes hasten to their end, / Each changing place with that which goes before, / In sequent toil all forwards do contend" (SON 60). That last line, with its pregnant adjective, could stand as a marvelous description of the throng competing for "place" at a Renaissance court.

The implication of Sonnet 64—that the "firm" place of the addressee is "confounded to decay" by the press of suitors—is more directly stated in another sonnet richly evocative of court life, Sonnet 67. Though the conceit is a hoary one from the "loud liar's" Petrarchan stock (that is, the Young Man's beauty bankrupts the rest of nature), its special interest here lies in its derisive meditation on the corrupt transactions that take place within the presence—and its meditation on the fierce impetus to *drain* for "advantage" that was felt by those admitted to this presence: "Ah wherefore with infection should he live, / And with his presence grace impiety, / That sin by him advantage should achieve, / And lace itself with his society?" (1-4). The "infection" of the first line is epidemiological kin to the "monarch's plague," flattery, of Sonnet 114, and the Young Man is cast as a patron of sin-infected courtiers, who adorn themselves (in aristocratic "lace") with his company. The following lines of this damning sonnet discover a further anatomy of the politics of the "presence": the cynosure of attention is surrounded by "false painting" that, to the speaker's eye, gives at best the effect of *nature morte* ("steal dead seeing"). The point is repeated when he calls the Young Man's attendants mere simulacra of virtue, "Roses of shadow." He is surrounded by bankrupt natures; hence their inability to blush ("Beggared of blood"). The Young Man is the only "exchequer" for these bankrupts, who arrogantly assume they can live "upon his gains." Fittingly, the sonnet's last line echoes the nostalgia for a golden age of "days long since, before these last so bad" that is often found in anticourt satire.

Sonnet 67 thus provides an observant (and rather self-righteous) bystander's view of the corrupting press at court. There are also among the Young Man sonnets many compelling expressions of the suitor's distresses that give us, as it were, a view from the inside. These sonnets capture some of the anxiety, self-questioning, and self-loathing to which earnest suitors could so easily fall prey. The ruling figure from Puttenham for these sonnets is not so much *paradiastole*, or "Curry-favell," as it is *meiosis*, or the "Disabler": "The abbaser working by wordes and sentences of extenuation or diminution . . . we call him the *Disabler* . . . and this is used to divers purposes, sometimes for modesties sake, and to avoide the opinion of arrogancie" and to make "a great matter seeme small, and of litle difficultie" (3:19).

An early and poignant instance of the disabling extenuation of ethical compromise occurs in Sonnet 35. Indeed, the method of the Disabler is candidly summarized in the second quatrain: "All men make faults, and even I in this, / Authorizing thy trespass with compare, / Myself corrupting, salving thy amiss." The psychological and ethical implications of this sonnet are disturbing, but as with many of the early Young Man sonnets the darkness is held back by the dexterity and exuberance of *compare*. The

Disabler works ever harder, and with increasingly obvious lack of success, as the sequence develops. Sonnet 88 represents something of a midpoint in the poet-suitor's efforts to extenuate the self-inflicted wounds of seeking the Young Man's favor. In this sonnet, the purpose of which is to confront a fear of rejection, the speaker swears: "Upon thy side against myself I'll fight, / And prove thee virtuous, thou thou art forsworn." Upon such promises courtly factions were built. In the following lines the speaker attempts to explain the advantages of this promise. The logic, archly and unconvincingly "disabling" though it is, does convey an essential public pose of the suitor: "The injuries that to myself I do, / Doing thee vantage, double vantage me. / Such is my love—to thee I so belong— / That for thy right myself will bear all wrong."

The pressures of this habitual extenuation explode impressively toward the end of the sequence, in Sonnet 119. The first two quatrains represent an ecstasy of revulsion at all the self-inflicted injury that has gone before in pursuit of the Young Man. "What wretched errors hath my heart committed, / Whilst it hath thought itself so blessèd ever!" But the sestet makes clear that the speaker has released this self-critical fury only to prepare for a triumphant disabling gambit, turning his "errors" into a kind of fortunate fall: "O benefit of ill, now I find true / That better is by evil still made better." Here is another plausible credo for the contemporary courtier, echoing Bacon's requirement of "good and evil arts" at court.

Sonnets 124 and 125 stand as farewells to the "ruffle" of court life. The loud and, for a Renaissance courtier, impossible boast of Sonnet 124—that the speaker is above the "accident" of courtly favor or disgrace—can only make sense if it is spoken by one who in his heart has chosen once and for all to leave the field (in the spirit of Wyatt's "Mine own John Poins" or Jonson's "To Penshurst"). The real agony of separation comes not in Sonnet 126, but in these two sonnets that stand so "hugely politic" in their imagery. They help to remind us that this idealized poetic construct of "mutual render" between a man of "public means" and an aristocrat takes place against the background of a very plausible representation of Renaissance courtly suit. Those who "bore the canopy" in ritual processions and honored superiors with their "extern" were everywhere, as were "suborned" informers. "Pitiful thrivers" gazed from many an antechamber or backstairs portal. We shall likely never plumb the personal identity of either the poet who speaks in the Sonnets or the Young Man, but the historical identity of the typical Renaissance suitor and Renaissance aristocrat is conveyed in Shakespeare's sequence with striking trenchancy.

This trenchancy cannot be fully appreciated without moving from all these general characteristics of courtly existence to more specific ones.

These, it seems to me, fall into categories encompassing the spatial, tactical, and psychological preoccupations of anyone—be he poet, scion, or upstart "not propp'd by ancestry"—drawn into the "tempest whirling in the court" (TIT 4.2.160).

☙

The suitor's spatial concerns focused on the *sine quibus non* for courtly thriving: "attending" in the outer chambers, gaining access to the powerful, competing with rivals, avoiding displacement from within the verge, and using unavoidable absences to advantage. "Waityng," as Churchyard noted, was the courtier's "trade," and every person within the verge except the monarch was "in waiting" in respect of one or many superiors.[22] This tedium of waiting finds powerful expression in Donne's mariner's parable of the "stupid calm" at court during which nothing happened, no hopes advanced. The extinction of mind induced by the boredom of waiting Donne bitterly expresses in the last lines of "The Calm": "We have no power, no will, no sense; I lie, / I should not then thus feel this misery" (200).

Time weighs heavily in the Young Man sonnets. It is no coincidence that the word *time* occurs about seventy times in them and not once in the Dark Lady sonnets. The speaker, of course, as a mere mortal and a true lover, resents "dear time's waste" and fears "time's tyranny," but it is also important to attribute this oppressing awareness of the "injury" of time in part to the Renaissance suitor's experience in waiting. Sonnet 61 may present the usual insomniac Petrarchan, but there is something of the suitor, too, in the speaker's willingness to "defeat" his own rest in order to "play the watchman" while the Young Man "dost wake elsewhere." The Sonnets contain much imagery of leasing, accounting, borrowing, bonding, auditing—all of which depends on the ticking off of "short-numb'red hours." It was inevitable for the suitor, as for all men, to hear time's winged chariot hurrying near. Perhaps for the suitor, ever fearful that his hopes (like the boy's beauty) would suffer a final quietus, time weighed especially heavily: he had so much of it to dispose of. Thus the pressure was great to strike for success at the privy chamber door while the iron was hot, and, hence, the special torture of any doldrums in this venue.

Shakespearean counterparts to "The Calm"—Sonnets 57 and 58—occur near that point in our archetypal suitor's career when he has become inured to waiting and is, perhaps, beginning to sense that his iron is cooling. In these sonnets we are vouchsafed views of the lives of a John Harington or a Boyet. These sonnets also hint, perhaps, why Shakespeare departed for the Globe Theater, where his honor (like that of Bertram's father in *All's Well*) could be in some way "clock to itself." Sonnet 57, indulging the figure of the curry-favor with a vengeance, is the "public" confession of a timeserver:

> Being your slave, what should I do but tend
> Upon the hours and times of your desire?
> I have no precious time at all to spend,
> Nor services to do till you require.
> Nor dare I chide the world without end hour
> Whilst I, my sovereign, watch the clock for you,
> Nor think the bitterness of absence sour,
> When you have bid your servant once adieu.
> Nor dare I question with my jealous thought,
> Where you may be, or your affairs suppose,
> But like a sad slave stay and think of nought
> Save where you are how happy you make those.

One cannot miss the profound self-reproach here. In the following couplet the temporizing speaker admits only that he is a "fool" for love. We must wait until Sonnets 124 and 125 to learn that he is here presenting himself as one of those obsequious "fools of time" the court inevitably produced and destroyed.

Sonnet 58 sounds the attending suitor's deep well of resentment with remarkable candor. In the second quatrain, for example, the speaker boasts of the patience necessary to be always on call; he also echoes the frequently paradoxical expressions of the first English courtly poet-agonist, Wyatt ("Alas, I tread an endless maze . . . And hope still, and nothing haze, / Imprisoned in liberties"[23]): "O let me suffer, being at your beck, / Th'imprisoned absence of your liberty— / And patience tame to suff'rance bide each cheek, / Without accusing you of injury." Sonnet 58 also drives home the impossibility of attaining the ideal of mutuality at a Renaissance court, for it remained wholly within the patron's power to "privilege" his time to his own "will." As the couplet, one of the Sonnets' best, plainly states, the clock belonged more properly in the outer chambers: "I am to wait, though waiting so be hell, / Not blame your pleasure, be it ill or well."

Timeserving at court produced special anxiety because the clock ticked loudly there. The "course of alt'ring things" (SON 115) was propelled at court by sudden changes in factional balances and in artistic or domestic fashions of all kinds. The poet-speaker of the Sonnets is keenly aware that time's whirligig may bring in its revenges and overtake his work. He worries that his "poor rude lines" will soon appear passé "with the bett'ring of the time" (SON 32) and that his "slight muse" will not survive "these curious days" (SON 38). In Sonnet 17 the poet-speaker fears his papers, "yellowed with their age," may "be scorned, like old men of less truth than tongue." This image of old age recurs in Sonnet 73: "That time of year thou mayst in me behold, / When yellow leaves, or none, or few, do hang." This poem's pathos derives partially from its implication that the court was a happier place for the young and vigorous. Even the most durable courtiers found that age brought with it feelings of estrangement and melancholy, and these feelings, of course, came sooner then. In 1592, when Bacon was roughly the age of the Sonnets' author, he wrote to Burghley, "I wax now somewhat ancient; one and thirty years is a great deal of sand in the hour-glass." Sonnet 73 perfectly expresses the "twilight" mood of a courtly attendant and is reminiscent of some lovely lines celebrating the retirement of Sir Henry Lea, the Queen's champion: "Time, with his golden locks to silver chang'd, / Hath with age-fetters bound him hands and feet."[24]

Having waited patiently and fortunately gained access to the audience chamber, the suitor turned his attention to riveting the (preferably un-divided) attention of the patron. This required real competitive skill and a certain egotistical verve. Many of the sonnets, of course, urge readers to view this skill primarily in terms of professional poetic rivalry. The note is first struck in Sonnet 21 ("So is it not with me as with that muse") and carries forward in many others, notably those associated with the Rival Poet. The speaker jealously carps at "every alien pen" (SON 78), frets that his "sick muse doth give another place" (SON 79), and with shameless self-service berates the "strained touches" of others' ornate verse.

But many of the Young Man poems offer an impressive if grim view of the fierce competition among *all* classes of suitors at court. The "world's eye" (SON 69), not just the poet's, viewed with sanguine cunning the profit to be gained from those at the top. The difficult task was to stand apart from, and then climb above, all others. The more or less limited resources of all patrons induced a powerful binary logic: If rivals "thrive," then the suitor must be "cast away" (SON 80). One was therefore obliged to become an expert boaster of one's own virtues (SON 55, 63, 81, and 107) and a satirist of the vices of others, imbuing them with "sin," "infection," and "false painting" (SON 67) and calling them thieves and parasites (SON 79). The harshest indictment of the patron himself in this context was thus bound to be that of failing to exclude *others* from grace: "thou dost common grow" (SON 69).

A great patron was a handsome prize and, apparently to no one's shock, elicited most ignoble stooping. Sonnet 86 finds the poet-speaker experienc-ing a temporary failure of his competitive instinct: "Was it the proud full sail of his great verse, / Bound for the prize of all too precious you, / That did my ripe thoughts in my brain inhearse . . . ?" Booth considers this image one of "an expedition in quest of treasure," but I think it has more to do with piracy: the patron as, possibly, a heavily laden Spanish galleon. Whether suitors came in "proud sail" or "saucy bark" (SON 80), the prize was too great to shy away from whatever piratical and cutthroat expedients might be necessary to heave him to for exploitation. After all, the patron's treasure, as Sonnet 97 implies, meant the difference between "rich increase" and "old December's bareness."

The seriousness and vigor of competition among suitors are reflected in the opening military imagery of Sonnet 46, which is based on the conceit of a Petrarchan lover's psychomachia. The eye and heart—like rival suitors—are locked in "mortal war," the question being: "How to divide the conquest of thy sight." The possible ways of reading this line are worth noting: the rivals are attempting to divide the spoils that derive from breaching the Young Man's presence and gaining a view of him (Booth sees a possible pun on "site" here); the Young Man's sight of the rivals itself confers victory in the suitors' war; and the Young Man is himself the object of conquest, a worthy object of military expedition. In any event, the eye refuses to divulge the "picture's sight" to the heart; the heart, feeling equally selfish and miserly, prefers to retain the image of the Young Man in "A closet never pierced with crystal eyes." Rivalry over the audience with the Young Man degenerates in the remainder of the sonnet into an elaborate comparison from that notorious form of Elizabethan loggerheads, a suit at law over real estate. The crassness of Shakespeare's image was not out of keeping with the venal atmosphere among rival suitors.

The crassness of competition and the almost neurotic fearfulness and suspicion it inspired are strikingly expressed in Sonnet 75:

> for the peace of you I hold such strife,
> As 'twixt a miser and his wealth is found;
> Now proud as an enjoyer, and anon
> Doubting the filching age will steal his treasure;
> Now counting best to be with you alone,
> Then bettered that the world may see my pleasure.

The pun on "the piece of you" may be, as Booth says, "logically and syntactically inadmissible" (263), but the positively reckless candor of it is wonderful. For the patron was as much a "piece" (that is, coin) or a source of pieces as he was a "prize" or "treasure." His favor was as good as money, as Falstaff's gulling of Shallow in 2 Henry IV makes clear. Because the patron's favor and resources were limited, though, a miser's instinct was encouraged among suitors, as was a constant worry that "filching" rivals might carry such favor and resources away. The suitor's ideal was to be the sole recipient of this favor, but part of the value of favor was to trade on it in public, as Falstaff seeks to do on the steps of Westminster Abbey. The suitor's life was rife with ambivalent feelings like these, as the remainder of Sonnet 75 succeeds in conveying. It was a full yet empty life: "Thus do I pine and surfeit day by day, / Or gluttoning on all, or all away." Competition made it so, the "strife" of "possessing or pursuing" never ceasing.

There were two natural consequences of the competition for favor, both tellingly reflected in the Young Man sonnets. One was the suitor's eagerness to be alone with the patron; the other, the necessity of accounting usefully for time spent while absent from the presence. The desire "to be alone with you" (SON 75) virtually amounted to a fantasy, given, as King James phrased it, the "uncessant swarme of suitors importunately hanging" on Renaissance aristocrats.[25] The fantasy element of this desire for exclusive intimacy can be seen in Sonnet 46's "closet never pierced with crystal eye" and Sonnet 48's "gentle closure of my breast," where the speaker wishes to "lock up" the Young Man and protect him from "every vulgar thief." The fantasy is most fully and, from the patron's perspective, suffocatingly elaborated in Sonnet 52, which begins, "So am I as the rich whose blessèd key / Can bring him to his sweet up-lockèd treasure, / The which he will not every hour survey, / For blunting the fine point of seldom pleasure." The speaker then likens his audience with the Young Man to "rare" feasts which, though often wished for, as Prince Hal notes, seldom come. The third quatrain reiterates the image of the patron as treasure trove: "So is the time that keeps you as my chest, / Or as the wardrobe which the robe doth hide / To make some special instant special blest, / By new unfolding his imprisoned pride." This was the deep-seated instinct: to encompass, isolate (imprison), and then exploit the patron's "pride" (Booth glosses this as splendor, ornament, fine clothes). The fantasy rarely lasted long in the real courtly world, and it does not in the Sonnets. In Sonnet 79 the poet speaks for all such suitors who harbored this fantasy: "Whilst I alone did call upon thy aid, / My verse alone had all thy gentle grace, / But now my gracious numbers are decayed, / And my sick muse doth give another place."

Except for those few souls capable of a true renunciation of court life, absence from the center of power incurred other kinds of anxiety. This was partly because, as Francis Walsingham wrote to Christopher Hatton, "In men's absence from Court envy oftentimes doth work most malicious effects"[26] and also because rustication was often occasioned by disgrace. Banished because of his affair with Mary Fitton, the Earl of Pembroke wrote to Cecil, "If the Queen continue her displeasure a little longer, undoubtedly I shall turn clown, for justice of the peace I can by no means frame unto, and one of the two a man that lives in the country needs must be."27 Clearly, absence from court resulted in anxiety because the tedium of court life compared very favorably with the tedium of country life. Harington wrote from his seat at Kelston in 1603, "Here now wyll I reste my troublede mynde, and tende my sheepe like an Arcadian swayne" (1: 180), but bored to tears, within a year he was planning his approaches to London and a new monarch.28

Sonnets that find the speaker coping with "injurious distance" (SON 44) from the Young Man are among the most distastefully strenuous in the sequence, perhaps because everyone at a Renaissance court recognized that absence was very likely to make the patron's heart grow less fond. Absence from the "torrid zone at Court, and calentures / Of hot ambitions" (Donne, 259) inevitably chilled a suitor's prospects: "How like a winter hath my absence been / From thee . . . What freezings have I felt, what dark days seen!" (SON 97). Absence from court elicited many an effusive letter, each seeking to make clear that this absence was not the result of attentions paid to other potential patrons. Thus, Sonnet 109's opening lines: "O never say that I was false of heart, / Though absence seemed my flame to qualify." Such accusations of betrayal were likely to be made when a patron-client relationship was indeed beginning to collapse. It is perfect timing for my parable of the suitor's life span that we find the speaker in Sonnet 117 reacting to such an accusation with a very lame conceit:

> Accuse me thus: that I have scanted all
> Wherein I should your great deserts repay,
> Forgot upon your dearest love to call,
> Whereto all bonds do tie me day by day;
> That I have frequent been with unknown minds,
> And giv'n to time your own dear purchased right;
> That I have hoisted sail to all the winds
> Which should transport me farthest from your sight.

The ideal for the absent suitor was to convince his patron of the incredible: that his "dear religious love" (SON 31) is unaffected by distance and that he has turned absence to ingratiating use: "O absence, what a torment wouldst thou prove, / Were it not thy sour leisure gave sweet leave / To entertain the time with thoughts of love" (SON 39). The "absence" sonnets bear such marks of inventive desperation as this. The speaker giddily wishes he could "leap large length of miles" to join the Young Man (SON 44) or describes the Young Man's appearance in a dream, "like a jewel hung in ghastly night" (SON 27).

∽

The court world, as we have noted, required from those who entered the verge a tactical flexibility and the prudent preparation of contingency plans. These characteristics led La Bruyère to liken courtiership to chess play: "Life at court is a serious, melancholy game, which requires of us that we arrange our pieces and our batteries, have a plan, follow it, foil that of our adversary, sometimes take risks and play on impulse. And after all our measures and meditations we are in check, sometimes in checkmate."[29] The Young Man sonnets show, obviously enough, a poet's extremely careful tactical maneuvering, but they also display many of the challenges to tactical flexibility that all suitors faced. Some are resolved on the level of etiquette. "O how thy worth with manners may I sing?" asks the speaker in Sonnet 39. And we are given the picture of a politely reticent suitor in the patron's entourage in Sonnet 85: "My tongue-tied muse in manners holds her still." Occasionally the speaker expresses a fear that he has overstepped the bounds of good taste: "Let not my love be called idolatry, / Nor my belovèd as an idol show" (SON 105). Such "manners" probably came naturally to most would-be suitors—the Armados, Malvolios and Ague-cheeks always excepted.

Learning the tactics of avoiding betrayal or, more likely, living with it was a far greater challenge, for "Courts are never empty of fained friend-ship and secret snares and subtilties."[30] The court, as Iago implies (1.1.61-65), was no place to wear one's heart on one's sleeve. Philibert admonishes with his usual sarcasm, "Those that with open hart declare and shewe themselves not willing to use fraude [at court] are reputed ignorant" (100). The courtly world was thus one of extreme circumspection in letters, elaborate ciphers, codes, spying, intrigue—all part of the background against which the speaker courts the Young Man. "True souls" were not infrequently "impeached." and it behooved one to take precautions against the "suborned informer" (SON 125). Ben Jonson said of spies: "You are the lights of state, but of base stuff" (52), and Shakespeare's speaker even suggests that spies are part of the Young Man's "state": "Is it thy spirit that thou send'st from thee / So far from home into my deeds to pry, / To find out shames and idle hours in me . . . ?" (SON 61).

Betrayal was endemic at court. The question was therefore (as it seems to be in the Sonnets) principally one of how to reconcile oneself to betrayal and contain its costs. Sonnet 41 ("Those pretty wrongs that liberty com-mits"), first of the love-triangle sonnets, provides an apt paradigm of the betrayed courtier's tactics. Its argument is as follows: the young patron is a "tempting" object and naturally attracts many rivals, among them one's own friends; only a "sour" patron would decline to pay attention to suitors other than the speaker; still, the speaker registers his hurt. But the main assumption of the sonnet—that betrayal is natural under the social circumstances—reflects a stark reality of court life: the powerful enjoyed the "liberty" to commit "wrongs" against suitors.

The tactic of Sonnet 41 is sugared acceptance of the inevitable. A tactic born of further unhappy experience,and therefore more desperate, is the emotional blackmail of Sonnet 92: "But do thy worst to steal thyself away." The speaker is able to recover from this risky bluff—"I see a better state to me belongs / Than that which on thy humor doth depend"—only by figuratively putting his life at the Young Man's disposal. Perhaps the most common tactic for the courtier, if swallowing one's pride and gracefully suffering ignominious treatment can be called a tactic, is exemplified in Sonnet 93: "So shall I live, supposing thou art true, / Like a deceived husband—so love's face / May still seem love to me, though altered new: / Thy looks with me, thy heart in other place." How apt these lines are to the real life of the Renaissance courtier, who perforce spent much time following "the false heart's history . . . writ in moods and frowns and wrinkles strange" of the time's grandees. This sonnet's eloquent grasp of the duplicities inherent in patron-client transactions is finely paralleled by the deceived yet open-eyed lover of Sonnet 138: "O love's best habit is in seeming trust."

Stephen Booth describes Sonnet 138 as an "exercise in logically improbable, unnatural, and uncomfortable unions that are also indivisible" (477). His shrewd summary applies alike to suitors, poets, and their patrons. He draws attention (as do SON 93 and 138) to the central tactical ability called for at court, the ability to live with compromise. "Silly honesty" and "neat integrity" inhibit flexibility, and Donne therefore warned against bringing them to court. Instead, as Daniel Javitch has written, the courtier needed "elasticity" and the willingness to "accommodate himself to the [ruler's] changing and unpredictable whims." Javitch cites Castiglione to underline his assertion: "I would have our Courtier bend himself to this, even if by nature he is alien to it, so that his prince cannot see him without feeling that he must have something pleasant to say to him; which will come about if he has the good judgment to perceive what his prince likes, and the wit and prudence to bend himself to this, and the considered resolve to like what by nature he may possibly dislike."[31] Such bending occurs often in the Young Man sonnets and is nowhere more elaborately or self-consciously expressed than in Sonnet 35. This sonnet's speaker has abandoned neat integrity. Booth's summary remark— "Everything about the poem . . . suggests *civil war*" (192)—resonates loudly in the courtly context: for the intercourse between patron and suitor, courteous though it may have seemed on the surface, encompassed much psychological warfare comparable to that in Sonnet 35. And its couplet is a prophetic intimation of the suitor's usual doom, which was the deprivation of wealth, hope, self-respect, and time: "I an áccessary needs must be / To that sweet thief which sourly robs from me."

The grim fact that "love" was not rendered mutually in a patron-client relationship is made clear in the lines of Sonnet 72. The speaker has often, as in Sonnet 35, indulged in "some virtuous lie" to give the Young Man a grace he may not deserve. Now, imagining himself dead, he begs the Young Man not to sully himself by uttering false praise; that would be beneath his station. To those around him, though, the urge toward false praise is irresistible, for the patron could do no wrong. We see this in Sonnet 95 ("How sweet and lovely dost thou make the shame") and notably in Sonnet 96:

> Thou mak'st faults graces that to thee resort.
> As on the finger of thronèd queen
> The basest jewel will be well esteemed,
> So are those errors that in thee are seen,
> To truths translated, and for true things deemed.

Such was the effect of the "strength of state" on truth at court. We here confront Puttenham's figure of extenuation at its most impressive. The suitor's life was grounded in extenuation. No wonder he expended so much effort trying by desperate conceits, "blenches," and "worse essays" (SON 110) to prove his patron was his "best of love." Poets, of course, trod the same path. Richard Brathwait's assertion in his satire "To the Poet-asters" was thus not an unfair one: "Such be our ranke of Poets now adayes, / As they adorne th'Immerited with praise / Above desert." [32]

The suitor's stratagems designed to make a wished-for patron into a genuine one can be seen in the "alchemy" by which the speaker of Sonnet 114 transforms courtly "monsters" into "cherubins." And it is seen in the "potions" the speaker distills from "limbecks foul as hell" to make something "more strong, far greater" of his "ruined love" in Sonnet 119. No, it was not by truth, virtue, or honesty that one was likely to succeed or survive at court. It was the rare person who left its verge for the last time without saying, or at least thinking ruefully of his paradox-laden life: "I have looked on truth / Askance and strangely" (SON 110).

The suitor's most difficult tactical decision was, perhaps, when to give up. One might think this an easy decision for those who, like Cecil, "sorrowed in the bright lustre of a Court" (*Nugae Antiquae* 1:263). But it was not. Chamberlain wrote in 1614: "The King is now at Audley-end [Essex house of the Earl of Suffolk] where some alteration or creation of new officers is expected, but I perswade my self the issue wilbe as in other things and times before, but men must please themselves with hopes from place to place and time to time, and will not geve over theyre hold though it be but by a twine thred" (1: 502). Sooner or later, however, the thread had to be cut. The sun in its "golden pilgrimage" must finally set, just as men must age and political power bend with the remover to remove: "But when from highmost pitch, with weary car, / Like feeble age he reeleth from the day, / The eyes ('fore duteous) now converted are / From his low tract and look another way" (SON 7). One imagines that the thought of withdrawal was never far from the minds of suitors, especially those who were merely treading water. In Sonnet 87 the speaker expresses this thought to the Young Man explicitly for the first time: "Farewell, thou art too dear for my possessing." This sonnet, not coincidentally, is the first in the sequence that extensively confronts and verbalizes the inequality of the patron-client relationship. Its couplet is a pregnant one for this discussion of the poor suitor's wakening to court's baseless and insubstantial pageantry: "Thus have I had thee as a dream doth flatter: / In sleep a king, but waking no such matter."

The threat of withdrawal in Sonnet 87 is a tactical gambit, one that is repeated more daringly in Sonnet 92's "I see a better state to me belongs." The real crisis of confidence—the point at which the "queasy pain / Of being beloved, and loving" (Donne, 200) erupts into genuine disease— comes later, in Sonnets 100-105. It is tempting to see this crisis as induced by the experience of Sonnets 93-96, in which the speaker betrays how difficult (impossible, some readers believe) it is for him to integrate his mixed feelings about the Young Man. At any rate, this crisis of confidence reinforces our paradigm of a typical suitor's experience. In Sonnet 100 the suitor's inspiration or hope (that is, the poet's muse) has become "forgetful" and "resty." He senses a diffusion of his "fury" on "base subjects"; his time, he now feels, has been "idly spent." In Sonnet 101 the muse is not merely forgetful but "truant." The tone of this sonnet may be gentler than that of Jonson's "To My Muse," but it is similarly self-deprecatory. Unlike Jonson, though, the speaker assesses *himself,* rather than his patron, as worthless. Beneath the lines is a terrible recognition: the Young Man has no vital need for the suitor's services, namely, the poet's "color," "pencil," or "praise". That which the suitor can offer in Sonnet 102 ("rich esteeming") is positively harmful in its suggestion that the client's "love is merchandised". The seasonal imagery that follows in this sonnet introduces a dragging, entropic melancholy to the deliberation: "Our love *was* new." The blithe aphorism of long before—"every fair from fair sometimes declines" (SON 18)—returns to haunt the speaker. The couplet of Sonnet 102 addresses as well one of the suitor's worst fears: that, as the spring never does, he may overstay his welcome and bore his patron: "I sometime hold my tongue, / Because I would not dull you with my song."

Sonnet 103, cast in the plain style of many Renaissance envois to court, finds the speaker in his worst slough of despair. He feels he can bring nothing of "worth" to the patron-client transaction. The diction is keen: *bare, blunt, disgrace.* This prostration reminds one of Sonnet 29 ("When in disgrace with fortune and men's eyes"), but there is here no lark ascending, no exhilarating thought of the patron. Sonnet 104 records the passage of three years. It would be hard to guess at the average life span of a suitor at the English court, but one might safely say three years was enough to evaporate the "April perfumes" of a suitor's first sanguine arrival at court. The suitor's crisis reaches a climax, if not a resolution, in Sonnet 105. He feels the full weight of keeping himself "to constancy confined" and fears that his unvarying "argument" will appear to be mere idolatry. Even as he writes, eyes may be gazing at him, accusing him of pitiful thriving. More subtle—and relevant to Shakespeare's eventual devotion to the stage—is Sonnet 105's allusion to the tedium of the courtier's life, which had to be (or at least had to seem to be) confined to constant loyalty and readiness to serve. If one line in the Sonnets holds the key to Shakespeare's renunciation of the poet's name, I believe it is in Sonnet 105: "One thing expressing, leaves out difference." In hindsight, no author appears to have been less fit than Shakespeare to spend his invention expressing one thing and leaving out difference.

A plausible consequence of a suitor's crisis of confidence in his patron, his hopes, or his effort was ever more desperate, unpredictable behavior. The later Young Man sonnets follow this pattern. As the speaker relinquishes his hope of avoiding the suitor's usual fate ("forfeit to a cónfined doom . . . " SON 107), his rhetorical and emotional excursions become more daring. Apex (SON 107) and nadir (SON 108) stand side by side. The speaker successively assumes the poses of confessional self-flagellation (SON 110), self-doubting timorousness ("my strong infection" SON 111), extravagant bravado (SON 116), resentfulness (SON 117), or righteous anger (SON 121). And several phrases barely conceal his disease: "replete with you" (SON 113), the "poisoned" palate for the Young Man (SON 114), "sick of you" (SON 118), and "madding fever" (SON 119).

There is dangerous language, and several dangerous feints, in these last two-dozen Young Man poems. In Henry's time a suitor who spoke with such temerarious candor might have found himself in the Tower, but in his daughter's time the failed suitor's end was more likely to be in the vein of Sonnet 126, the last one addressed to the Young Man. There is no melodrama in this moving and graceful parting of the ways. The speaker's "quietus" is to render the Young Man back to that life in which, he now recognizes, he can no longer take a satisfying part, or from which he can no longer expect sufficient "recompence." Having spoken his final gentle warning, the speaker quietly takes his leave from the privy chamber and exits via one of the many gates opening into a teeming world elsewhere. In effect, the speaker is following the advice of Du Refuge in *A Treatise of the Court:* "It is farre more honourable to descend silently and peacefully by the staires and doore, then to stay till we are enforced out of window" (2: 188). It appears that Shakespeare himself took a similar sensible leave early in his London career.

Certain important psychological dimensions of the suitor's life are apparent in and between the lines of the Young Man sonnets. Principal among these is how the man of "public means" copes with the charisma of great power. It was an electric confrontation in a rigidly hierarchical primogenitary society, which conferred "proud titles" according to bloodlines rather than merit. And merit in the nobility, as the Princess mordantly observes in *Love's Labour's Lost,* was often rather ascribed than possessed. The speaker's salutatory opening lines in Sonnet 26 bear a touch of Armado's unction ("sole dominator of Navarre, my soul's earth's god . . . "), but they also express the mental posture of deference that charismatic power demanded: "Lord of my love, to whom in vassalage / Thy merit hath my duty strongly knit, / To thee I send this written ambassage, / To witness duty, not to show my wit." A celebrity like the Young Man, who is viewed by "the world's eye" (SON 69), is a powerful magnet for "love" of all kinds. For one thing, this love gives the poet-suitor of the Sonnets his great expressive energy, gives him Venus's aspiring "spirit all compact of fire." But awe of power can quickly transform to nerves when the powerful come near. Shakespeare casts such nervousness in terms of stage fright in Sonnet 23:

> As an unperfect actor on the stage,
> Who with his fear is put besides his part
> . . . .
> So I for fear to trust forget to say
> The perfect ceremony of love's rite,
> And in mine own love's strength seem to decay,
> O'ercharged with burthen of mine own love's might.

The playwright was to capture such anxiousness of the "meaner sort" in the "presence majestical" in the Nine Worthies pageant of *Love's Labour's Lost* and in the tedious, brief play in *A Midsummer Night's Dream*.

There is nothing comic, however, about the probing of the Young Man's charisma in the latter part of the sequence. Whence comes this power of favor (*charisma*'s Greek root = to show favor)? "What is your substance, whereof are you made, / That millions of strange shadows on you tend?" This rhetorical question that opens Sonnet 53 hangs like a pall over all that comes afterward. It is a question that must have been asked often (silently, of course) by those who danced attendance at a Renaissance court. Certainly it is a question that would occur to the tired speaker of Sonnet 66, who has beheld "desert a beggar born, / And needy nothing trimmed" in aristocratic "jollity." Sonnet 78 means to be complimentary, but in order for the conceit (the patron is the real creative "influence" on the verse) to work, the Young Man's lack of discrimination must be asserted: his charisma imparts grace both to "ignorance" and to "learning." Not only is the charismatic person himself undiscriminating here; he also ruins the powers of discrimination in those who come within his bewitching presence: "Some say thy fault is youth, some wantonness, / Some say thy grace is youth and gentle sport; / Both grace and faults are loved of more and less; / Thou mak'st faults graces that to thee resort" (SON 96). The charisma of power causes the sordid translation of "truths" into "errors." Awesome power imbued the great at court, as the speaker goes on to suggest in Sonnet 96, echoing that self-conscious wielder of this power, the Princess of France: "How many gazers mightst thou lead away, / If thou wouldst use the strength of all thy state!"

The diction of these two lines brings us to the two climactic anatomies of charisma residing under the canopy of state, Sonnets 124 ("If my dear love were but the child of state") and 125 ("Were't ought to me I bore the canopy"). The strength of state that induced "gazing" among the pitiful thrivers at court was ineluctable. There was no "if" about it: Everyone at a Renaissance court was a "child of state" and subject to the accidents of whim among the powerful. Elizabeth was supremely mercurial, and her chief peers surely aped her, if in less spectacular ways. The levy of power on the suitor was overwhelming, and no poems from the period convey his "sequent toil" more powerfully than Sonnets 124 and 125.

Coming to terms with the charisma of power was balanced by a corollary coming-to-terms with the devastation of self-worth. Jonson counted among the cardinal virtues at court *Storge*, or "allowable selfe-love" (4: 166), but very little overt self-love was allowable to a Renaissance suitor. Again, a kind of binary logic reigned: "I love another," wrote Wyatt in paraphrase of Petrarch, "And thus I hate myself" (80). The virtual absence of self-love is apparent in the Young Man sonnets. When the speaker ventures to admit that the "sin of self-love possesseth all mine eye" (SON 62), it is simply for conceit's and compliment's sakes. Sonnet 62's lavish mock confession of self-love and independence of spirit ("And for myself mine own worth do define") is finally subverted in the tenth line when the speaker looks at his "beated and chopped" face in the mirror. He concludes that "self so self-loving were iniquity" and in the couplet translates his error into flattering but literally cosmetic "truth": "'Tis thee, myself, that for myself I praise, / Painting my age with beauty of thy days." This repulsive poem's denial of self in order to render praise reminds one of the Princess's remark about those moments when, "for praise, an outward part, / We bend to that the working of the heart" (LLL 4.1.32-33). Although the Princess is thinking of seeking praise, the point applies as well to the bending heart of the flatterer in Sonnet 62.

Phrases conveying the bending of the heart stud the Young Man sonnets. In Sonnet 35, for instance, the speaker becomes an "accessary" to one who "sourly robs" from him and (most unimaginably to an Elizabethan) becomes a litigant against himself. A typical but more elaborate expression of self-devastation for the sake of praise occurs in Sonnet 40. While the ostensible subject may be the alleged love triangle, the sonnet also reflects on the exploitative uses to which patrons put suitors: "I cannot blame thee for my love thou usest; / But yet be blamed, if thou thyself deceivest / By wilful taste of what thyself refusest. / I do forgive thy robb'ry, gentle thief." Such was the suitor's frequent fate: to be left in "poverty" of spirit and means by the "sweet thief" of courtly aspiration. The tone and ultimate conceit of the poem are ingratiating. Donne, however, looked on essentially the same situation with more acerbity in his fifth satire (the reference to lust is pertinent to the Young Man's alleged behavior):

> All men are dust,
> How much worse are suitors, who to men's lust
> Are made preys. O worse than dust, or worm's meat,
> For they do eat you now, whose selves worms shall eat.
> They are the mills which grind you, yet you are
> The wind which drives them; and a wasteful war
> Is fought against you, and you fight it; they
> Adulterate law, and you prepare their way
> Like wittols [that is, cuckholds]; th'issue your own ruin is. [171]

Something like a self-awakening to the harsh truths Donne expresses here occurs in the later Young Man poems. In Sonnet 110 the suitor, "gored with [his] own thoughts," confesses that he has made a fool of himself and has "sold cheap what is most dear." This sonnet represents the crisis of a suitor confronting the reality of his self-humiliation and feeling the oppression of idolizing "a god in love, to whom I am confined." Certainly Sonnet 110's miserably lame couplet is unable to counter the first three quatrains' tremendous weight of resentment. In fact, Sonnet 110 is, in a fascinating way, a counterpart to Sonnet 129 ("Th'expense of spirit in a waste of shame"), the speaker confessing to the expense of his poetic fury in a waste of invention and false compare.

Subsequent sonnets move further toward Donne's satiric bluntness and indignation. The devastation of self-worth becomes self-poisoning in Sonnet 114, a blanketing artistic apologia in Sonnet 115 ("Those lines that I before have writ do lie"). Sonnets 117 through 121 are rent with awareness of self-inflicted psychological and moral wounds ("bitter sauces," "potions . . . of siren tears," "my transgressions," "my abuses"). Part of the ironic power of the rhetorical question in the second quatrain of Sonnet 125 is that it implicates the speaker himself: "Have I not seen dwellers on form and favor / Lose all and more by paying too much rent, / For compound sweet forgoing simple savor, / Pitiful thrivers, in their gazing spent?" The speaker has thrived pitifully too . . . in all those "sweet" compounds which *were* the early Young Man sonnets. Only toward the end of his suitor's life span does he come to recognize that these sonnets are becoming "eager compounds" (SON 118; Latin *aeger* = bitter).

The Renaissance court was filled with many "gazers" and a few true seers. King Lear makes this point in his sarcastic fury: "Get thee glass eyes, / And like a scurvy politician, seem / To see the things thou dost not" (4.6.170–72). The suitor begins to see through real rather than glass (that is, Petrarchan) eyes as, in the later Young Man sonnets, he begins to convalesce from "the distraction of this madding fever," which is courtly aspiration (SON 119). In the last three sonnets, the suitor is incapable of further gazing, but sees clearly what he has hitherto been unable to grasp, whether out of infatuation, genuine emotional engagement, "policy," or sanguine self-delusion. The fine irony, which I hope the present chapter has served to emphasize, is that Shakespeare was not so unperspicuous as his gazing persona when he wrote the Young Man sonnets. He was decidedly a *seeing* observer of the courtly economy of form and favor.

The final psychological challenge I will note here—the challenge to integrate deeply mixed feelings—derived inevitably from the suitor's subjection to the charisma of power and his consciousness of self-injury. As we observed in chapter 4, the Renaissance experience of courtly life, both fictional and historical, often found expression in equivocal figures such as the paradox and the oxymoron. To this can be added the figure *amphibole*, which Abraham Fraunce says occurs "when the sentence may be turned both ways, so that a man shall be uncertain what to take."[33] Court life was deeply affected by the figure *amphibole*, for the courtier was constantly pressed to "turn both ways." I can think of no poem from the English Renaissance that better captures this racking anxiety of not knowing which way to turn than a sonnet attributed to Wyatt:

> Driving to desire, adread also to dare,
> Between two stools my tail goeth to the ground.
> Dread and desire the reason doth confound,
> The tongue put to silence. The heart, in hope and fear,
> Doth dread that it dare and hide that would appear.
> Desirous and dreadful, at liberty I go bound.
> For pressing to proffer methinks I hear the sound:
> "Back off thy boldness. Thy courage passeth care."
> This dangerous doubt, whether to obey
> My dread or my desire, so sore doth me trouble
> That cause causeth for dread of my decay.
> In thought all one; in deeds to show me double,
> Fearful and faithful! Yet take me as I am,
> Though double in deeds, a inward perfect man.[34]

Donne gives a pithy and oxymoronic synopsis of this anguished poem in his comment on the court: "Suspicious boldness to this place belongs" (213). A conflicted mind such as that displayed by Wyatt is often apparent in the Sonnets.

In 1611 one John Seller published *A Sermon against halting betweene two opinions*. Shakespeare's poetry and plays—monuments, one might say, to the figure of *amphibole*—are supreme testimony that he was not of Seller's mind. Confronted with the "great contradiction and opposition of the worlde," Shakespeare seems to have been constitutionally unable to avoid halting between two (sometimes more) opinions when the book of nature or of society urged him to do so.[35] The Young Man sonnets, in particular, manifest Shakespeare's sensitivity to the contradictory feelings a lover, suitor, or poet might have for the object of his affection, or for himself. In this respect, a line from that sonnet which so thoroughly evokes mixed feelings may serve as a touchstone for the entire sequence: "Such civil war is in my love and hate" (SON 35). I have already drawn attention to much in the Sonnets that expresses the speaker's psychomachia. To underline the point, it is perhaps worth remembering all of the oxymoronic phrases that betray the coincidence of a suitor's love and hate: "beauteous niggard" and "unthrifty loveliness" (SON 4), "sweet thief" (SON 35, 99), "gentle thief" and "lascivious grace" (SON 40), "pretty wrongs" (SON 41), "loving offenders" (SON 42), "darkly bright" (SON 43), "thievish truth" (SON 48), "virtuous lie" and "niggard truth" (SON 72), then finally "pitiful thrivers" (SON 125). The difficulty of integrating mixed feelings can also be emphasized by returning for a moment to Sonnet 119, in which the speaker desperately tries one last time to reconcile his "wretched errors" and his "love." He attempts to resolve the octave of recrimination by resorting in the sestet to the ultimate oxymoronic concept of the *felix culpa:* "O benefit of ill, now I find true / That better is by evil still made better." Sonnet 119, one might say, is an oxymoron written large, and thus a formal image of the courtier's "civil war."

The same can be said of that most vexing and vexed sonnet of all, Sonnet 94 ("They that have pow'r to hurt, and will do none"), which so clearly halts between two opinions at the break between octave and sestet. Many critical observations about Sonnet 94 serve to nominate it as the archetypal expression of the courtier's hard task of integration. It is the capstone to G. Wilson Knight's "integration pattern," while Patrick Cruttwell sees it as betraying a personality experiencing "deep envy, a reluctant admiration, and a suppressed distaste." And Lever says that the sonnet "stands back from the group much as a contemplative soliloquy does from the dialogue of a play." [36] Such a view has caused some to point to another deeply conflicted courtier and his soliloquizing efforts at integration: "To be or not to be." Sonnet 94 is, of all the Sonnets, the most apt counterpart to the Wyatt poem quoted above: Both help to suggest, I think, what a next-to-impossible task it was for a Renaissance courtier to achieve a serene integrity. Both speakers are "desirous and dreadful," "fearful and faithful," at the same time. Resolving these mixed feelings into something approaching comfort was the great challenge. Both poems suggest that there was no easy way to meet it. Perhaps this is why L. C. Knights looked at Sonnet 94 and concluded, "This is the attitude . . . of *Measure for Measure.*" [37] That is, Shakespeare halting between two opinions, presenting rather than resolving the challenging dilemmas of human experience.

It remains, before leaving the Young Man sonnets, to comment on the importance in them of the art of dissembling—an art, we have seen, that courtly life encouraged one to refine. Elizabeth's personality, for instance, encouraged this art: "She did oft ask the ladies around hir chamber, If they lovede to thinke of marriage? And the wise ones did conceal well their liking thereto; as knowing the Queene's judgment in this matter" (Harington, *Letters*, 124). There is a lifetime of circumspection in Harington's careful description of his queen: "she *said* she loved us" (*Letters*, 125; emphasis added). It was hard to *know* anything at court. Anyone who, like Hamlet, professed to "know not 'seems'" would have felt greatly out of joint there.

Much of the more psychologically complex literature of the Renaissance derives from this courtly impetus toward concealment behind various masks and roles—what Hamlet calls "ambiguous giving out" (1.5.178). The Young Man poems rest fundamentally on the art of dissembling, just as the Dark Lady sonnets seem to rest on the impetus toward truth-telling directness. It was a rare courtier who would bluntly admonish his superiors as the speaker does the Dark Lady in Sonnet 139: "Use pow'r with pow'r, and slay me not with art." For "art," notes Philibert, was the decorum at court: "The semblances and apparaunces of all things cunningly couched are the principall supporters of oure [courtier's] Philosophie" (56). Nor would the courtier (or the speaker of the Young Man sonnets?) ever have dared to say aloud to his patron: "do not press / My tongue-tied patience with too much disdain" (SON 140). Such a warning was unthinkable, as was the aggressively heterodox "No, I am that I am" of Sonnet 121. Rather than appear as he was, the courtier was always urged in the direction of "ambiguous giving out."

The Young Man poems are a tour de force of dissembling. The speaker's boast in Sonnet 125 that his "oblation . . . knows no art" is easily the most stunning bit of "loud lying" in the entire sequence. Attention has already been drawn to instances of dissimulation, but an apt way of summarizing and concluding is to search in the Young Man sonnets for the various roles of that chameleonic role-player identified in chapter 4, the poet-at-court. Virtually all of the roles are discernible.

First, the *false suitor*. Samuel Daniel wrote that "Love hath few Saints, but many confessors," and the lover of the Young Man is no saint. He, like most courtly lovers, has ulterior motives. We have already identified many of these motives, but they can also be discerned in the thoroughly "merchandised" commercial, fiduciary, and legal imagery of the Sonnets. The speaker is, to borrow again from Daniel, guilty of many "mercynary lines."[38] Many phrases suggest that the speaker's view of the Young Man as his "treasure" is not entirely figurative:

> plead for love and *look for recompense*
> thy sweet love rememb'red *such wealth brings*

> while I think on thee, dear friend,
> *All losses are restored*
> my love engrafted *to this store*
> I *in thy abundance* am sufficed

The *poet-as-stylist* is much in evidence, especially in the earlier sonnets. He has his fine moments: Sonnet 18 has the grace and polish of Berowne at his best. But he has his dismal moments as well: Sonnet 24 is nearly as bad as those intentionaly ghastly poems composed by the men in *Love's Labour's Lost*. At times this stylist labors hollowly for invention (SON 52 and 68, to name but two) or feels himself in a rut (SON 76). Sonnet 35, though, best displays the poet-as-stylist, for he was in real life but an "accessary" at the luxurious pageant. So, as the Young Man sonnets progress, the pleasantry and delight of being a courtly stylist begin to wane, and the poet gradually devolves from a Berowne into a Boyet. As in Sonnet 96, where the speaker, esteeming "base jewels," begins looking more abjectly askance at truth.

The *jester-fool* is the speaker's least successful role. Some of his humor, like Armado's, was not intended, as he ruefully admits in Sonnet 110: "Alas, 'tis true, I have gone here and there, / And made myself a motley to the view." This is because, being so manifestly an enthusiastic participant in the social economy, he cannot attain to the usual Shakespearean clown's detachment from the comic scene presented to him. Nor is the speaker "licenced" with the intellectual or social freedom to stand apart, and so cannot achieve the ironic perspective necessary for satisfying foolery. Quite the contrary, he is to "constancy confined." He wants to be a Kent or, failing that, a Horatio; he can therefore never be a Fool.

The role of *entertaining cohort* is also sometimes assumed by the speaker, notably in the witty, punning, male-bonding humor (worthy of Mercutio) of Sonnet 20 ("A woman's face with nature's own hand painted"). The entertainer is also suggested in both the high-wrought conceit of Sonnet 46 ("Mine eyes and heart are at a mortal war") and the impressive variation on *tempus edax rerum* in Sonnet 55 ("Not marble nor the gilded monuments"). But, as with the jester, real success in the role of witty companion can come only with more freedom of spirit and casual flippancy than the speaker of the Young Man sonnets can muster. Perhaps as a result, the most purely comedic Shakespearean sonnets are found in the Dark Lady sequence (SON 128, 130, 135, and 143).

The presence of the *poet-as-upstart* requires no further elaboration. In Sonnet 111 the speaker confesses his humble origins. He presents himself as hitherto chid by the "guilty goddess" fortune, elsewhere as "made lame by fortune's dearest spite" (SON 37). He is poor in hope (SON 29), and his "poverty" is consistently counterpoised with the Young Man's "treasure." Sonnet 23, we have noted, presents the speaker—among such company as Armado and Aguecheek—as a neophyte on the court's stage.

As in Shakespeare's plays, the role of *poet-as-satirist* in the Sonnets is the most intriguing. There are but slight hints of him in the first two-thirds of them, however: in the subversion of Petrarchism in Sonnet 21 ("So is it not with me as with that muse") and in Sonnet 66 ("Tir'd with all these, for restful death I cry"), which summarizes with Jaques' world-weary tone the agenda of Renaissance satire. But the tone of 66 is genteel; genuine *saeva indignatio* of the Juvenalian sort does not appear until after the collapse of the speaker's efforts at integration in Sonnet 94. With this pivotal sonnet a seemingly involuntary urge toward ostracism grows ever more powerful. One can almost sense the removal of velvet gloves and the appearance of the satirist's mailed fist in Sonnet 95 ("How sweet and lovely dost thou make the shame") and in Sonnet 96 ("Some say thy fault is youth, some wantonness"), as the speaker pursues his anatomy of corrupting flattery at court. In Sonnet 100 the poet announces he will write a "satire to decay," should time mar the Young Man's face, but this sonnet, we have observed, is in fact a satire on the decay of his own muse. In subsequent sonnets we sense the speaker moving, as the satirist-at-court was always compelled to do, further and further to the side of the stage. He turns a harsher eye on himself and on court life in general (especially in SON 110, 117, 118, 119), finally bowing from the stage altogether in Sonnets 124 and 125.

The most compelling of the speaker's performances as a satirist is the bitter Sonnet 121 ("'Tis better to be vile than vile esteemed"). If Sonnet 94 is the Hamlet sonnet, this is surely the Coriolanus sonnet, its "No, I am that I am" echoing the proud Roman's "Rather say, I play / The man I am" (3.2.15-16). I suggested in the preceding chapter that Coriolanus represents the satirist who banishes himself from the social stage, and this is precisely what a courtier would be doing were he to speak in the tone and language of Sonnet 121. He would be bidden to leave and return with better music. Castiglione warned the courtier not to "contrarie every man spitefully without respect" (107). But Coriolanus and the speaker of Sonnet 121 do just that. In Sonnet 121 the speaker turns away from the world of politic ingratiation and the "ruined love" (SON 119) it bequeaths him, just as Coriolanus turns his back on the "falling fabric" of Rome.

❦

The anarchic impulses of Coriolanus and the speaker of the later Young Man sonnets recall Arthur Mizener's observation that, in the "soft focus" of its figurative language, Shakespeare's poetry is "always wantoning on the verge of anarchy."[39] Perhaps Mizener's phrasing can help us speculate in another way about Shakespeare's early exit from the arena of rival courting poets. For there are many pressures toward anarchy in the Sonnets: pressures against the decorum of "false-fac'd soothing" that Coriolanus associates with "courts and cities"; against the unambiguous, "hard focus" clarity of denotation; against the laborious constraints of the evaporating fashion of sonneteering; and against the "idolatry" of addressing to a powerful aristocrat poem after poem confined to variations on "Fair, kind, and true." These sonnets are in many ways, to use a Shavian epithet, unpleasant. They are freighted with discomforting awarenesses that make it easy to imagine why their author might eventually choose to leave what Drayton termed the "nice and Narrow way of Verse" to seek a writer's world elsewhere.[40]

Such a choice faced all Renaissance poets, though not all summoned the nerve to make it. Daniel wrote in *Delia* Sonnet 48, boasting: "No no my verse respects nor Thames nor Theaters, / Nor seekes it to be knowne unto the Great." But of course it was Daniel's decision to be known to the great, especially Queen Anne, whom he served for years. He led a sheltered courtly life, and for many critics this is explanation enough for his dull stuff.[41] In the same sonnet, Daniel speaks of "myne unambitious Muse," which it truly was. Shakespeare's muse, like his speaker's, appears to have been more "resty" and inclined to strain the reins to tautness. This muse, it appears, led Shakespeare to make the one choice Daniel specifies that forced him (Coriolanus-like) outside the walls of city, court, and legal jurisdiction. Shakespeare, in Daniel's words, chose finally to respect in his verse the "Theaters," declining at the same time either to respect the "Thames" and become a city poet or to seek to be known "unto the Great" and ratify himself as a courtly denizen. The more spectacular ambition, then, was not Daniel's to be a close "accessary" to the powerful, but Shakespeare's to free himself of a poet's name. He chose to avoid the path trod by the ingratiating and tedious Daniel—whom Edmund Gosse called "a Polonius among poets"—and chose instead the path of a Coriolanus, banishing himself to the South Bank (in the "liberty" outside the city walls) where he could contemplate, and continue describing, the "acclamations hyperbolical," "praises sauc'd with lies" and "smiles of knaves" of the other bankside from a distancing perspective.[42]

The instincts of the speaker of the later Young Man sonnets are those of a Coriolanus; for all their superficial dialogue of compliment, they also betray a distinct "lack of stooping" (COR 5.6.28). These sonnets also exude a tense pressure against the constraints of decorum, as when Coriolanus chides with heavy sarcasm: "What custom wills, in all things should we do't, / The dust on antique time would lie unswept, / And mountainous error be too highly heap'd / For truth to o'erpeer" (2.3.117-21). Custom called Shakespeare, at his career's inception, to the vocation of courting poet, then so heavily dusted by "antique time." I hope the preceding discussion has revealed in his Sonnets some intimations that Shakespeare was beginning to recognize that, if he was not himself a Coriolanus, he did have a character like Coriolanus within his creative powers. The truths Shakespeare observed did indeed o'erpeer the nice and narrow way of verse. This narrow way was not for a writer whose greatest dramatic achievements were to be, in their various ways, as Aufidius says of Coriolanus, "rough, unswayable and free." He therefore sought elsewhere a world—imaginative *worlds*—unconfined to courtierly constancy.

Statues and Breathers

The court is like an edifice of marble; I mean it is
composed of men who are very hard, but very polished.
—La Bruyère

OVER a generation ago allegorical interpretations of *Antony and Cleopatra*
were in fashion, the Roman-Alexandrian axis representing to different
critical eyes the conflict between Reason and Intuition, the World and the
Flesh, or Power and Love.[1] By way of concluding this exploration of the
Renaissance poet's life in Shakespeare's works and reiterating my speculations about his transformation from a "profest" into a "scenicke" poet, I
would like to suggest another allegorical approach to the play. This will
require us to look at *Antony and Cleopatra*, for the moment, with a view to its
potent and enlivening anachronism.

It is not the only Shakespearean play whose profound contempo-
raneity is worthy of notice. *Julius Caesar* rests fundamentally on the arrogance and treacheries of Elizabethan political life. *A Midsummer Night's
Dream* gives us a fair sense of the period's kersey- and lace-collar styles of
living. The two parts of *Henry IV* splendidly capture the ambiance of life in
the Elizabethan royal palace, tavern, and Gloucestershire countryside.
And *Timon of Athens* glosses much of what we learn from Lawrence Stone's
Crisis of the Aristocracy. But *Antony and Cleopatra* is the play that can most
aptly help me to speculate in a last, admittedly impressionistic, way why
Shakespeare may have retired from the professional courting poet's re-
gimen to that of the tiring-house and stage. Consider, then, that Rome and
Alexandria represent, respectively, aristocratic London (the corridors of
power and venues of public pomp) and the city's disreputable Liberties. For
example, the Clink Liberty, where the Globe Theater stood and where
Shakespeare was eventually to make his name and fortune. In other words,
consider that an ambitious young writer tired of the elaborate obliqueness
and uncertain rewards of following in trains of the powerful at Whitehall or
Westminster—and enticed by the entrepreneurial possibilities of the Bankside—might well have thought to himself, "I' th' East my pleasure lies."

It is difficult to imagine the members of an audience at a performance of *Antony and Cleopatra* in the Globe Theater failing to sense that, by their very presence on the Bankside, they had cast their lot for the "pleasure," "mirth," and "voluptuousness" of Shakespeare's Alexandria. By journeying into one of the notorious "Suburbs without the Walles," the audience displayed its desire to escape, if only temporarily, from the decorous, customary, and legal restraints of City and Court which, we shall observe, are elaborately shadowed in the play's Roman scenes.[2] Rome is the locus of "office and devotion" (1.1.5), "imperious show" (4.15.23), "studied" thought (2.2.137), and "graver business" (2.7.120). Rome is where the political stakes are high, where the few great power holders bask as cynosures of vulgar attention, and where mercurial shifts of "scrupulous faction" (1.3.48) never cease. Rome is also where "cunning" (3.2.31), cool forensics, expedience, and the "ostentation" of love (3.6.52) rather than love itself are all *de rigueur*.

This, as contemporary witnesses and subsequent historians have unanimously shown us, is the world of the English Renaissance courtier. It must have registered in a Globe audience, if only subliminally, that the "high Roman fashion" (4.15.87) was very much the high Tudor and Stuart fashion. Shakespeare makes virtually no effort either to "Romanize" his diction or mask a decidedly anachronistic projection of styles of government. This diction is more akin to what we find in modern studies of English Renaissance political and legal economy than to Roman history. We hear, for instance, of *authority, mandate, power, name, presence, honor, faction, dismission, scutcheon, lieutenancy, lordliness,* and *train* (that is, entourage). Only once, with *lictors* (5.2.214), does Shakespeare indulge in an authentic epithet, and, while Caesar, Antony, and Lepidus are triumvirs, the word never occurs in the play (though *triumpherate,* suggesting a false etymology, occurs at 2.6.28). Nor is there a single legal or commercial epithet that a Globe audience would have considered exotic: *business, petition, process* (that is, summons), *bond, article, oath, property, taints, tributaries, revenue, deputation.* Shakespeare's imaginary Rome, in short, greatly resembles the real-life London of serious, solemn "business" hours and *gravitas,* where the wisest measure was "narrow" (3.4.8) and where straightness and order reigned. Antony's imagery is apt when he promises his new Roman wife, "I have not kept my square, but that to come / Shall all be done by th' rule" (2.3.6-7).

Conversely, Shakespeare's Alexandria is cast in terms that would make a Bankside audience feel completely at home. It evokes that part of London where "gaudy night" (3.13.182) was its gaudiest, where *levitas* and "private stomaching" (2.2.9) reigned. Caesar captures the posture of a proper City father disgusted at the enticements of the Bankside when he says, "our graver business / Frowns at this levity" (2.7.120-21).[3] It was also a masterstroke to introduce us to Alexandria through the appalled eyes of the Roman Philo (1.1.1-10), who sounds like nothing so much as a City father damning errant apprentices, fops, or roaring boys for frequenting the stews, bear-baitings, taverns, and theaters of the Liberties. Indeed, one is tempted to think that Shakespeare depended more on the traditional libertinism of Southwark than on Plutarch for the sense of "rioting" and "surfeits" that his Egyptian scenes convey. As David Johnson observes in *Southwark and the City*, the Bankside was for a very long time known for its "loose manorial local government," its "cosmopolitan character," and its "concentration of men and women of uncertain social status and even more dubious morals." Stow underscores this reputation in his *Annales* when he lists among Southwark's "houses most notable" the Tabard ("an Hosterie, or Inne"), "the Stewes," and the "Beare-Gardens," in addition to no fewer than five prisons. Stow later observes that "the *Bordello*, or Stewes," are "for the repaire of incontinent men to the like women."[4]

Antony and Cleopatra, the most famously incontinent pair of the English-speaking stage, take part of their identity from this low caste. Respectively, they are heroic avatars of the marauding courtier who has ferried over from Whitehall Steps or the Strand and of the Bankside prostitute who beckons him eastward to "lascivious wassails" (1.4.56). Their Alexandria is a seamless blend of Bankside tavern and whorehouse. John Earle says of "A Taverne" in his *Micro-cosmographie* (1628) that "It is the Torrid Zone" (Dv) and "the idle mans businesse" (D2v): Cleopatra and her city are Antony's torrid zone, just as idleness is his Alexandrian business. "Ten thousand harms," he admits, "My idleness doth hatch" (1.2.129-30), and he famously calls Cleopatra "idleness itself" (1.3.93). The carousal aboard Pompey's galley off the coast of Naples is a thinly disguised tavern scene, perhaps the most boisterous Shakespeare ever wrote. "Fill till the cup be hid," cries Pompey there. (2.7.87). And some of the later interviews between the lovers are punctuated with commands worthy of Sir Toby Belch or Falstaff and perfectly suitable to the Garter or the Boar's Head:

> Some wine, within there, and our viands! [3.11.73]
>
> Fill our bowls once more;
> Let's mock the midnight bell. [3.13.183-84]
>
> Let's to-night
> Be bounteous at our meal. [4.2.8-9]
>
> Well, my good fellows, wait on me tonight.
> Scant not my cups. [4.2.20-21]

> Let's to supper come,
> And drown consideration. [4.2.44-45]

Egypt is the land of "bacchanals," where wine rather than soldiery is "conquering" and the real monarch is the "monarch of the vine" (2.7.104, 113).

Our Globe audience would also have quickly associated Cleopatra with denizens of the stews that prospered in the vicinity. Cleopatra, as she accurately observes, is susceptible to judgment in "the posture of a whore" (5.2.221), and she is called this by both Caesar (3.6.67) and Antony (4.12.13). Elsewhere she is a strumpet (1.1.13) and a trull (3.6.95). Shakespeare must have expected that not only Plutarch's Cleopatra but also the prostitutes of Southwark would contribute to his heroine's infinite, titillating variety . . . and provide his audience with an agreeable shock of recognition. For in Renaissance London, as Steven Mullaney concludes, "brothel and playhouse [were] indissolubly linked in the cultural imagination, making the two virtually synonymous."[5]

Finally, the Globe Theater's very marginality to the solemn business of Court and City is shadowed in the Alexandrian courtship of the noble general and the foreign queen, whose thespian identity and abilities are reiterated often in the play. Just a few years after Burbage built London's first theater, the preacher John Stockwood railed against men who would build such "Houses" on purpose in the Liberties, "as who woulde say, 'There, let them [that is, the City's governors] saye what they will say, we will play.'"[6] Situated likewise on the margins of the Roman empire, Antony and Cleopatra act on this same motto of recreational contempt for the higher values of the polity. Say what Caesar will, they will play.

Early in the play, the Bankside world of surfeiting on sex, food, drink, and entertainment is caught by Caesar when he chides Lepidus for indulging Antony's behavior:

> Let's grant it is not
> Amiss to tumble on the bed of Ptolomy,
> To give a kingdom for a mirth, to sit
> And keep the turn of tippling with a slave,
> To reel the streets at noon, and stand the buffet
> With knaves that smells of sweat. [1.4.16-21]

Which is to say, behave as if one were on a Bankside debauch. And Cleopatra, imagining the treatment she will receive if taken alive to Rome, strikes precisely the City attitude toward, and ballad-mongers' sensational exploitation of, Southwark prostitutes: "Nay, 'tis most certain, Iras. Saucy lictors / Will catch at us like strumpets, and scald rhymers / Ballad 's out a' tune" (5.2.214-16).

Antony and Cleopatra allegorizes the tense, indissoluble complementarity that existed between the high- and low-life environs of London divided by the Thames. West and north of Southwark lay the London of "office" and "business," where "firm security" (3.7.48) waited to be won by traditional commercial and political means. Those who believed, in Coriolanus's derisive words, that "what custom wills, in all things should we do't" (2.3.118) became the powerful within the walls—whether of royal palace, Parliament, Guildhall, or the City itself. Those who, like Coriolanus himself, rejected "aged custom" and found the bonds of duty and propriety oppressive were drawn inevitably to the liberty, not to say license, of the Liberties. Not "firm security" but "present pleasure" (1.4.32) was to be found there . . . and found by means of "chance and hazard" (3.7.47). The tension between Rome and Alexandria occurs in any great metropolis. "High order" and "great solemnity" (5.2.366) will always rest tantalizingly, nervously side by side with "rioting" and "vacancy." The distance between Rome and Alexandria is thus in one sense very short—as short as the width of the Thames or the distance between New York City's Park Avenue and Forty-second Street or London's Belgrave and Leicester squares.

This dialectic can be expressed in a final way that will draw us to the present purpose of this brief excursion. Cleopatra inquires how Antony's new wife, Octavia, comports herself, and the messenger replies: "She creeps; / Her motion and her station are as one; / She shows a body rather than a life, / A statue, than a breather" (3.3.18-21). The comparison is invidious but, as our experience of Octavia verifies, accurate. The statuesque Octavia ideally embodies all of the conventional values, as Maecenas (a Roman, of course) observes: "If beauty, wisdom, modesty, can settle / The heart of Antony, Octavia is / A blessed lottery" (2.2.240-42). But all of this—and let us add poise, dutifulness, and sincerity to the list—stales in contrast to Cleopatra's infinite if also dangerous variety. Octavia is at best a Micaëla to the Egyptian queen's Carmen.

This distinction between statues and breathers runs through the entire Shakespearean dramatis personae, and it is telling how often the notable "statues" also appear to be the most impressively (or oppressively) socialized: Malvolio, John of Lancaster, Bullingbrook, the Lord Chief Justice, Theseus, Polonius, Volumnia, Jaques (the ultimate in cynical civility), and even, I would venture, Prince Hal. The notable "breathers" are just as frequently the ostracized, the self-exiled, or, at least, the unbecomingly or daringly outspoken: Petruchio, Juliet's Nurse, Mercutio, Bottom, Quickly, Falstaff, Emilia, Kent, Alcibiades, Coriolanus, and Paulina.

The distinction between statues and breathers resonates historically, too. Westminster, Whitehall, the great houses along the Strand, the Guildhall, and the Inns of Court—these were the venues for circumspection, concealment, masking reticence, and indirection. These were the venues, in short, for showing a body rather than a life, as the portraiture of Holbein or of the artists gathered in Roy Strong's *English Icon: Elizabethan and Jacobean Portraiture* might serve overwhelmingly to suggest. Aristocratic and affluent London was, too, quite literally the venue for London statuary, which in Shakespeare's time was almost entirely confined to expensive funeral monuments. There is, thus, a sharp contemporary bite to the messenger's distinction: a mortuary lifelessness in Octavia is contrasted with Cleopatra's vitality.

If Holbein or the anonymous monumental sculptor brings us the typical representation of London's "statues," then the style of, say, Frans Hals is surely most apt to the "private stomaching" of London's "breathers." Holbein might have done much justice to Shakespeare's great concealing, or "masked," characters such as Hamlet, Hal, or Iago, but only a Hals could one imagine rising to the challenge of such sitters as Falstaff, Quickly, Bardloph, Doll Tearsheet, Pistol, Peto, or Poins—that band of "irregular humorists" who epitomize the Bankside's clientele. The Bankside was where "breathers" congregated or where erstwhile "statues" ventured in order to aspirate more freely. This was where one might go, after dark, simply to people-watch. Alexandria, Antony tells us, is also such a place: "All alone, / To-night we'll wander through the streets, and note / The qualities of people" (1.1.52-54).

By now the reader may have guessed at the speculative leap for which I have been preparing. The professional soldier and the professional poet have much in common. The noble general who turns the "office and devotion" of his eyes from the high Roman fashion shadows the poet who, early in his London writing career, turned his eyes from the high aureate fashion of sonnets, epyllions, and *amour courtois* custom to become—on the Bankside—the supreme theatrical observer of "the qualities of people." Antony, let us imagine for a moment, is Shakespeare.

Antony and Cleopatra is perhaps the last and most poignant of Shakespeare's shadowed renunciations of the courting poet's life . . . a life that, as Puttenham suggests, is ultimately one of putting a high marmoreal gloss on one's statuesque creations. Puttenham, in his *Arte*, describes the

"Gorgious," which is the "principall figure of our poetical Ornament": "For the glorious lustre it setteth upon our speech and language, the Greeks call it *Exargasia* [and] the Latine *Expolitio*, a terme transferred from these polishers of marble or porphirite, who after it is rough hewen and reduced to that fashion they will, set upon it a goodly glasse, so smooth and cleere, as ye may see your face in it" (3:20). Being an artist notably uninterested in, or soon tired of, seeing his own face in his creations, Shakespeare turned away from the richly narcissistic and self-advertising impositions of the courting poet's life. He appears to have relinquished the "smooth and cleere" deployment of his poetic power (unlike Jonson, he did not value it as "neat and clean") in favor of the more rough-hewn authorial challenges of the stage. He relinquished the obligation to set a gloss on the London world's Octaviuses, for whom his works betray such a keen distaste.

Shakespeare gave up, in other words, the marmoreal world of *The Rape of Lucrece*—Lucrece and and Octavia are hewn from similar blocks!—in favor of the infinite variety of such breathers as Cleopatra, who becomes "marble-constant" (5.2.240) only at her highly theatrical end. This infinite variety was too great for Drayton's "nice and Narrow way of Verse." Cleopatra's story required the liberty, the "witchcraft" of the stage; it also required the Liberty. Shakespeare forces this recognition on us when he has Cleopatra utter one of his typically reflexive speeches. Here she predicts the condescension with which she will be treated in Rome, and the picture she imagines reflects precisely what a Globe audience would experience at a performance of *Antony and Cleopatra*:

> The quick comedians
> Extemporally will stage us, and present
> Our Alexandrian revels: Antony
> Shall be brought drunken forth, and I shall see
> Some squeaking Cleopatra boy my greatness
> I' th' posture of a whore. [5.2.216-21][7]

Shakespeare, as I have several times suggested in the preceding chapters, appears to have left the arena of fashionable poets for that of "quick comedians," thinking (whether as he stood in the streets outside Whitehall, in the Strand, or in an outer chamber of Southampton House in Holborn?) that his professional pleasure and profit might lie in the east. It is possible, too, that his acquaintances, aware of the decision he was contemplating and still taken by his "mellifluous & hony-tongued" poetic voice, may have lectured him as Enobarbus lectures Antony for his subjection to Cleopatra:

[You] leave unexecuted
Your own renowned knowledge, quite forgo
The way which promises assurance, and
Give up yourself merely to chance and hazard,
From firm security. [3.7.44-48]

To which Shakespeare could have responded with the Retort Curt: the antechambers of the powerful are filled with eager, frustrated wishers, and wishers are ever fools. Or the Retort Cynical: since when did "smiling pomp" offer obsequious authors firm security? Or the Retort Philosophical: firm security at Court may not "promise assurance" to artists of true genius (and then he might have pointed to the example of Daniel, who had a tedious *Cleopatra* to his credit). The paradox, of course, is that we can see from hindsight that, by casting his lot with the theatrical profession, Shakespeare was escaping from a literary world of chance and hazard and assuring himself a secure retirement to Stratford.[8] One need merely contrast the declining years of Shakespeare with those of Jonson, who never relaxed his grasp on the hopes of climb-fall court, to appreciate the wisdom of Shakespeare's choice.

The professed poet sought a world elsewhere. It would be folly to suggest either that he did so without profoundly mixed feelings or that the world of the theater was a carefree one. Doubtless, on many occasions Shakespeare must have felt about Thalia, Melpomene, or Clio much as Antony does about Cleopatra: "Would that I had never seen her!" However, Enobarbus's shrewd and eloquent rejoinder applies not only to Cleopatra but to all the hitherto undiscovered theatrical countries Shakespeare would explore after leaving behind the title *poet:* "O, sir, you had then left unseen a wonderful piece of work, which not to have been blest withal would have discredited your travel" (1.2.152-55).

Exemplary Front Matter

For discussion of these dedications, see pages 87-88.

A. John Hind, *The most excellent historie of Lysimachus and Varrona* (1604)

TO THE RIGHT
Honourable *Henry Wriothesly*, Earle of
Southampton, and Baron of *Titchfield:*
J.H. *wisheth encrease of all vertuous*
and Honourable resolutions.

Report (Right Honourable) that hath enobled your singular, and manifold vertues, by nature and fortune, to the Worldes recommendation, hath induced mee, to thrust into the open light this my abortive issue, to be shrowded under the shadowe of your Lordships winges, the fruite of some idle houres, sith after many thoughts I could not excogitate any more pleasing recreation, whereon I might bestow times of leysure. The argument, I confesse, is of too base consequence to procure your liking, or deserve your allowing. Neverthelesse the force of dutie, and zeale, possessing the chiefest portion of mine interests, overrule my thoughts and resolutions, in hazarding the entertainment thereof, at your favourable courtesie, and construction. And if I may perceive that your Lordship affoords the countenance, to grace my papers with the demonstration of the extreamest degree of good liking, I shall be emboldned to raise my Muses note, that now yeelds harsh musick, to an higher key, a fairer fruite, of my better ordered vacant houres, and manifest my dutie to your Honour, in some matter of greater import, then a superficiall toy. But fearing to grow offensive through tediousness, I commit this simple work to your Lordships patronage, and your Honour to the Almighties protection: for the preservation of which, I will pray continually. I ende

> *Your Lordships most firmely devoted*
> *in all serviceable endevours.*
> J.H.

B. Thomas Dekker, *The Wonderfull Yeare* (1603)

To the Reader

And why to the *Reader?* Oh good Sir! theres as sound law to make you give good words to the *Reader,* as to a *Constable* when hee carries his watch about him to tell how the night goes, tho (perhaps) the one (oftentimes) may be served in for a *Goose,* and the other very fitly furnish the same messe: Yet to maintaine the scurvy fashion, and to keep *Custome* in reparations, he must be honyed, and come-over with *Gentle Reader, Courteous Reader,* and *Learned Reader,* though he have no more *Gentilitie* in him than *Adam* had (that was but a gardner), no more *Civility* than a *Tartar,* and no more *Learning* than the most errand *Stinkard,* that (except his owne name) could never finde any thing in the Horne-book.

How notoriously therefore good wits dishonor, not only their *Calling,* but even their *Creation,* that worship *Glow-wormes* (in stead of the *Sun*) because of a litle false glistering? In the name of *Phoebus* what madnesse leades them unto it? For he that dares hazard a pressing to death (thats to say, *To be a man in print*) must make account that he shall stand (like the olde Weathercock over Powles steeple) to be beaten with all stormes. Neither the stinking Tabacco-breath of a *Sattin- gull,* the *Aconited* sting of a narrow-eyde *Critick,* the faces of a phantastick Stage-monkey, nor the *Indeede-la* of a Puritanicall Citizen, must once shake him. No, but desperately resolve (like a French Post) to ride through thick & thin: indure to see his lines torne pittifully on the rack: suffer his Muse to take the *Bastoone,* yea the very stab, & himselfe like a new stake to be a marke for every *Hagler,* and therefore (setting up all these rests) why shuld he regard what fooles bolt is shot at him? Besides, if that which he presents upon the Stage of the world be *Good,* why should he basely cry out (with that old poeticall mad-cap in his *Amphitruo*) *Ionis summi causa clare plaudite,* beg a *Plaudite* for God-sake! If *Bad,* who (but an Asse) would intreate (as Players do in a cogging *Epilogue* at the end of a filthie Comedy) that, be it never such wicked stuffe, they would forbeare to hisse, or to dam it perpetually to lye on a Stationers stall. For he that can so cosen himselfe, as to pocket up praise in that silly sort, makes his braines fat with his owne folly.

But *Hinc Pudor!* or rather *Hinc Dolor,* heeres that Divell! It is not the ratling of all this former haile-shot, that can terrifie our *Band* of *Castalian Pen-men* from entring into the field: no, no, the murdring Artillery indeede lyes in the roaring mouthes of a company that looke big as if they were the sole and singular *Commanders* over the maine Army of *Poesy,* yet (if *Hermes* muster-booke were searcht over) theile be found to be most pitifull pure fresh-water souldiers: they give out, that they are heires-apparent to *Helicon,* but an easy *Herald* may make them meere yonger brothers, or (to say troth) not so much. Beare witnes all you whose wits make you able to be witnesses in this cause, that here I meddle not with your good Poets, *Nam tales, nusquam sunt hinc amplius,* If you should rake hell, or (as *Aristophanes* in his Frog sayes) in any Celler deeper than hell, it is hard to finde Spirits of that *Fashion.* But those Goblins whom I now am conjuring up, have bladder-cheekes puft out like a *Swizzers* breeches (yet beeing prickt, there comes out nothing but wind) thin-headed fellowes that live upon the scraps of invention, and travell with such vagrant soules, and so like Ghosts in white sheetes of paper, that the Statute of Rogues may worthily be sued upon them, because their wits have no abiding place, and yet wander without a passe-port. Alas, poore wenches (the nine Muses!) how much are you wronged, to have such a number of Bastards lying upon your hands? But turne them out a begging; or if you cannot be rid of their Riming company (as I thinke it will be very hard) then lay your heavie and immortall curse upon them, that whatsoever they weave (in motley-loome of their rustie pates) may like a beggars cloake, be full of stolne patches, and yet never a patch like one another, that it may be such true lamentable stuffe, that any honest

Christian may be sory to see it. Banish these *Word-pirates* (you sacred mistresses of learning) into the gulfe of *Barbarisme:* doom them everlastingly to live among dunces: let them not once lick their lips at the *Thespian* bowle, but onely be glad (and thanke *Apollo* for it too) if hereafter (as hitherto they have alwayes) they may quench their poeticall thirst with small beere. Or if they will needes be stealing your *Heliconian Nectar,* let them (like the dogs of *Nylus*) onely lap and away. For this *Goatish* swarme are those (that where for these many thousand yeares you went for pure maides) have taken away your good names, these are they that deflowre your beauties. These are those ranck-riders of Art, that have so spur-gald your lustie wingd *Pegasus,* that now he begins to be out of flesh, and (even only for provander sake) is glad to shew tricks like *Bancks* his Curtall. O you Booke-sellers (that are Factors to the Liberall Sciences) over whose Stalles these Drones do dayly flye humming; let *Homer, Hesiod, Euripides,* and some other mad Greekes with a band of Latines, lye like musketshot in their way, when these Gothes and Getes set upon you in your paper fortifications; it is the only Canon, upon whose mouth they dare not venture, none but the English will take their parts, therefore feare them not, for such a strong breath have these chese-eaters, that if they do but blow upon a booke, they imagine straight tis blasted: *Quod supra nos, Nihil ad nos,* (they say) that which is above our capacitie, shall not passe under our commendation. Yet would I have these Zoilists (of all other) to reade me, if ever I should write any thing worthily: for the blame that knowne-fooles heape upon a deserving labour, does not discredit the same, but makes wise men more perfectly in love with it. Into such a ones hands therefore if I fortune to fall, I will not shrinke an inch, but even when his teeth are sharpest, and most ready to bite, I will stop his mouth only with this, *Haec mala sunt, sed tu, non meliora facis.*

Notes

INTRODUCTION

1. My discussion of the sonnets will rest on the consensus as to date of composition expressed by Hallett Smith in *The Riverside Shakespeare* (1974): "The period of 1592 to 1596, with the possibility of occasional later sonnets, would seem satisfactory to most Shakespearean scholars" (1745).

2. Robert Pricket, *Honors Fame* (1604), A2r.

3. Richard Barnfield, *Poems in divers humors* (1598) E2v; John Weever's epigram "Ad Gulielmum Shakespeare" (*Epigrammes* [1599] iv.22) also refers specifically only to the two long poems.

4. Richard Poirier, *The Performing Self: Composition and Decomposition in the Language of Contemporary Life* (1971), 111.

5. Quoted in ibid., 92.

6. Ibid., 87.

7. Richard Helgerson, *Self-Crowned Laureates: Spenser, Jonson, Milton and the Literary System* (1983), 13.

8. Giovanni Della Casa, *The Galateo of Maister John Della Casa* (STC 4738; 1576), 19, 27.

9. Jorge Luis Borges, Preface to *El otro, el mismo* (1969), in *Selected Poetry: 1923-1967*, ed. Norman Di Giovanni (1972), 279; interview in *Writer's at Work*, ed. George Plimpton (4th ser., 1976), 135.

10. Michael Drayton, "To M. John Davies, My Good Friend," *Works*, ed. J.W. Hebel (1961), 1:499.

11. Alvin Kernan, *The Playwright as Magician* (1979), 46. Kernan's views quoted here are discussed more fully on page 163.

12. John Donne, *Letters to Severall Persons of Honour* (1651), 103; *Sir Thomas More* (3.2.216-18, 229), in *The Shakespeare Apocrypha*, ed. C.F. Tucker Brooke (1908; reprint, 1967), 401; cf. Jonson's epigram "To my Lord Ignorant": "Thou call'st me poet, as a term of shame: / But I have my revenge made, in thy name" (*Complete Poems*, ed. George Parfitt, (1975), 37, and his observation of the "practise" in his day of giving poetry

"diminution of Credit, by lessening the Professors['] estimation, and making the Age afraid of their Liberty" (8:633).

13. Samuel Taylor Coleridge, *Coleridge's Writings on Shakespeare*, ed. Terence Hawkes (1959), 55. Coleridge also noted that "with approved powers as a poet Shakespeare commences a dramatist" (47).

14. Oscar Wilde, *The Works of Oscar Wilde* (1909), 9:198, 207. This 1885 essay was later published as "The Truth of Masks" in Wilde's *Intentions* (1891); it carries this later title in *The Works*.

15. Kenneth Muir, "Shakespeare's Poets," in *Shakespeare the Professional and Related Studies* (1973), 22-40; Shakespeare's attitudes toward poetry and the question of "just how far Shakespeare himself shared in the skepticism of his characters toward poetry" (3) are the subject of Philip Edwards's *Shakespeare and the Confines of Art* (1968).

16. Quoted from Jonathan Goldberg's formulation in *James I and the Politics of Literature* (1983), xv.

17. Joel Fineman, *Shakespeare's Perjured Eye;* see below pp. 164; 209 n 11; 218, n 10; 227, n 42.

18. G.K. Hunter, "Spenser's *Amoretti* and the English Sonnet Tradition," in *A Theatre for Spenserians*, ed. Judith Kennedy and James Reither (1973), 126.

1. "THOU THING MOST ABHORRED"

1. Richard Lanham, *The Motives of Eloquence: Literary Rhetoric in the Renaissance* (1976), 102 (original emphasis). The parallel drawn from *All's Well* is made by A.C. Hamilton in *The Early Shakespeare* (1967), 163-64; quotations from *Venus and Adonis* cited hereafter in this chapter by line number will be made from the Arden edition by F.T. Prince (1960).

2. See p. 189 for a discussion of a characteristic Wyatt poem.

3. John Chamberlain, *The Letters of John Chamberlain*, ed. Norman McClure (1939), 1:133-34; subsequent citations from these letters will be made in the text by volume and page number.

4. Baldassare Castiglione, *The Book of the Courtier* (1528; trans. Thomas Hoby, 1588; 1928 edition), 96; all subsequent citations from this edition will appear in the text.

5. Chapter 5 explores more fully the observations made here.

6. Kernan, *Playwright as Magician*, 26.

7. Puttenham, *Arte*, (3:7, emphasis added). According to Puttenham, Venus and, to a lesser extent, Adonis are "pleaders." Who then is the judge? Not the narrator, according to Lanham: "What does the narrator think of Venus and Adonis? He does not think at all" (*Motives*, 90). Lanham calls the two characters "disputants" (87), but he might have used the more contemporary term *pleaders*. The judge, then, is the reader: "We are," Lanham writes, "also meant to weigh the arguments of each of the characters" (91).

   I have found the following essays on *Venus and Adonis* especially illuminating: Norman Rabkin, "'Venus and Adonis' and the Myth of Love," *Pacific Coast Studies* (1973): 171-86; Lucy Gent, "'Venus and Adonis': The Triumph of Rhetoric," *MLR* 69 (1974): 721-29; William Sheidley, "'Unless it be a boar': Love and Wisdom in Shakespeare's 'Venus and Adonis,'" *MLQ* 35 (1974): 3-15. In Heather Dubrow's *Captive*

Victors: Shakespeare's Narrative Poems and Sonnets (1987), Venus is referred to along with "that other impresario Prospero" (26).

8. Thomas Heywood, *An Apology for Actors* (STC 13302; 1612), C3v.

9. Sir Philip Sidney, *The Defence of Poesy*, ed. Geoffrey Shepherd (1965), 142; further citations from this edition will be made in the text by page.

10. Samuel Butler, *The Note-Books*, ed. H.F. Jones (1917), 192. Butler also wrote of the two Shakespearean epyllions, "They teem with fine things, but they are got-up fine things."

11. S. Schoenbaum, *Shakespeare and Others* (1985), 64, 41. Though Joel Fineman's language and methods in *Shakespeare's Perjured Eye* are vastly different from my own, he writes likewise of the poet-speaker's loss of identity in the Young Man sonnets. For example, he addresses the speaker's identity as "an identity of ruptured identification, a broken identity that carves out in the poet's self a syncopated hollowness that accounts for the deep personal interiority of the sonnets' poetic persona" (25). Several of the premises underlying my discussion of the Sonnets in chapter 5, I discovered with some surprise, appear to be shared by Fineman.

12. John Day, *The Works of John Day*, ed. A.H. Bullen (1881), 37. On the poet as "torchbearer of civilization," see Eckhard Auberlen, *The Commonwealth of Wit*, (1984), 48-54, 56-57, 62-65, 74-91.

13. Ronald Levao argues provocatively that Sidney's *Defence*, in its extroverted poetical style, renders ambiguous the author's real attitude toward poetry: "Sidney does praise the courtier who finds a style 'fittest to nature' and who 'doth according to art, though not by art,' and contrasts him to the pedant who uses 'art to show art, and not to hide art.' But Sidney is not that courtier. Little is hidden by the style of the *Apology*. His adopted role is announced as an adopted role, and nearly all his persuasive tricks and witty anecdotes are relished as persuasive tricks and demonstrations of wit" ("Sidney's Feigned *Apology*," *PMLA* 94 [1979]: 231); see also Arthur Marotti's "'Love is not Love': Elizabethan Sonnet Sequences and the Social Order," *ELH* 49 (1982): 396-428.

14. Erasmus, *In Praise of Folly*, trans. Clarence Miller (1979), 81.

15. Poirier, *Performing Self*, 87.

16. John Stephens, *Satyrical Essayes, Characters and Others* (STC 23249;1615), 111.

17. In 1591 Thomas Nashe referred to "this golden age," but only because it was "so replenisht with golden Asses of all sortes" (prefatory essay to *Astrophil and Stella*). By the 1620s, though, memories were already turning roseate. In 1622 Henry Peacham wrote of "the time of our late Queene *Elizabeth*, which was truly a golden Age (for such a world of refined wits, and excellent spirits it produced, whose like are hardly to be hoped for, in any succeeding Age)" (*The Compleat Gentleman* [STC 19502], 95).

18. William Barley, *A New Booke of Tabliture*, ed. Wilburn Newcomb (1966), 5.

19. Levao, "Sidney's Feigned *Apology*," 232.

20. On Wyatt in this respect see Raymond Southall, *The Courtly Maker: An Essay on the Poetry of Wyatt* (1964), and Donald Friedman, "The Mind in the Poem: Wyatt's 'They flee from me,'" *SEL* 7 (1967): 1-14. The Sidney poems that I have found particularly reflexive are *Astrophil and Stella* 1-3, 6, 15, 28, 40, 50, 55, 57, 58, 63, 69, 70, and 90; Shakespeare's sonnets of this kind are discussed later in this chapter and more fully in chapter 5. See also Anne Ferry, *The 'Inward' Language* (1983); Ferry makes a case for the influence of the *Astrophil and Stella* sequence on Shakespeare, focusing on sonnets

in which "some disinction is drawn between the poet-lover's social behavior and his simultaneous preoccupation with a private, inward experience" (195).

21. *Longinus on the Sublime*, ed. and trans. W. Rhys Roberts (1935), 95. In this same vein John Marston counterposes honesty and eloquence in his epistle "To the Reader" for *The Malcontent* (STC 17479; 1604): "I am an ill Oratour; and in truth, use to indite more honestly then eloquently, for 'tis my custome to speake as I think, and write as I speake" (A3v).

22. Della Casa, *Galateo 75*.

23. C.L. Barber, *Shakespeare's Festive Comedy* (1959), 87; G.K. Hunter, *John Lyly: The Humanist as Courtier* (1962), 334. In chapter 1, quotations from *Love's Labour's Lost* will be made in the text from the Arden edition by Richard David (1951).

24. Walter Oakeshott, *The Queen and the Poet* (1960), 109. In the present discussion and in the subsequent discussion of the play in chapter 3, I have sought to avoid traversing ground already covered by William Carroll in *The Great Feast of Language* (1976). Our differing approaches will be apparent to anyone who compares my use of Puttenham's *Arte* in the following pages with his in *The Great Feast*. Carroll focuses on several rhetorical figures not of present concern (*antanaclasis, antimetabole, auxesis, synonymy*), and whereas Carroll is interested in showing with Puttenham's aid how *Love's Labour's Lost* addresses several popular topics of the Renaissance "philosophy" of poetry (imitation, art- vs.-nature, the "garment" of style, *ut pictura poesis*, and decorum), I focus on implications in the *Arte* for the more mundane, practical task of deploying one's art in society. Nor have I moved toward the sophisticated linguistic analysis in chapter 5 of Trousdale's *Shakespeare and the Rhetoricians* (1982), which is devoted to "Shakespeare's most rhetorical play" (113). Trousdale views *Love's Labour's Lost* as "a play whose very life seems bound up with the nature of poetic language as the Elizabethans imagined it to be" (95); whereas my concern is with the nature of the poetic *life* and with the (nature of poetic language only insofar as it affected perceptions about such a life.

25. Philibert de Vienne, *The Philosopher of the Court* (STC 19832), 13; Thomas Dekker and Henry Chettle, *Patient Grisill* (STC 6518), Cv. John Earle, in *Micro-cosmographie* (STC 7439; 1628), describes "A down-right Scholler" as of "good mettal in the inside, though rough & unscour'd without, and therefore hated of the Courtier, that is quite contrary" (E8v); the humor of Navarre's "academe" is founded on Earle's stereotype.

26. Stephen Gosson, *The School of Abuse* (STC 12097; 1579), fol. 34 (mispaginated 33). The ladies view the men as mere "dumb pictures" of potential husbands. Gosson's mortuary image, I think, is reflected in the pun on *still* as in stillborn in the King's description of the academy as "Still and contemplative in living art" (1.1.14; Shakespeare uses *still-born* at 2H4 1.3.64 and *still-breeding* at R2 5.5.8). The pun on miscarriage is "completed" toward the end of the play by the Princess's comment on "great things laboring [which] perish in their birth" (5.2.516). The 1587 edition of Gosson's work is, fittingly, dedicated to the person who most successfully combined the *vita contemplativa* and *vita activa*: Sidney.

27. Oscar Wilde, "Phrases and Philosophies for the Use of the Young," *The Complete Works* (1966), 1205.

28. Puttenham's imagery in this description of *exargasia* is worth quoting more fully. He notes that this figure is related to "*Expolitio . . .* or otherwise as it fareth by the bare and naked body, which being attired in rich and gorgious apparell, seemeth to the common usage of th'eye much more comely and bewtifull than the naturall" (3:20). The

clothing image is particularly apropos for the references to clothing in *Love's Labour's Lost* and may help to explain why, of all Shakespeare's comedies, it is to my mind the least susceptible to performance in non-Elizabethan costume. Thomas Middleton could well have had in mind a play like *Love's Labour's Lost* when, in 1611, he made this trenchant sumptuary comparison: "The fashion of play-making I can properly compare to nothing so naturally as the alteration in apparel; for in the time of the great crop-doublet, your huge bombasted plays, quilted with mighty words to lean purpose, was only then in fashion: and as the doublet fell, neater inventions began to set up. Now, in the time of spruceness, our plays follow the niceness of our garments; single plots, quaint conceits, lecherous jests, dressed up in hanging sleeves: and those are fit for the times" ("To the Comic Play-readers," in *The Roaring Girl, The Dramatic Works*, ed. A. H. Bullen [1984], 4:7).

29. Sidney *Defence*, 137. The full quotation is pertinent: "If I were a mistress, [I] would never persuade me that they were in love; so coldly they apply fiery speeches, as men that had rather read lovers' writings and so caught up certain swelling phrases." However, one must draw attention to an almost as brilliant periphrasis on the subject of sleep in *Astrophil and Stella* Sonnet 39.

30. Robert Greene, *Greenes Groatsworth of Wit* (STC 12245; 1592), F1.

31 This is the "false" beauty of cosmetics that Shakespeare often associates with false rhetoric. In *Love's Labour's Lost* see 2.1.13-16; 4.1.17-19; and 4.3.235-36; also see Sonnets 21, 53, 68, 82, 83, 101, and 146.

32. Giles Fletcher, *Licia, or Poemes of Love* (STC 11055; 1593), A3r.

33. The two master pun words in *Love's Labour's Lost* are *fair* and *will*. The term *fair* Shakespeare particularly associated with the ornate ethos (see SON 21.1-4), the word's incidence being a kind of litmus test for its presence. *Fair*, for instance, occurs twenty-three times in *Romeo and Juliet's* first act, which Shakespeare works hard to give a steamy Petrarchan ambience; the word occurs but twenty-one times throughout the remainder of the play. The man who wrote the sonnets on "will" (135 and 136) clearly wrote *Love's Labour's Lost*; see, for example, 2.1.34-36, 49-50, 96-100, and 212. *Will*, incidentally, is the single pun word that occurs in the canon so often (5,295 times) that the Harvard Concordance omits presentation of specific instances.

34. Nietzsche, aphorisms 145 ("Against Images and Similes") and 148 ("The Grand Style and Something Better"), in "The Wanderer and His Shadow," in *Human, All-too-human* (1880), trans. Paul Cohen (1909-11; reissue 1964), 3:266.

35. Note the irony of Shakespeare's snobbish Ovidian epigraph for *Venus and Adonis*: "Let base-conceited wits admire vile things, / Fair Pheobus lead me to the Muses' springs" (Marlowe's translation).

36. In a fashion even more sober than Sidney's, Roger Ascham associates lack of inward touch with indulgence in poetry; his description of agile-tongued young courtiers in *The Schoolmaster* deserves quotation here, so richly does it reflect the characterization of the men in *Love's Labour's Lost*:

Quick wits commonly be . . . more quick to enter speedily than able to pierce far, even like oversharp tools, whose edges be very soon turned. Such wits delight themselves in easy and pleasant studies and never pass far forward in high and hard sciences. *And therefore the quickest wits commonly prove the best poets but not the wisest orators—ready of tongue to speak boldly, not deep of judgment either for good counsel or wise writing.* Also, for manners and life quick wits commonly be in desire newfangled, in purpose unconstant; light to promise anything, ready to forget everything. . . . In youth also they be ready scoffers, privy mockers, and ever over light and merry. . . . They be like trees that show forth fair blossoms and broad leaves in springtime, but bring small and not lasting fruit in harvest time. [Lawrence Ryan ed. (1967), 21-22; emphasis added]

Ascham's criticism seems almost cordial in comparison with much of the opprobrium heaped on poets of the time. Consider, for example, what John Webster (who was willing to defend and praise actors) has to say of "A Rimer": "He is a Juggler of words. . . . There is no thing in the earth so pittifull, no not an Ape-carrier; he is not worth thinking of, and therefore I must leave him as nature left him: a Dunghill not well laide together" (*Works*, ed. F.L. Lucas [1927], 4:44).

37. Granville-Barker, *Prefaces to Shakespeare*, 1st series (1927), 2.

38. Ascham, *The Schoolmaster*, 115; Francis Bacon, *The Advancement of Learning*, in *Works*, ed. James Spedding (1859; facsimile reprint, 1963), 3:284.

39. Sonnets 35 and 69 are also specially relevant to the satire on courtly praise in *Love's Labour's Lost*. For the dating of the Sonnets on which my discussion is based, see n.1 to the introduction.

40. Sir Philip Sidney, *The Countess of Pembroke's Arcadia*, ed. Maurice Evans (1977), 437. Subsequent citations from this edition will be made in the text.

41. James Calderwood, "A Wantoning with Words," *Studies in English Literature* 5 (1965): 325.

42. Adena Rosmarin comments interestingly on the "vulnerability" of the Sonnets in "Hermeneutics versus Erotics: Shakespeare's Sonnets and Interpretive History," *PMLA* 100 (1985): 20-37. Rosmarin writes, "The Sonnets recognize their vulnerability to the charges of insincerity and artifice, and they defend themselves by stage-managing this recognition: dwelling on it, dramatizing it, and, frequently, denying it. . . . By taking artifice and sincerity as their topics, the Sonnets remake themselves into a more difficult kind of writing, a poetry that is more properly and usefully termed philosophic as well as—or, even, rather than—amatory" (27).

43. Henry Peacham the Elder, *The Garden of Eloquence* (1593), title page.

44. Eustache Du Refuge, *A Treatise of the Court* (STC 7367; English translation 1622), 1:124. Subsequent citations will appear in the text. *Love's Labour's Lost* is a thoroughly fashionable satire on fashion and has suffered for its topicality. Reviews of new productions of the play, therefore, often begin with a caveat comparable to the following: "*Love's Labour's Lost* is plugged into its period as into a life-support system. Pulled out of topical context, most of its jokes expire. And even in context, batteries of footnotes are needed to galvanize the play's petrified guyings of defunct absurdities back to life. . . . With its pastiche and its parody so rooted in a specific cultural phase, much of the comedy has an unavoidably antiquarian look" (*Times Literary Supplement*, 9 January 1985, 64).

45. John Davies, "In Ciprium," in *The Poems of John Davies*, ed. Robert Krueger (1975), 138.

46. Samuel Daniel, *A Defence of Ryme* (STC 6259), Ir. Jonson's mordant description of the public's brief powers of concentration provides a corollary to Daniel: "Expectation of the vulgar is more drawn, and held with newness, than goodness; we see it in fencers, in players, in poets, in preachers . . . so it be new, though never so naught, and depraved, they run to it, and are taken. Which shows, that the only decay, or hurt of the best men's reputations with the people, is, their

wits have outlived the people's palates" (*Discoveries*, 387). Jonson lived long enough to suffer precisely this fate.

47. Thus, the suppression of the 1609 quarto hypothesized by so many commentators have may occurred not because Shakespeare objected to the invasion of his privacy but because, several years after the sonnet craze had waned, he thought his sequence would appear "richly suited, but unsuitable" and perhaps even detrimental to his reputation as a popular playwright. Barbara Everett, taking into account the very few surviving copies of the quarto and the utter absence of contemporary allusions to it (except for Alleyn's notation that he bought a copy for five pence), speculates along these lines: "It may be that Shakespeare had been strongly unwilling to publish the contents of the 1609 volume because (among other reasons) he knew that it would fail: and it did. Few copies survive because few sold, and those that did sell were not cherished and preserved." Everett ventures further: "It seems to me vital that our image of Shakespeare should widen and deepen to include a man whose poems failed. The 1609 *Sonnets* failed because the poems were too good, too difficult, and perhaps even too defeated: beyond a certain point they refused to 'keep company' with the writer's public." ("Mrs Shakespeare," *London Review of Books*, 18 December 1986, 9). Antisocial impulses in the Sonnets are discussed in the concluding pages of chapter 5.

48. John Florio, *First Fruits* (STC 11096), 71r.

49. Orlando Gibbons, *The First Set of Madrigals and Mottets of 5 Parts* (STC 11826; 1612), A3v.

50. King James, *His Majesties speech . . . at Whitehall* (STC 14395; 1607), Br.

51. William Fennor, "Description of a Poet," in *Fennors Descriptions* (STC 10784; 1616), B2r.

52. This notion of leaving behind the ornate style for a more theatrical idiom is pregnantly underscored by the hero and his foil in *The Taming of the Shrew*. Throughout the action the ornate style inhibits Lucentio's development as a character, so that at the very end he is bitterly undeceived when his Bianca turns shrew. Petruchio, on the other hand, has not remained "at home, / Where small experience grows" (1.2.51-52) in the Petrarchan style, but thrusts beyond it with consummate plain-style, and hence highly theatrical, vigor. Brian Morris, recent Arden editor of the play, "would like to think [it is] the first play Shakespeare wrote after arriving in London" (65). Could Lucentio be the author's first hint of where his professional allegiance would eventually rest?

53. "To sum up: Shakespeare was living in St. Helen's parish, Bishopsgate, at some date before October 1596; perhaps as early as the winter of 1596-97, but certainly no later than 1599, he had taken up residence in the Liberty of the Clink in Southwark. In other words Shakespeare crossed the river around the time that his company did" (S. Schoenbaum, *William Shakespeare: A Compact Documentary Life* [1977], 223).

54. The reference to his *arte Maronem* (that is, Virgilian art) in the Gheerart Janssen funeral monument scarcely identifies Shakespeare as a lyric or recreational poet. It is an irony worth noting that the epitaph that was hung on a pillar near Sidney's grave in St. Paul's also failed to carry the title *poet*; see William Bond, "The Epitaph of Sir Philip Sidney," *Modern Language Notes* 58 (1943): 253-57.

55. "the force of Demosthenes [rather] than the transport of the poet" (101). Ascham is drawing on Cicero's *Brutus* here: "Sulpicius [121-88 B.C.] indeed was of all orators whom I have ever heard the most elevated in style, and, so to speak, the most theatrical [*tragicus orator*]. His voice was strong and at the same time pleasing and of brilliant timbre, his gesture and bodily movement extraordinarily graceful" (trans. G.H. Hendrickson [1926], 173).

My suggestion that Shakespeare's exclusion (whether at his own or others' urging) from the world of courting poets helped to open up his greater achievements on the stage has recently been reiterated by Barbara Everett. Trying to suggest "by what processes Shakespeare far surpassed his age," she summarizes: "The greatest developments in the Elizabethan literary arts don't take place at the center of power, within the Court—however hard all writers struggled to get in. The real breakthroughs were with the excluded; they were acted out not in the Court but on the despised public stage; and of course depended above all on Shakespeare" ("Mrs Shakespeare," *London Review of Books*, 18 December 1986, 9). Harry Levin shares my conviction that, of Shakespeare's plays, *Love's Labour's Lost* represents a crucial stage in its author's artistic coming of age. In the last paragraph of "Sitting in the Sky (*Love's Labour's Lost*, 4.3)," in *Shakespeare's "Rough Magic,"* ed. Peter Erickson and Coppélia Kahn (1985), Levin observes, "Shakespeare's homeopathic task [in LLL] was to overmaster . . . rhetoric, to commandeer artifice as a weapon against artificiality. It was incidentally fun, since it allowed him to have his cake while eating. . . . What had been so labored, so laborious, so overelaborate well deserved to be lost, along with the transitory courtships of Navarre and his book-men. What Shakespeare won was his own courtship of the English language and his accession to artistic maturity" (129). Similarly, Coleridge viewed *Love's Labour's Lost* as "the link between [Shakespeare's] character as a Poet, and his art as a Dramatist" (*Shakespearean Criticism*, ed. Thomas Raysor [1930], 2:128).

2. "DEDICATED WORDS"

1. Thomas Nashe, "Epistle Dedicatorie," in *The Unfortunate Traveller* (1594).

2. Anthony Munday, *A Courtly controversie, betweene loove a. learning* (1581); to be fair, Munday's epistle is attractively short: seventy-five words. Compare John Reynolds's note to the reader for his translation of Du Refuge's *A Treatise of the Court* (1622): "It was my desire, and withall my resolution not to have afforded thee the bare *Complement* of an *Epistle*, although the affectation & iniquity of our times . . . rather make it Customarie, then Commendable" (A8r).

3. John Taylor, *The eighth wonder of the World, or Coriats Escape* (1613).

4. This epistle is discussed at the end of this chapter and is reproduced in full in Appendix B.

5. Thomas P. Roche, "Autobiographical Elements in Sidney's *Astrophil and Stella,*" *Spenser Studies* 5 (1985): 218.

6. Was Shakespeare perhaps given a hint for his first poetical venture by the last line in Nashe's essay prefixed to *Astrophil and Stella?*—"Now I will leave you to survey the pleasures of *Paphos*, and offer your smiles on the Aulters of *Venus.*" In *Shakespeare's*

Perjured Eye, Joel Fineman refers to Sidney's sequence as "the inaugural moment of the Elizabethan sonnet" (2).

7. See the chapter "Aesthetic Elitism" in my *Shakespeare and the Courtly Aesthetic* (1981), 107-18.

8. All quotations from Nashe in this passage are from *The Unfortunate Traveller* (1594), A2 and were written within months of *Venus and Adonis*'s first appearance in print. Indeed, it may be that Shakespeare's dedication inspired Nashe's own choice of a dedicatee, for he writes: "A dere lover and cherisher you are, as well of the lovers of Poets, as of Poets themselves."

9. John Heath varied this theme in "To the Bookseller" for *The House of Correction* (1619): "Nay, feare not *Bookeseller*, this Booke will sell: / For be it good, as thou know'st very well, / *All will goe buy it*; but say it be ill, / *All will goe buy it too*: thus thou sel'st still."

10. Michael Drayton, *The Tragicall Legend of Robert, Duke of Normandy* (1596).

11. Barnaby Rich, Epistle "To the Curteous and friendly Reader," in *A New Description of Ireland* (1610). There is a reference in *Coryats Crudities* (1905 ed.) to "the unmeasurable abundance of bookes of all artes, sciences, and arguments whatsoever that are printed in this learned age wherein we now breathe, in so much that me thinks we want rather readers for bookes than bookes for readers" (1:7).

12. This difficulty is manifest in the case of Thomas Thorpe (fl.1604-24), long the most notorious printer of unauthorized material; more recently, Katherine Duncan-Jones has argued for a revision of the allegation of underhand behavior in his printing of the Sonnets ("Was the 1609 *Shakes-speares Sonnets* Really Unauthorized?" *RES* n.s. 34 [1983]:151-71).

13. John Day, *The Parliament of Bees* (circa 1608), in *Works*, 36.

14. Thomas Dekker, "Not to the Readers: but to the Understanders," in *A Strange Horse-Race* (1613).

15. Barnaby Barnes, *A Divine Centure of Spirituall Sonnets* (1595); Thomas Nashe, *The Terrors of the Night* (1594); Thomas Dekker, *The Wonderfull Yeare* (1603); Barnaby Rich, *A New Description of Ireland* (1610).

16. Matteo Aleman, *The Rogue* (1623); Peter Woodhouse's *The Flea* (1605) contains an "Epistle Dedicatorie . . . To the giddie multitude."

17. Gascoigne here elaborates on what it means to advance in knowledge of the unknown: "So that not onely his travaile and paine are very commendable (who out of sundrie Authorities woulde gather one reasonable conjecture) but also the worke is not to be thought bareine, although it does not fully proove so much as may be expected, since he that plougheth in a flintie fielde, speedeth well if he reape but an indifferent crop." Gascoigne's charming apology is especially germane to criticism, like the present study, which plows the flinty field of speculation about Shakespeare's artistic biography.

18. Alfonso Ferrabosco, in "To the world," *Lessons for 1. 2. and 3. Viols* (1609). J.W. Saunders' "The Stigma of Print," *Essays in Criticism* 1 (1951), 139-64, remains an important discussion of this aspect of Renaissance publishing.

19. Robert Anton addressed the Howard "constellation of brotherhood": "Right Honourable branches of a fayre and spreading family, under whose shades my best fortunes ruminate. . . . " (*Moriomachia*, 1613).

20. Wright, *The Passions of the Mind* (1604); Heywood, *Pleasant Dialogues and Drammas* (1637).

21. John Day observed that "ill-tutord jacks" could, by indecorously addressing great ones, "Poyson the fame of Patrons" *(Bees*, 33). I found no title addressed to Pembroke that would fall into this demeaning category.

22. See Barbara Lewalski's extensive discussion of this important patroness: "Lucy, Countess of Bedford: Images of a Jacobean Courtier and Patroness," in Kevin Sharpe, Steven Zwicker, eds., *Politics of Discourse* (1987), 52-77.

23. This observation is pursued further in chapter 5.

24. The popularity of a play in the theater was usually a prominent selling point included on quarto title pages. In an epistle to the reader for his 1604 edition of *The Malcontent*, Marston admits that he is afflicted "to thinke that Scenes invented, meerely to be spoken, should be inforcively published to be read." But he concludes with the hope that "this trifle . . . may bee pardoned, for the pleasure it once afforded you, when it was presented with the soule of lively action." For thoughts on the *Troilus* preface, see Leslie Fiedler, "Shakespeare's Commodity-Comedy: A Meditation on the Preface to the 1609 Quarto of *Troilus and Cressida*," in *Shakespeare's "Rough Magic*," ed. Peter Erickson and Coppélia Kahn (1985), 50-60.

25. Dedication to Lady Walsingham for the conclusion to *Hero and Leander* (1598).

26. Jones's address "To the Gentlemen" for Breton's *Arbour of Amorous Devises* (1597); Case, epistle to Breton, for Breton's *The Pilgrimage to Paradise* (1592).

27. Webbe, *A Discourse*, 17; Cornwallis, *Essayes* (STC 5775; 1600), H7r. In an appendix to a 1596 edition of the *Defence of Poesy* (STC 22534X), reference is made to "the precedent Pamphlet" (Aar). Fulke Greville concluded in his *Life of Sir Philip Sidney* that his works "were scribled rather as pamphlets, for entertainment of time, and friends, than any accompt of himself to the world" (ed. Nowell Smith, [1907], 17). Perhaps more relevant to *Venus and Adonis* is Amorphus's comment to the courting neophyte Asotus in Jonson's *Cynthia Revels:* "Put case they doe retaine you [at Court] . . . to read them asleep in afternoones upon some pretty pamphlet" (4:83). Other occurrences include the following: Churchyard observes in a dedication to Essex of his *Musicall Consort* (1595) that "A greater boldness cannot be committed . . . than to present Pamphlets and Poetrie to noble Counsellors"; in *A Floorish upon Fancie* (1577) Nicholas Breton included some "pretie Pamphlets for pleasant heads to passe away idle time withal"; Thomas Bradshaw offered his paraphrase of *Theocritus* (1591) as "this sillie Pamphlet"; W. Bettie offered *Titana and Theseus* (1608) as "this imperfect Pamphlet."

28. Thomas Newman to Frauncis Flower, Esq., *Syr P.S. His Astrophel and Stella* (1591); Lyly to the Earl of Oxford, *Euphues* (1586); Thomas Robinson to James, *The Schoole of Musicke* (1603).

29. See Stephen Booth's note on Sonnet 76.8 (265) for other Shakespearean and non-Shakespearean natal references.

30. "Shakespeare's Dedication" (1929), in *John Clare and Other Essays* (1950), 46. Murry ventures that *dedicate* "was one of Shakespeare's favorite words" (47); his explanation for the fact that the word "turns to ashes" in Shakespeare's mouth in *Timon* is the hypothesis that his former dedicatee was the person responsible for releasing the Sonnets manuscripts for publication.

31. Arthur Mizener, "The Structure of Figurative Language in Shakespeare's Sonnets," in *A Casebook on Shakespeare's Sonnets*, ed. Gerald Willen and Victor Reed (1964), 223. For a discussion of the anarchic impulses in the Sonnets, see pp. 193-94.

32. Chapman, "To the Lady Walsingham," conclusion to *Hero and Leander* (1598).

3. POET'S LABORS LOST

1. *A Discourse* . . . (STC 25172), A2r-A3v. All quotations from *Love's Labour's Lost* and *Timon of Athens* in this chapter are from the Arden editions by Richard David and H.J. Oliver, respectively.

2. *The Life and Works of George Peele*, ed. David Horne (1952), 245-47. One J.M. repeats the assertion in *A Health to the Gentlemanly Profession of Servingmen* (1598): "The liberall Maister is a rare Phenix" (Er). So does Brathwait in 1614: "So rarely is *Pallas Shield* borne by the Noble, or supported by such whose eminence might revive her decaied hopes, as *Brittaines Pernassus* . . . is growen despicable in her selfe, because protected by none but her selfe" (*Medley*, A2r). So does Heywood in 1637: "this Age affording more Poets than Patrons (for nine Muses may travell long ere they find one Meceonas)" (*A Curtaine Lecture*, A2r). Alvin Kernan, in *Playwright as Magician*, ventures this extremely pessimistic conclusion: "There is not, I believe it is accurate to say, a single case of a totally satisfactory poet-patron relationship in the time of Elizabeth and James" (26). Kernan's view is wittily supported in Thomas Thorpe's dedication "To his Kind and True Friend: Edward Blunt" for Lucan's *Pharsalia* (1600): "One special virtue in our Patrons of these days I have promised myself you shall fit excellently, which is to give nothing." See also Richard Barnfield's *Complaint of Poetrie, for the Death of Liberalitie* (1598). Relevant studies are: Patricia Thomson, "The Literature of Patronage, 1580-1630," *Essays in Criticism* 2 (1952), 267-83; Arthur Marotti, "John Donne and the Rewards of Patronage," and Leonard Tennenhouse, "Sir Walter Raleigh and the Literature of Clientage," both in *Patronage in the Renaissance*, ed. Stephen Orgel and Guy Fitch Lytle (1981), 207-34, 235-58. Robert C. Evans' *Ben Jonson and the Poetics of Patronage* (1989) appeared too late to figure in the present discussion.

3. *Gabriel Harvey's Marginalia*, ed. G.C. Moore Smith (1913), 190.

4. Edmund Spenser, *Mother Hubberds Tale* (1591), ll. 667, 701, *Works* (1947), 7 (Part 2): 123-24. Thomas Greene, "The Flexibility of the Self in Renaissance Literature," in *The Disciplines of Literature*, ed. Peter Demetz *et al.* (1968), 258.

5. *Nugae Antiquae [of] Sir John Harington*, ed. Thomas Park (1804; reprint, 1966), 1:346; all subsequent citations from this work will appear in the text by volume and page number. Quotations from *The Letters of Sir John Harington*, ed. Norman McClure (1930), will be cited as *Letters*.

6. Harrington, 1:338. A similar conclusion appears in Jonson's *Discoveries*: "Poetry, in this latter age, hath proved but a mean mistress, to such as have wholly addicted themselves to her, or given their names up to her family. They who have but saluted her on the by, and now and then tendered their visits, she hath done much for, and advanced in the way of their own profession (both the Law, and the Gospel) beyond all they could have hoped or done for themselves, without her favor" (393).

7. A.D.B. *The Court of the most illustrious* . . . *King James* (STC 1022; 1619), 9.

8. Antonio de Guevara, *A Looking Glass* (Eng. translation, 1575), fol. 44v; Thomas Churchyard, *A Pleasant Discourse* (STC 5249), A3r; Henry Wotton, *The Elements of Architecture* (facsimile reprint), ed. Frederick Hard (1968), Av. For references to Prospero's island as a maze and discussion of related allegorical significations, see my *Shakespeare and the Courtly Aesthetic* (1981), 219-23.

9. A.D.B. *The Court*, A2v; Nicholas Faret, *The Honest Man* . . . (STC 10689), 6.

Du Refuge speaks of "the *Ocean* of these *Court* affaires" in *A Treatise of the Court* (STC 7367; Eng. translation, 1622), 1:4.

10. Daniel Javitch, *"Il Cortegiano* and the Constraints of Despotism," in *Castiglione: The Ideal and the Real in Renaissance Culture,* ed. Robert Hanning and David Rosand (1983), 19; Patricia Thomson, *Sir Thomas Wyatt and His Background* (1964), 29. Compare Javitch's similar conclusion in his *Poetry and Courtliness in Renaissance England* (1978): "In their style and in their temperament the courtiers at Urbino display a marked intolerance and distrust of absolute or even settled convictions" (32). Joel Fineman's study of the Sonnets, *Shakespeare's Perjured Eve,* focuses on Shakespeare's deployment of the "paradox of praise" (29) and the "variability, the brittle instability, of paradoxical intention" (33). See also Javitch's "The Impure Motives of Elizabethan Poetry," in *The Power of Forms in the English Renaissance,* ed. Stephen Greenblatt (1982), 225-38.

11. Quoted in Joan Simon, *Education and Society in Tudor England* (1966), 352.

12. *The Countess of Pembroke's Arcadia,* ed. Maurice Evans (1977), 199.

13. "The Elizabethan Laureate: Self-Presentation and the Literary System," *ELH* 46 (1979): 193-220. See also Helgerson's *Self-Crowned Laureates: Spenser, Jonson, Milton and the Literary System* (1983).

14. Katharine Duncan-Jones attempts to upset this generalization in "Was the 1609 *Shake-speares Sonnets* Really Unauthorized?" RES n.s. 34 (1983): 151-71.

15. Samuel Daniel, "Musophilus" (ll. 440-41), *Complete Works,* ed. Alexander Grosart (1885), 1:239; Muriel St. Clare Byrne, ed., *The Lisle Letters* (1981), 2:3; John Donne *The Courtier's Library,* ed. Evelyn Simpson (1930), 40-41; Philibert, *Philosopher,* 29-30. See Daniel Javitch's *"The Philosopher of the Court:* A French Satire Misunderstood," *Comparative Literature* 23 (1971): 97-124. In *Cynthia's Revels,* Asotus, the courting neophyte, says he will "give out my acquaintance with all the best writers, to countenance me the more," and his mentor Amorphus warns, "Rather seeme not to know 'hem, it is your best" (4:83). This cavalier attitude toward book learning extended notably to Inns of Court students. Henry Peacham wrote in *The Complete Gentleman* (1622) that they have "no further thought of studie, then to trimme up their studies with Pictures, and place the fairest Bookes in openest view, which, poore Lads, they scarce ever opened or understood not" (33).

16. Lawrence Stone, *The Crisis of the Aristocracy* (1965), appendix 37, p. 794; Phoebe Sheavyn, *The Literary Profession in the Elizabethan Age* (2d rev. ed. by J.W. Saunders, 1967), 155. See also Sears Jayne's *Library Catalogues of the English Renaissance* [i.e., 1500-1640] (1965); Jayne defines as a library any collection of fifteen or more separately named works, with an overwhelming percentage of these libraries belonging to men associated with Oxford and Cambridge. See generally J.W. Saunders, *The Profession of English Letters* (1964), especially the chapter on "The Renaissance Professionals."

17. Rowse, *The Elizabethan Renaissance: The Life of Society* (1971), 32; Hunter, *John Lyly: The Humanist as Courtier* (1962), 30-31.

18. From a letter by John Harington quoted in L.G. Black, "A Lost Poem by Queen Elizabeth I," *Times Literary Supplement* 23 May 1968, 535.

19. John Neale, *Queen Elizabeth* (1934), 390.

20. John Nichols, *The Progresses, Processions, and Magnificent Festivities of King James the First* (1828), 4:1134-35.

21. Allan Westcott, *New Poems of James I of England* (1911), lxix.

22. "To My Muse" (54). Eckhard Auberlen contributes a valuable discussion of Jonson's unique experience of, and attitudes toward, patronage, as well as a shrewd

comparison of Daniel's and Jonson's styles of clientage, in the fourth chapter of *The Commonwealth of Wit* (1984), 107-32.

23. *Virgidemiarum* (STC 12716; 1597), 57.

24. *Wonderfull Yeare*, B2r.

25. *The Book named the Governor*, (1531) ed. S.E. Lehmberg (1962), 107. It is precisely this gift of affability that Iago so skillfully exploits in *Othello*. He is, to borrow a phrase from *Timon of Athens* (3.6.91), an affable wolf.

26. Sir Robert Naunton, *Fragmenta Regalia, or observations on the late Queen Elizabeth, her times and favorites* (1641; 1985 ed. by John Cerovski), 65. Naunton says further of Perrot: "He had the endowment of courage and height of spirit, had it lighted on the alloy and temper of discretion. The defect thereof, with a native freedom and boldness of speech, drew him on to a clouded setting, and laid him upon the spleen and advantage of his enemies."

27. Javitch, *"Il Cortegiano,"* 28. There is something of this sentiment in Shakespeare's Sonnet 96: "So are those errors that in thee are seen, / To truths translated, and for true things deemed."

28. *Directions for Speech and Style*, in *The Life, Letters, and Writings of John Hoskyns*, Louise Osborn ed. (1937), 125. Puttenham defines *catachresis* as when a word "neither naturall nor proper" is chosen and "[we] do untruly applie it to the thing which we would seeme to expresse" (3:17).

29. Allusions to Mercury as cheater occur twice in Shakespeare: TN 1.5.97-98 and WT 4.3.24-28. The richly antithetical significances of the Mercurial figure in the Renaissance are often observable. Robert Anton alludes to his dark side when he refers to "the *Mazes* of slie Mercurie" in *The Philosopher's Satyres* (STC 686) (60); Jonson alludes to his bright side when he dresses *Euphantaste* ("well conceited Wittinesse"), one of the cardinal virtues at court, in "a *Petasus*, or *Mercuriall* hat" (4:166-67). Mercury is also at hand in a passage from the *Arcadia* that is highly reminiscent of the courting in LLL. Phalantus "at least for tongue-delight" sets himself to woo Artesia and uses "the phrase of his affection in so high a style that Mercury would not have wooed Venus with more magnificent eloquence" (155). Artesia eventually treats Phalantus rather as the women treat the men in LLL: "She took the advantage one day, upon Phalantus' unconscionable praising her and certain cast-away vows how much he would do for her sake, to arrest his word as it was out of his mouth" (154; cf. the Princess's "We arrest your word" [LLL 2.1.160]).

30. Antonio de Guevara, *A Looking Glasse* (STC 12448), 33v; *The Life of Edward, First Lord Herbert of Cherbury*, ed. J.M. Shuttleworth (1976), 28. This is the same lesson that we, now influenced by deconstructionist criticism, are in danger of failing to remember: "Our ability to identify a perverse use of terms *as* perverse depends on the assumption that there is such a thing as calling things by their right names, and this in turn depends on the assumption that there is a common world and that language's relation to it is not wholly arbitrary" (Gerald Graff, *Literature Against Itself* [1979], 90).

31. Such toadying for social intimacy is ridiculed by Barnabe Rich in *Faultes, Faults, And nothing else but Faultes* (STC 20983; 1606): "By these steps of soothing, our Courtiers seeke to climbe; and if a noble man doe but vouchsafe him a nodde he waxeth so drunken with joy, that he that should but marke his demeanour, woulde thinke him to be raised againe with *Lazarus*" (55v).

32. Greene, "Flexibility of the Self," 263.

33. *Crisis of the Aristocracy* (1965), 748-49. Compare Francis Markham's comment

on "Dunghill, or Carpet-Knights" in *The Booke of Honour* (STC 17331; 1625); "Truck-Knights, whose Honors have no other assent or Scale to rise by, but onely their wealth and purchase, trucking and bargaining with gold or other merchandise" (69). The English publication of Giovanni Nenna's *Discourse whether a nobleman by birth, or a gentleman by desert is greater in nobilitie* in 1600 was very well timed.

34. See Robert Miola, "Timon in Shakespeare's Athens," *Shakespeare Quarterly* 31 (1980): 21-30. Miola notes that "the conception of Athens as a city of licence and disorder became proverbial" (22) in Shakespeare's time. See the discussion of *Timon* in Gail Paster's *The Idea of the City in the Age of Shakespeare* (1985), 91-109.

35. Lawrence Stone's analysis of conspicuous consumption is, I think, pertinent to *Timon of Athens:* "Conspicuous consumption satisfies three deep-seated psychological needs present in every human being: the instinct for aggression and competition, which sometimes can find no other outlet; the compulsion to work, be it only by performing in some futile, costly, and time-consuming ceremonial; and the urge to play . . . As the playwrights never tired of telling their audience, this was an age of exceptionally prodigal living, made possible by the rising tide of luxury imports and stimulated by a desire to imitate the opulent Renaissance courts of Europe." Stone continues, "conspicuous consumption serves a social function as a symbolic justification for the maintenance or acquisition of status. So long as their position is secure and unchallenged, old-established families are usually unostentatious in their spending. It is new wealth which sets the standard of novelty, of fashion, and of opulent display, simply because wealth is not a sufficient source of honor in itself. It needs to be advertised, and the normal medium is the purchase of obtrusively expensive capital goods, equipment, and services" (184-85).

36. Page 450. Apemantus's glosses on Stone's summary occur at 4.3.213-16 and 243-50. For his 1608 edition of *A Poetical Rapsody*, Davison added this "character" of "The Courtier" by John Davies (ed. Robert Kreuger [1975]:

> Long have I liv'd in Court, yet learn'd not all this while
> To sell poore suitors smoke; nor where I hate to smile;
> Superiors to adore, inferiors to despise,
> To flie from such as fall, to follow such as rise,
> To cloake a poore desire under a rich array,
> Nor to aspire by vice, though 'twere the quicker way. [238]

37. Guevara, *Looking Glasse*, 35r.

38. Very similar is the implication of Hamlet's "I eat the air, promise-cramm'd" (3.2.94). The Painter's comment accurately reflects on Tudor and Stuart court life, as Donne suggests in his astonished reaction to a courtier who actually made good on his promises: "In good faith he [Lord Hay] promised so roundly, so abundantly, so profusely, as I suspected him, but performed what ever he undertook . . . so readily and truly, that his complements became obligations, and having spoke like a Courtier, did like a friend" (*Letters to Severall Persons of Honour* [1651], 125).

39. "An Account of the Revenue, the Expences, the Jewels, &c. of Prince Henry," *Archaeologia* 15 (1806): 23.

40. *Ibid.*, p. 22.

41. *Calendar of State Papers*, Venetian 11 (1607-10), par. 954; Franklin Williams, *Index of Dedications and Commendatory Verses in English Books Before 1641* (1962). See in

general J.W. Williamson, *The Myth of the Conqueror: Prince Henry Stuart: A Study of 17th Century Personation* (1978). See also Elkin C. Wilson, *Prince Henry and English Literature* (1946) and Roy Strong, *Henry, Prince of Wales & England's Lost Renaissance* (1986).

42. *Calendar of State Papers, Venetian 12 (1610-13), par. 159.*

43. Thomas Birch, *The Life of Henry Prince of Wales* (1760), 390; George More, *Principles for yong Princes*, 26v-27r.

44. Sir Charles Cornwallis, *The Life and Death of our late most Incomparable and Heroique Prince, Henry* (1641), 100-101.

45. "Particulars of the Expences of the Royal Household," *Archaeologia* 12 (1796): 80-86.

46. *Myth of the Conqueror*, 122.

47. Ambassador quoted in ibid., 120; Birch, *Life*, 399.

48. For a discussion of the influence of the Jacobean court masque on *The Tempest*, see the present writer's *Courtly Aesthetic*, 134-45, 223-25.

49. Williamson, *Myth of the Conqueror*, 31.

50. Trumbull's manuscript is reproduced in Herford and Simpson, 10:522-3.

4. "CHAMELEON MUSE"

1. Greene, "Flexibility of the Self," 258. Greene quotes from chapter 9, book 3 of Machiavelli's *Discourses*. This was a Machiavellian theme. In a letter of January 1513 to Piero Soderini, Machiavelli observed that since "men in the first place are short-sighted and in the second cannot command their natures, it follows that Fortune varies and commands men, and holds them under her yoke." On improvisation as "a central Renaissance mode of behavior" see Stephen Greenblatt, *Renaissance Self-Fashioning* (1980), 229ff.

2. *The Poems of Sir John Davies*, ed. Robert Krueger (1975), 125. Davies applied the compliment to himself in a dedicatory sonnet to Sir Anthony Cooke (a cousin of Cecil and Bacon) attached to the manuscript for his "Gullinge Sonnets": "Here my Camelion Muse her selfe doth chaunge / To divers shapes of gross absurdities" (163). Edward Topsell's remark in an essay "Of the Chamaeleon" in his *History of Serpents* (STC 24124; 1608) is also pertinent: "hence also commeth another proverbe . . . more mutable than a *Chamaelion*, for a crafty, cunning, inconstant fellow, changing himselfe into every mans disposition" (115).

3. George Chapman, *Mounsieur D'Olive* (1606), E3.

4. Letter to Robert Markham, 1606 (original emphasis), Harington, *Letters*, 124.

5. Compare also these lines from Donne: "Courts are theatres, where some men play / Princes, some slaves, all to one end, and of one clay" (214). Donne repeats the idea in 11:185-86 of his fourth satire (169). Thomas Churchyard wrote of the court in *A Pleasant Discourse of Court and Wars* (STC 5249; 1596) as "The platform where all Poets thrive / The stage where time away we drive" (Br), and Du Refuge that "the *Court* is an emminent and conspicuous *Theatre*" (*A Treatise*, 1:3).

6. Chapman, *D'Olive*, B2v.

7. Raymond Southall, *The Courtly Maker* (1964), 69.

8. Drayton, *Works*, ed. J.W. Hebel (1961), 1:173. Samuel Rowlands associates the

sea-god with courtiership in his epigram, "Proteus": "Time serving humour thou wrie-faced Ape, / That canst transforme thy selfe to any shape: / Come good *Proteus* come away a pace . . . " (*Humors looking glasse* [STC 21386; 1608], C4v). Philibert specifically compares and praises the courtier's and sea-god's abilities in *The Philosopher of the Court:* "This facilitie of the Spirite is not therefore to be blamed which makes man according to the pleasure of others to chaunge and transforme hymselfe. For in so doing he shall be accounted wise, winne honour, and be free of reprehension every where: which *Proteus* knewe verie well, to whom his diverse Metamorphosis and oft transfiguration was verie commodious" (101). Praise suitable to the role-changing courtier was, quite naturally, also suitable to the stage actor: Thomas Heywood, in his "Prologue to the Stage at the Cock-pit" for Marlowe's *The Jew of Malta*, exalted Edward Alleyn as a "Proteus for shapes" *(Complete Plays*, ed. Irving Ribner [1963], 178).

Another article by Thomas Greene is relevant here: "Ben Jonson and the Centered Self," *Studies in English Literature* 10 (1970): 325-48. Greene writes, "In this disoriented world of Jonson's comedies, the most nearly successful characters seem to be the chameleons, the Shifts and Brainworms and Faces who refuse to be centered, who are comfortable with the metamorphoses society invites" (336). Greene also ventures that "the subject of *Volpone* is protean man" (337). In chapter 15 of *Biographia Literaria*, Coleridge wrote of Shakespeare as a "Proteus of the fire and flood . . . [who] becomes all things, yet for ever remaining himself" (2:20). See Michel Grivelet's "A Portrait of the Artist as Proteus," in *Interpretations of Shakespeare*, ed. Kenneth Muir (1985), 27-46. On the myth of Proteus see A. Bartlett Giamatti's chapter, "Proteus Unbound: Some Versions of the Sea God in the Renaissance," in *Exile and Change in Renaissance Literature* (1984), 115-50. Proteus and the chameleon are also discussed together in Jonas Barish, *The Anti-Theatrical Prejudice* (1981), 100- 112.

9. The figures here are drawn from the manuscript entitled "The State of England, 1600," written by one Sir Thomas Wilson. It was edited by F.J. Wilson and published in the *Camden Miscellany*, 3rd series, 52 (1936), 1-43. How Wilson arrived at his figures is not always clear, but they do not seem unreasonable. Wilson does admit that "it were too impossible a matter" (16) to guess at England's entire population; this figure I have supplied from the *Encyclopedia Britannica* (1968).

It is perhaps worth rehearsing Wilson's stratification of English society. There are five classes: *Nobiles, Cives, Yeemani, Artisani*, and *Opifices rusticorum*, with the nobility subdivided into two classes. The major nobility consists of *marchiones* (of which he notes there are two), *comites* (that is, earls, 18), *vicecomites* (2), *barones* (39), and *episcopos* (26); the minor nobility comprises *equites* (knights, 500), *armigeros* (about 16,000), *generosos* (gentlemen), *ministros* (clergymen), and *literatos omnes qui gradus aliquos in Academiis acceperunt*. On the demography of the period see the discussion and other works cited by Ann Jennalie Cook in *The Privileged Playgoers of Shakespeare's London* (1981), 49-51.

10. "Place and Patronage in Elizabethan Politics," in *Elizabethan Government and Society: Essays Presented to Sir John Neale* (1961), 106.

11. *Memoirs of the Life and Times of Sir Christopher Hatton*, ed. Harris Nicholas (1847), 304-305; Donald Friedman, "The Mind in the Poem: Wyatt's 'They flee from me,'" *SEL* 7 (1967): 13; Muriel St. Clare Byrne, ed., *The Lisle Letters* (1981), 1:435.

12. Stefano Guazzo describes this competitive atmosphere in *The Civile Conversation of M. Steeven Guazzo* (Eng. translation 1574; reprint, 1925): "If you once set your foote in the Court of some Prince . . . you shall see an infinite number of Courtiers assemble together, to talke and devise of many matters, to understande the news of the

death or confiscation of the goods of some one, to seeke to obtaine of the Prince, either promotions, goods, pardons, exemption, or priviledge for them selves or others . . . and to practise the favour of the Secretaries, and other Officers. And you shall have there besides, other good fellowes, conspiring together, and secretly devising howe to bring some Officer into the disfavour of his Prince, that hee may bee put from his office, and some other placed in his roome" (1:117). This, setting in Cyprus notwithstanding, is the psychosocial locus of *Othello;* see the discussion of Iago at pp. 155-58. See also J.E. Neale's essay on "The Elizabethan Political Scene," in *Essays in Elizabethan History* (1958), 59-84.

13. The Old Lady appears in scenes (2.3 and 5.1) that are usually ascribed to Shakespeare by students of this problematic text. Posthumus, in *Cymbeline*, echoes her sense of the futility of suit when he observes that to be "as good as promise" is to be "most unlike our courtiers." He concludes, "Poor wretches that depend / On greatness' favor as I have done, / Wake and find nothing" (5.4.136-37, 127-29).

14. William Webbe, *A Discourse of English Poesie* (STC 25172, 1586; facs. rpt. 1966), 95. The Greek word is anomalously spelled (wrongly transcribed or set, perhaps); it appears to be a form of the Greek *krypts‡* = hidden, secret, occult.

15. *The Book named the Governor*, ed. S.E. Lehmberg (1962), 46. Subsequent citations from this work will appear in the text. Compare this "Character of the Author" from Thomas Coryat's *Odcombian Banquet* (STC 5810; 1611): "He is a great and bold Carpenter of words, or . . . a *Logodaedale*" (B2r).

16. Quoted in David Willson, *King James VI and I* (1956), 195.

17. Naunton, *Fragmenta Regalia* (1641), 32.

18. Elyot, *The Governor*, 107; Castiglione, *The Courtier*, 107; Philibert. *Looking Glasse*, 108; Daniel, "Musophilus," *Works*, 1:227-28. Shakespeare makes comic use of "Singularitie" at court with Malvolio (he is urged by an anonymous letter to put himself "into the trick of singularitie" for Olivia—TN 2.5.152, 3.4.71) and tragic use with Coriolanus, whose salient character flaw is seen by observers as "his singularity" (1.1.278).

19. Prefatory letter to Thomas More, *The Praise of Folly*, tr. Clarence Miller (1979), 2; *Gabriel Harvey's Marginalia*, ed. G.C. Moore Smith (1913), 155-56. The preeminent exploration of this subject is Stephen Greenblatt's *Renaissance Self-Fashioning* (1980); see also Frank Whigham's *Ambition and Privilege: The Social Tropes of Elizabethan Courtesy* (1984).

20. Alessandro Pascolato, ed., *Re Lear e Ballo in maschera: lettere di Giuseppe Verdi ad Antonio Somma* (1902), 71.

21. "Epistle Dedicatory" to *Man and Superman*, *Collected Plays* (1974), 2:522. Stendhal observed in "Racine and Shakespeare" (1823) that *"Coriolanus* belongs to the world of comedy" *Oeuvres Complètes* (1954), 16:83 n.

22. *The Schoolmaster*, ed. Lawrence Ryan (1967), 21-22.

23. The remark, with final italics added, is from Booth's promptbook (1878) and is quoted in the note for 3.3.486 of the Arden *Othello* (1958), edited by M.R. Ridley. Laurence Olivier approached Iago similarly against Ralph Richardson's Othello: "I played Iago entirely for laughs . . . terribly sweet, and as charming as can be" (*On Acting* [1986], 101). Arrigo Boito, in the published *Disposizione Scenica* for *Otello*, insists that the artist playing Iago "must be handsome and appear jovial, frank, and almost good-natured" (5; my translation).

24. *Magic in the Web: Action and Language in Othello* (1956), 25-30.

25. Barnaby Rich, "Of Apolonius and Silla," in *Riche his Farewell to Militarie Profession* (STC 20996; 1581), G2. Resonating behind my entire discussion of Iago is Greenblatt's assertion in *Renaissance Self-Fashioning* (252) that this villain is one of "the playwright's . . . representation[s] of himself."

26. "There was great irregularity in obtaining access, and suitors 'swarmed about his Majesty [James] at every back gate and privy door, to his great offence.' Charles decreed at his accession that suitors 'must never approach him by indirect means, by back stairs or private doors leading to his apartments, nor by means of retainers or grooms of the chambers, as was done in the lifetime of his father'" (Willson, *King James*, 195). S. Schoenbaum is eloquent on the extent to which this complex political atmosphere—"labyrinthine, remorselessly unsentimental, dangerous, and ego-centered—lurks everywhere in the Shakespeare canon" (*"Richard II* and the Realities of Power," in *Shakespeare and Others* [1985], 94).

27. Elyot, *The Governor*, 104.

5. "FEARFUL MEDITATION"

1. "Those who have never tried to court a friend in power think it is pleasant; one who has tried dreads it" (Epistle 18, Book 1 [ll. 86-87]).

2. *Biographia Literaria* (1817), ed. John Shawcross (1907), 2: 14-16 (original emphasis).

3. *Naive and Sentimental Poetry*, tr. Julian Elias (1966), 106.

4. Here I am relying on Isaiah Berlin's precis of Schiller in "The Naivete of Verdi," in *The Verdi Companion*, ed. William Weaver and Martin Chusid (1977), 3. Twain's praise for *Venus and Adonis* occurs in *Is Shakespeare Dead* (1909), 42.

5. C.S. Lewis wrote of the poem that it "reads well in question, but I have never read it through without feeling that I am being suffocated" ("Hero and Leander," in *Elizabethan Poetry: Modern Essays in Criticism*, ed. Paul Alpers [1967], 236-37). W.B.C. Watkins wrote that "One suspects that his head is in the poem but not his heart" (*Shakespeare and Spenser* [1950], 6). Mark Van Doren observed, "Desperate, indeed, is the word for 'Venus and Adonis' . . . there is strain, there is conceit, there is bad taste" (*Shakespeare* [1938], 8). Douglas Bush, saying the poem is not "a living thing," complained that the two characters are "an unattractive pair . . . remote from humanity" (*Mythology and the Renaissance Tradition* [1932], 139, 146). But perhaps William Hazlitt was the most withering, calling the two long poems "a couple of ice-houses. They are about as hard, as glittering, and as cold" (*Characters of Shakespeare's Plays* [1955], 272).

6. A caveat—perhaps an unnecessary one at this late date in Sonnets criticism—is worth making here, one similar to the editorial credo that Stephen Booth announced discreetly in a long note on Sonnet 112: "The commentary I offer in this edition is designed to counter a tendency in editors, critics, and students to assume that an obvious expository coherence precludes other less important or unimportant coherences" (370). The best one can hope for, in other words, is that one's own "expository coherence" will be given a considered attention, a temporary rather than a permanent privileging.

7. *Playwright as Magician* (1979), 46. The reader is urged to consult Kernan's chapter, "From the Great House to the Public Theater: Shakespeare's Sonnets and the Failure of Patronage" as a complement to the present discussion. In some respects we agree; in others we part company. Kernan's conclusion that Shakespeare took the step

from great house to theater "with great reluctance at leaving a golden past" (48) is perhaps the one most strenuously challenged in the following pages.

8. *The Mutual Flame* (1955; reprint, 1962), 127.

9. Thomas Greene, "Pitiful Thrivers: Failed Husbandry in the Sonnets," in *Shakespeare and the Question of Theory*, ed. Patricia Parker and Geoffrey Hartman (1985), 237.

10. J.W. Lever, *The Elizabethan Sonnet* (1956; reprint 1966), 206.

11. *Renaissance Self-Fashioning*, 162.

12. *Fennors Descriptions* (STC 10784; 1616), B2r.

13. Francis Peck, *Desiderata Curiosa* (1979), 49.

14. *Crisis of the Aristocracy*, 224.

15. The quoted phrase comes from an unpublished essay by Frank Whigham; his *Ambition and Privilege* (1984) is complementary to much of the following discussion.

16. *A Poetical Rapsody* (1602), ed. Hyder Rollins (1931), 1:21.

17. These quotations are reminiscent of Wolsey's career in *Henry VIII*; note especially the s.d. at 3.2.203: "Exit King, frowning upon the Cardinal." Not surprisingly, *eye(s)* occur more frequently in the Sonnets than in any other Shakespearean work.

18. "Aspects of the Short Poem in the Renaissance," in *Forms of Discovery* (1967), 60. See also Arthur Marotti's discussion of Sonnet 29 on pages 410-11 in the article cited in note 13 of chapter 1.

19. *The Life of Sir Walter Raleigh Together with his Letters*, ed. Edward Edwards (1868), 2:257.

20. The quoted phrase and lines are from two verse letters, both addressed to Sir Henry Wotton (215, 213).

21. *The Booke of Honour* (1625), 70. The conceit was hardly new. Compare Horace's *Hic ego rerum / fluctibus in mediis et tempestatibus urbis* ("Here [at Rome], amid the waves of life, amid the tempests of the town. . . . " [Epistle 2 from Book 2, ll. 84-85; Fairclough, translation 430-31]).

22. Thomas Churchyard, *A pleasaunte Laborinth called Churchyardes Change* (STC 5250; 1580), llr.

23. Ballade 75 (121); compare sonnet 160 (226) and epigram 164 (228), both attributed to Wyatt.

24. This is the text of the poem "Far from triumphing court" set to music by John Dowland, in his *Second Booke of Songs* (STC 7095; 1600); it also appears in Robert Dowland's *A Musicall Banquet* (STC 7099; 1610). The Bacon letter is included in Spedding (8:108).

25. James I, condoling Buckingham in *A Meditation upon the Lord's Prayer* (STC 14384; 1619), A5v.

26. Letter dated 22 December 1582, in *The Memoirs of the Life and Times of Sir Christopher Hatton*, ed. Harris Nicolas (1847), 296. La Bruyère wrote in his fourth aphorism "Of the Court," "A man who leaves the court for a single moment renounces it forever; the courtier who was there in the morning must be there at night, and know it again next day, in order that he himself may be known there" (trans. Henri van Laun [1885], 184).

27. *Calendar of the Manuscripts of the . . . Marquis of Salisbury*, Historical Manuscripts Commission, Part 11 (1906), 361. "Pray, if I write idly, pardon me," Pembroke adds, "for I have as little to do here as any man living."

28. On the longueurs of country life, see Stone *(Crisis of the Aristocracy,* 391f): "In country house after country house could be heard the yawns and sighs of boredom and loneliness."

29. This maxim is quoted by Norbert Elias, in *Power and Civility, Volume 2: The Civilizing Process* (1939; Eng. translation Edmund Jephcott, 1982), 270. Elias's chapter on "The Muting Drives: Psychologization and Rationalization" in part two of this volume ("Towards a Theory of the Civilizing Process") will be found pertinent to English Renaissance court life. Indeed, Elias's enumeration of the necessities of court life describes clearly the constrictions surrounding poetical suitors: "Continuous reflection, foresight, and calculation, self-control, precise and articulate regulation of one's own effects, knowledge of the whole terrain, human and non-human, in which one acts, become more and more indispensable preconditions of social success" (271).

30. A.D.B., *Court of . . . James, the First,* 146. Court life grew gradually less dangerous in sixteenth-century England. Thomas Hannen describes Henry VIII's court as "a place of deadly serious intrigue where each faction plotted against every other for royal favor. Behind the artificial frivolity and the macabre mask of charm, every word or deed was weighed for the information it could yield. . . . It was a company in which duplicity and secrecy were a necessity if one was to avoid the wrong move that often meant death" ("The Humanism of Sir Thomas Wyatt," in *The Rhetoric of Renaissance Poetry*, ed. Thomas O. Sloan and Ramond Waddington [1974], 43). The change with Elizabeth was marked, and A.L. Rowse captures it in *The Elizabethan Renaissance* (1971): "The reserve in the faces painted by Holbein is reserve in the face of omnipresent danger, the reserve of fear. This is not present in Elizabethan Court-portraits: there was no fear for life, but an open-eyed civilized wariness. Behind Henry's one sees the law of the jungle; behind Elizabeth's, the slippery ladder of favor, the competitiveness, the exhibitionism encouraged at the top, a world of flattery" (32-33). Such a world led Lord Burghley to give his son this sad advice: "Trust not any man with thy life, credit or estate. For it is meer folly for a man to enthrall himself to his frend, as though, occasion being offered, he should not dare to become the enemie" *(Desiderata Curiosa* [1779], 49). Raleigh's advice to his son was similar: "Publicke affaires are rockes, private conversacions are whirlepooles and quickesandes" (quoted by Agnes Latham in "Sir Walter Raleigh's *Instructions to his Son,"* in *Elizabethan and Jacobean Studies Presented to Frank Percy Wilson* [1959], 207). In *Ambition and Privilege* (1984), 137-39, Frank Whigham presents lengthy quotations from Castiglione and Guazzo on the dangers of courtly friendship. Lacey Baldwin Smith's *Treason in Tudor England: Politics and Paranoia* (1986) compendiously explores the "black poison of suspect" (Jonson) in the English Renaissance courtier's world.

31. Javitch, *"Il Cortegiano,"* 20. Javitch's quotation here is from the Charles Singleton translation (1959).

32. *A Strappado for the Divell* (STC 3588; 1615), 22.

33. *The Lawiers Logicke* (STC 11343; 1588), fol. 27v. Puttenham includes *amphibologia* among "vices in speaches and writing [that] are alwayes intollerable" (257). This figure he defines as "when we speak or write doubtfully and that the sence may be taken two wayes" (267).

34. *Complete Poems* (226). The editor's note to this poem: "Muir and Thomson, who introduced this poem into the Wyatt canon [in their 1969 edition], apparently doubt that it is by him because of its unusual amount of alliteration." The poem certainly captures in a spectacular way the "crisis of the divided mind" that Southall finds at the heart of

Wyatt's poetry (*Courtly Maker*, 76). The courtier's "divided mind," I have already remarked (91-92, 174), is also powerfully conveyed in Donne's "The Storm" and "The Calm." In his recent study, *John Donne: Coterie Poet* (1986), Arthur Marotti calls these "especially powerful poems of self-examination and self-criticism" as a courtier (114). Pertinently for my dark view of the Sonnets, Marotti summarizes thus his impression of the writings from Donne's courting years: "One finds in the verse and prose letters of the late nineties an extended exploration of disillusionment, set against the background of Donne's growing courtly involvement" (113).

35. John Sellar, *A Sermon* (STC 22182), 8. An important recent and extensive exploration of this Shakespearean characteristic is Norman Rabkin's *Shakespeare and the Problem of Meaning* (1981). Adena Rosmarin addresses the contradictory nature of the Sonnets from the perspective of recent advances in critical theory in "Hermeneutics versus Erotics: Shakespeare's Sonnets and Interpretive History," *PMLA* 100 (1985): 20-37. Rosmarin writes, "As E.H. Gombrich observes [of floor mosaics at Antioch], it is practically impossible to keep such patterns fixed because they present 'contradictory clues. The result is that the frequent reversals force our attention to the plane.' The Sonnets also force our attention to the plane, teaching us to see word as word, phrase as phrase, poem as poem" (29).

36. Knight, *Mutual Flame*, generally; Patrick Crutwell's chapter on "Shakespeare's Sonnets and the 1590s," in *The Shakespearean Moment* (1954; reprint 1970), 31; Lever, *Elizabethan Sonnet*, 216-17.

37. "Shakespeare's Sonnets" (1934), in *Explorations* (1958), 54.

38. *Hymen's Triumph*, in *The Complete Works*, ed. Alexander Grosart (1885), 3:339; *Delia*, Sonnet 48, *Poems and A Defence of Ryme*, ed. A.C. Sprague (1965), 34.

39. "The Structure of Figurative Language in Shakespeare's Sonnets," in *A Casebook on Shakespeare's Sonnets*, ed. Gerald Willen and Victor Reed (1964), 223. This article, which originally appeared in the *Southern Review* 5 (1940): 730-47, focuses on Sonnet 124; Booth calls this article "the most illuminating single comment on the Sonnets" (419).

40. Drayton, *Works*, 1:499.

41. J.W. Saunders speaks of the "placid Daniel" who was "always the professional secure in a backwater of patronage" in "Donne and Daniel," *Essays in Criticism* 3 (1953): 113-14.

42. The Gosse remark is from *The Jacobean Poets* (1894; reprint 1970), 14; The quoted phrases are spoken by Coriolanus (1.9.51-53, 3.2.115). For a study of "the marginality of Elizabethan drama" and civic jurisdiction, see Steven Mullaney's *The Place of the Stage: Licence, Play, and Power in Renaissance England* (1988).

Precisely the kind of distancing I suggest here may have occurred as Shakespeare set about revising his sonnets of the 1590s for publication in 1609. Gary Taylor has recently proposed this theory of revision in a comparison of several manuscript versions of Sonnet 2 with the 1609 version (*Times Literary Supplement*, 19 April 1985, 450). Taylor concludes, "Cumulatively, the variants in the 1609 edition characterize the youth economically but vividly. They also *ironically distance poet from patron*. No longer another Aeneas, the incarnation of mythological virtues, the youth becomes a flawed, specific mortal" (emphasis added). As well, certain of Joel Fineman's assertions suggest that Shakespeare's sonnets act Coriolanus-like toward received poetic "custom." Fineman writes that the Sonnets "truly speak against a strong tradition" and "markedly distance themselves from the tradition of idealizing poetry" (*Shakespeare's Perjured Eye*, 15, 187).

EPILOGUE: STATUES AND BREATHERS

1. See S.L. Bethell, *Shakespeare and the Popular Dramatic Tradition* (1944); J.D. Danby, *Poets on Fortune's Hill* (1952); Harold Goddard, *The Meaning of Shakespeare* (1951). An important, more recent book-length study of the play is Janet Adelman's *The Common Liar* (1973).

2. The quoted phrase is from John Stow's *Annales, or Generall Chronicles of England* (1618 ed.), 791.

3. Caesar's sober view is seconded in one of Francesco Guicciardini's maxims, which captures the essence of Antony's career in the play: "I believe there is nothing worse in this world than levity. For lighthearted men are ready instruments of any party, no matter how bad, dangerous, or pernicious. Therefore, flee from them as you would from fire" (*Maxims and Reflections*, ed. Mario Domandi [1955], 83).

4. David J. Johnson, *Southwark and the City* (1969), 64; Stow, *Annales*, 770-71. The Globe Theater was built within the old boundaries of the Clink Liberty, the name deriving from the Bishop of Winchester's prison in that vicinity; see, generally, Steven Mullaney's *The Place of the Stage* (1988) on the social marginality of the Liberties. See also Leah Marcus, *Puzzling Shakespeare: Local Reading and Its Discontents* (1988).

5. *The Place of the Stage*, 144. The pun on *queen/quean* (= whore) looms behind the play's action.

6. *A Sermon Preached at Paules Crosse* (1578; STC 23284), 134. Mullaney writes, "the public playhouses were not a minor irritation to London; they represented a threat to the political well-being and stability of the city" (53). Antony's debauchery in Alexandria represents a similar threat to Rome.

7. The intermingling of the worlds of tavern, brothel, and theater achieved in *Antony and Cleopatra* can also be found in Jonson's *Every Man in his Humor* (1601):

> He makes my house as common as a *Mart*,
> A *Theater*, a publike receptacle
> For giddie humor, and diseased riot,
> And there (as in a Taverne, or a stewes)
> He, and his wilde associates, spend their houres,
> In repetition of lascivious jests,
> Sweare, leape, and dance, and revell night by night. [3: 214-15]

The contemporary association of the theaters and prostitution is discussed in Ann Jennalie Cook, "'Bargains of Incontinencie': Bawdy Behavior in the Playhouses," and Wallace Shugg, "Prostitution in Shakespeare's London," *Shakespeare Studies* 10 (1977), 271-90, 291-313.

8. By the end of the sixteenth century Shakespeare must already have been well on the way to firm financial security. For in the sole extant letter addressed to him (but apparently never sent), one Robert Quiney in October 1598 asked to borrow the huge sum of £30. See S. Schoenbaum, "Looking for Shakespeare," in *Shakespeare and Others* (1985), 36-37.

Index

+22   18/03